SUCCESSFUL
WRITING

Third Edition

SUCCESSFUL WRITING

Third Edition

MAXINE C. HAIRSTON
The University of Texas at Austin

W. W. NORTON & COMPANY
New York   London

Copyright © 1992, 1986, 1981 by Maxine C. Hairston. All rights reserved. Printed in the United States of America.

The text of this book is composed in Sabon, with the display set in Avant Garde Gothic. Composition by New England Typographic Service. Manufacturing by Courier Westford.

Library of Congress Cataloging in Publication Data
Hairston, Maxine.
   Successful writing / Maxine C. Hairston.—3rd ed.
     p. cm.
   Includes index.

   1. English language—Rhetoric. I. Title.
PE1408.H297   1992
808′.042—dc20   91-40992

   ISBN 0-393-96204-0

W. W. Norton & Company, Inc., 500 Fifth Avenue, New York, N.Y. 10110
W. W. Norton & Company, Ltd., 10 Coptic Street, London WC1A 1PU

1 2 3 4 5 6 7 8 9 0

Contents

---

5 ◇ DRAFTING YOUR PAPER   69

---

6 ◇ REVISING   91

12 ◇ WRITING ON THE JOB   221

Preface

This third edition of *Successful Writing* maintains the focus established in the earlier editions, that of giving practical, concise advice to student writers who have mastered the elements of usage and mechanics and can write readable prose. Now they are ready to learn more about the craft of writing: how to find their topics, develop ideas, write for different purposes to different kinds of readers, and how to revise, polish, and edit their writing into clear, forceful prose that will engage as well as inform their readers.

Such writers may be in second-semester or honors freshman courses or in sophomore or upper-division courses in or out of English departments. Whatever their classification or their major, most of them find they have to write more and more in all their courses, and they realize they will continue to write, both by themselves and collaboratively, after they leave college and become professionals. Many of them also want to become better writers just for the sheer fun of it. That may be the best motivation of all.

This third edition responds to all these needs with direct and accessible suggestions about generating and organizing material and an expanded chapter on revision that emphasizes revision as a creative, rewarding, and interactive process that is distinct from editing. To make the book conform more directly to actual writing practice, that chapter on revising now appears directly after the chapter on drafting a paper. Chapters focused on improving style follow the chapter on revision. The editing process is now handled in a separate chapter, new to this edition. In keeping with the field's focus on workshop pedagogy, this edition also puts new emphasis on writing as a social act and provides special guidelines for students working in groups as well as suggestions for many writing activities to be carried out in groups.

Chapter 1, "Writing in College," has been expanded to accommodate a larger, more-specific section on what professors expect of students who write papers, and it includes a new, informative student paper on *film noir*. Chapter 2, "What is Good Writing?," is now more focused on academic writing, bringing in new assignments and new examples. Chapter 3, "What Happens When People Write?," expands on the theory that writers vary their writing processes according to the kind of writing they are doing and introduces new terms, *explanatory* and *exploratory*, to describe and clarify these approaches. The chapter also includes fresh material on using computer programs for generating material and for outlining.

Chapter 4, "What Is Your Writing Situation?," has been extensively revised to put greater emphasis on audience awareness; it now includes succinct, carefully focused guidelines for analyzing audience, purpose, and persons. Chapter 5, "Drafting Your Paper," remains essentially the same but offers fresh examples and new writing activities. Chapter 6, "Revising," has been reorganized and tightened to give students realistic and workable suggestions about revising; it now includes specific advice to help students work on their revising in peer groups. The chapter provides two response sheets for giving students feedback on drafts, one for large-scale revision and one for small-scale revision. It also shows the development of a new student paper, "The Roots of Country Music," through three drafts and includes comments on that development.

Chapter 7, "Holding Your Reader," has an expanded section on writing strong leads; Chapter 9, "Crafting Paragraphs," expands its coverage of beginning paragraphs and now gives more specific advice and guidelines for writing closing paragraphs. Chapter 10, "Editing," is a new chapter, conceived as a reference for advanced students who need succinct advice on overcoming common stumbling blocks in usage and mechanics. It underscores the key role editing plays in appealing to readers and makes suggestions for improving the visual impact of a paper. It helps students set priorities about errors and documents this advice with results of a survey asking business and professional people what errors they find most offensive. *Successful Writing* is the only advanced-composition text with this pragmatic feature.

Chapters 11 and 12, "The Research Paper" and "Writing on the Job," are essentially unchanged from the second edition. Chapter 11 is designed to help students whose research tasks may take them beyond traditional library sources; chapter 12 gives students advice they may need for some academic writing tasks and later on the job when they must write case studies, grant proposals, abstracts, and other kinds of working documents.

This edition, like the previous two, retains distinctive features that make it a particularly useful text for advanced writing courses:

- All student writing examples come from the papers of students in advanced courses.

- Writing activities and assignments are based on topics that range across the curriculum and stress the importance of audience and purpose in every writing situation.
- Special guidelines help students draft, revise, and evaluate their own papers; additional guidelines help them work with their peers and in collaborative writing situations.
- Several chapters include self-teaching prompts designed to make students careful critics of their own work.
- Advice about usage and writing conventions is pragmatic and sets priorities. It is based on an actual survey of how readers respond to lapses in usage and mechanics.

The underlying premises of this third edition of *Successful Writing* remain unchanged from previous editions:

1. Writing is a dynamic social process that can be taught and learned.

2. People grow as writers by learning to draft, revise, and polish their writing by working in a variety of situations for a variety of readers.

3. Learning to interact and work with other writers is an important part of every writer's development.

I believe in these principles as strongly now as I did ten years ago when the first edition of *Successful Writing* appeared.

MAXINE HAIRSTON

Acknowledgments

I received encouragement, support, and valuable advice on this book from a number of colleagues and friends, but I want to express my special appreciation to Professor Michael Keene of the University of Tennessee. I owe him a great deal. I also wish to thank Mary Trachsel for her assistance in rewriting the chapter on research papers.

I also want to express my thanks to the following people who made useful and enlightening suggestions at all stages of manuscript preparation: Douglas Atkins (University of Kansas), Martha A. Bartter (The Ohio State University—Marion Campus), Mary Bly (University of California, Davis), Linda Cades (University of Maryland), Edward P. J. Corbett (The Ohio State University), Toby Fulwiler (University of Vermont), Richard Gebhart (Findlay College), William Harmon (University of North Carolina), E. D. Hirsch, Jr. (University of Virginia), Paula Johnson (University of Wyoming), Andrea Lunsford (The Ohio State University), Donald P. McNeilly (University of Maryland), Susan Miller (University of Utah), Amy Richards (Wayne State University), Robert Rudolf (University of Toledo), Joseph Trimmer (Ball State University), Steven J. Vander Weele (Calvin College), and John Walter (University of Texas) and John Webster (University of Washington).

1 ◇ Writing in College

WRITING AS A WAY OF LEARNING

If you are like most college students, writing papers is a way of life for you. In fact, the further along you get in your studies, the more papers you will probably have to write, not only in courses such as history, philosophy, and English but also in courses you had not thought of as writing courses, such as engineering and accounting and astronomy. That's not surprising because in recent years, more and more faculty in widely varied disciplines have come to believe that students benefit from writing in college courses in a number of ways. Here are some of those benefits:

• Writing helps us absorb and master new information. When we write about a topic we have to engage with it and become active learners, not simply sponges for information. Writing also forces us to organize our ideas more carefully and put them in explicit form. Thus we understand material better and retain it longer when we write about it.

• Writing helps us to discover what we know. Writing about a topic stimulates our thinking, and as we write we tap into our store of knowledge and remember relevant experiences and anecdotes. Writing also helps us generate new ideas because when we write we often make connections, see relationships, and draw parallels that would not have occurred to us if we hadn't started to write.

• Writing promotes critical thinking. When we write, we put our ideas into tangible form so we can distance ourselves from them and see them more objectively. When we write something down we are more apt to ask ourselves, "Is this worth saying? Will this idea stand up to scrutiny? Can I support this claim?" Writing also helps us to spell out

1

problems and see their parts so we can consider how we might go about solving them.

In short, writing is a powerful tool for learning, one that plays a crucial role in education and in your later career. It is also a highly satisfying craft to have at your command. It just feels good to know you can write clearly and effectively and that whatever writing task you face, you're equal to it. The purpose of this book is to help you develop the habits and strategies that will give you that sense of control and make you a confident and competent writer in any situation.

STRATEGIES FOR WRITING PAPERS IN COLLEGE COURSES

Some kinds of college writing assignments are so highly specialized that you may need to take a course in scientific and technical writing in order to do them well, but in most courses in the liberal arts or social sciences, you will get off to a good start on your papers if you follow a few general guidelines for planning and roughing out a first draft. You will find initial guidelines in this chapter, and you can then consult other chapters in the book to learn more about developing and refining your paper.

Analyzing Your Writing Situation

Before you start to write, take the time to think about your writing situation and to analyze what's involved. Begin by asking these questions about the three factors that control any writing situation.

- What is my purpose? What am I trying to accomplish? What is the main point I want to get across?
- Who are my readers? What assumptions should I make about my readers? What questions do they want me to answer?
- What limitations am I working under? What resources (information, library facilities, and so on) do I have to work with? How much time do I have to write? How long is the paper supposed to be?

It's a good idea to take time to jot down preliminary answers to these questions before you start to write even a rough draft. Writing down answers will serve two purposes.

First, it will help you to focus your paper and keep it under control by reminding yourself not to take on more than you can manage. For instance, if you're writing a short paper or you have only a week to do the research, don't be too ambitious. Choose a relatively narrow topic or one on which you already have a good deal of information.

Second, writing out the answers to these questions will help you get started on your paper. Like brainstorming, such preliminary writing helps your mind to lay down tracks on which you can start moving to generate ideas.

Here is an example of how one might go about answering these questions and establishing the context for a specific paper.

MODEL TOPIC

WRITER: Cindy Nolan

THE COURSE: Upper-division writing course

THE ASSIGNMENT: Write an informative paper focusing on some special area within your general topic. (In this course, all students chose a general topic and wrote several papers on various aspects of it.) Your article should be directed toward the readers of a specific magazine.

Cindy's general topic for the semester was "film"; her specific topic for this paper was the French concept of "*film noir*" and its impact on American movies.

Working Title: A Touch of Noir: It's Still a Matter of Style

QUESTION 1: Cindy decided she would write a paper about film that would both inform and entertain. She wanted to explain the concept *film noir*, show where it came from, illustrate its typical style and techniques, and show how it has influenced American movies. She wanted to give her readers a better understanding of some major films they had seen and help them get more out of films in the future.

QUESTION 2: Cindy chose readers of *Premiere* magazine (a magazine about films and the movie industry) as her audience because she wanted to write for an audience who was already interested in film and would be familiar with most of the films she wanted to mention. Cindy assumed that her readers would have heard of *film noir* but wouldn't necessarily know its origins or how it fits into the current movie scene. Some of their questions might be these: What is the idea behind *film noir*? What are some films that fit this category? What are typical characteristics?

Cindy's immediate audience—her writing professor—will also have those questions but in addition will want to see how clearly Cindy explains her concepts, how well she illustrates them, and how well she adapts her writing to the audience she has chosen. Another important audience is her classmates, some of whom she will be working with in a small group as she drafts and revises her paper.

QUESTION 3: The paper should be about 1,000 words, because that is the average length of articles in *Premiere* magazine. Cindy had three weeks to draft and revise this paper, which gave her enough time to look again at some of the films she wanted to write about. Because she had taken two film courses and knew many other people interested in film, she already had considerable background information and knew where to look for specific examples to support her ideas.

Guidelines for Limiting a Paper Topic

Some of the worst problems with college papers come about because students choose topics that are too broad for them to deal with adequately in a paper of the assigned length or in the time available. If you pick a broad topic such as "Illiteracy in Texas" or "The Politics of Abortion" and try to write about it in only four or five pages, you will inevitably wind up with a collection of generalities. When you stake out too much ground to cover, you can't bring in those details that give a topic life and make it worth writing about. You're not likely to learn much from writing the paper, and you certainly won't impress your professor.

Deciding how much one can expect to handle responsibly in a paper of a specific length is tricky, even for experienced writers, but these rough guidelines may help.

Four-to-six page paper: A short paper, probably one of several for the course. Your thesis should be a narrow one in which you make only one or two important points but support those points with specific examples. For example, "Joe Christmas's obsession with moral guilt in *Light in August* goes back to his fundamentalist religious upbringing." Or this: "For good reason, the British government disputes the Greeks' claim that the Parthenon Marbles rightly belong to them." Although an expert might write at length on either topic, each can also be handled responsibly with specifics in a short paper.

Ten-to-twelve page paper: A paper in which you can treat a limited topic in some detail, giving examples and quoting from sources. This length is too short to let you write about a broad topic such as art in the Renaissance, or a major philosophical movement such as Existentialism, without being superficial, but you could write on some subtopic within the larger topic, such as "The Influence of Van Dyke as Court Painter for Charles I" or "The Existentialist Hero in Camus's novel *The Plague*." Other topics that one could cover adequately in ten to twelve pages:

Plato's Treatment of Poets in *The Republic*.
The Role of the Grand Jury in the County Judicial Process.

Eighteen- to twenty-page paper: A paper that gives you enough space to treat a limited but complex topic in detail. Usually the professor who assigns a twenty-page paper expects you to do some research for it because he or she wants material from outside sources and wants you to evaluate that material and draw conclusions. You still need to be careful not to pick a topic so broad that it would require a master's thesis to do it credit. Some topics of the kind that might be suitable for a twenty-page paper:

Three Recent Supreme Court Decisions That Have Affected Freedom of the Press in the United States.

The Impact on the Federal Deposit Insurance Corporation of the 1989 Savings and Loan Scandal.

GENERAL CRITERIA FOR ACADEMIC WRITING

Academic writing is hardly a precise term—after all, in college, a student may do a dozen different kinds of writing, ranging from personal experience papers in freshman English and case studies in experimental psychology to reflective critical essays in an ethics course and technical reports in an engineering class. It's all academic writing, yet the professor of experimental psychology expects a paper very different from the reflective essay written for the ethics course. The rules for choosing and presenting evidence vary greatly from one discipline to another as do the conventions for writing style and even documentation. So I can't give any clear-cut instruction for "How to Write a College Paper." It's not that simple.

Nevertheless, as I point out in the next chapter, there is such a thing as good writing, and I believe it is possible to outline some useful ground rules for what constitutes good writing in college. Professors do make up a special kind of audience, and whatever their specialities, they tend to expect—and reward—certain characteristics in papers they get from their students. I'll divide those features into content and form.

Matters of Content

- *If you have a choice of topics, write on something that's fresh and interesting to you.* Find an approach to your topic that gives you a chance to explore new material and to say something new. Professors get tired of reading the same old comments on traditional topics, and although they don't expect students to have original insights in an area in which they're not experts, they welcome new ideas and interpretations. They're likely to notice the student who teaches them something, who picks a focused topic and digs in to find new material.

- *Don't overstate your case.* When you make sweeping claims that go far beyond what your evidence will support, you undermine your credibility. So be careful about using those treacherous words *everyone, all, never,* and *always*—they can get you into trouble. Statements like "*Everyone* in the popular music industry is corrupt" or "Wolves have *never* been the menace that cattlemen claim they are" can be proved wrong if your readers know even one contradictory example. But if you write, "The popular music industry seems riddled with corruption" or "Wolves have seldom been the menace the cattlemen claim they are," you've still made strong statements, but you haven't gone beyond what you can document.

- *Support your claims.* Most professors are skeptical readers who expect all writers, not only you, to back up claims with solid evidence and reasonable arguments. If you write, "Alcoholism in the United States was worse 100 years ago than it is now," be sure you have figures and comparisons to back up your claim. If you write, "The growing number of women doctors promises to change the practice of medicine in this country," be ready to give figures and to frame your argument. As you draft your paper, try to anticipate when your professor might have questions such as "Who says so?" "Why do you say that?" and "How do you know?"

- *Argue logically and avoid highly connotative language.* Although opinion has it place in college writing, especially if you are asked to interpret a work of literature or counter an argument, most of the time instructors prefer that you maintain an objective tone and bolster your claims with traditional arguments such as cause and effect, induction, assertion and support, and so on. Rely on the weight of facts rather than on emotional appeal, and try to write a structured, reasonable argument (see the section on Toulmin logic in Chapter 5).

Matters of Form

- *Choose an accurate title that reflects the content of your paper.* Your title introduces you and your paper so be sure it gets you off to a good start with your reader (See pp. 111–13).

- *Organize your points so they are easy to follow and mark them clearly.* Because professors read a great many papers, and they have to read them quickly, they welcome the paper with a clear introduction that forecasts the argument, then leads them through it with *first, second, consequently,* and so on.

- *Document your sources.* You don't necessarily have to use formal notes or attach a "Works Cited" page, but let your reader know where your information came from. Try to anticipate places where your reader might ask "How do you know that?" and never let the question go unanswered for more than a few moments. For research papers, invest in an APA or MLA style sheet—they'll save you a lot of guesswork. (Chapter 11 also provides basic guidelines for documentation; see pp. 204–20.)

• *Turn in a double-spaced, carefully corrected, and proofread paper that is typed or printed on quality paper.* If you're writing with a computer, run the spell checker on your computer if you have one. Get a second reader to check for errors. Leave good margins and number your pages. Garner all the points you can from good appearance—it costs too much not to.

The student paper that follows is a good example of a paper that meets all the criteria for content and form and is fresh, engaging, and informative.

A Touch of *Noir*: It's All a Matter of Style

by Cindy Nolan

Have you ever thrilled to the labyrinthine intrigue of one of those old hard-boiled detective movies of the forties and fifties? Or melted under a close-up of the seductive gaze of a femme fatale, sighing, "They just don't make 'em like that any more?" The Humphrey Bogart/ Lauren Bacall prototypes of the French-labeled "*film noir*," a B-movie genre of the post–World War II era, are well-known icons of American culture, recreated and caricatured in television shows, commercials, cartoons, etc. But what about movies? Do they make 'em like that anymore? A working definition of what *film noir* is, thematically and stylistically, should provide us with some clues.

Thematically, *film noir* is a paranoid reflection of the changes, fears, and tensions wrought in American culture by the war years and the ominous circumstances of nuclear warfare. The apocalyptic possibilities of the A-bomb and the fact of the devastation wrought at the hands of the American government directly challenged characteristic American feelings of optimism, security, and trust in government based on humanistic principles. This was the dark side of America, stigmatized by hypocrisy and inhumane tyranny, the side that *film noir* inhabited. *Noir* drew its story line from the detective novels of the thirties, of which Raymond Chandler was the archtypical author. The protagonist was the two-bit detective—an average Joe, a little seedy, but possessing an unfailing sense of justice. On false pretenses, he is drawn into a maze of deception, where clues don't add up, people are not what they claim to be, and everyone but him seems to be in on some secret.

The person who got him into all this trouble in the first place was, significantly, a woman—the famed femme fatale. In *noir* thematics, the femme fatale was a symbol of the changing roles that women were now beginning to demand. The servicemen returned after the war to a nation of women who had become the work force. It was the women who had melted the steel and fashioned and assembled what was the most sophisticated weaponry in the annals of war history. They worked hard, as hard as men, and they enjoyed working. They were more than a little reluctant to give up their new freedom and experience to return to the subservient domain of the house.

The men, of course, had expected to return home to a hero's welcome and an adoring little housewife. You could say that they felt more than a little threatened when confronted by their more autonomous and assertive wives when they attempted to reestablish the old order. The femme fatale was a symbol of that threat. She was glamorous and smoked. She was seductive and duplicitous. She often was the villain. She was the embodiment of evil, and it was the hero's job in the course of the investigation and its incumbent dangers to straighten her out, resisting her attempts to sully him, and restore the "natural" order of things.

A movie could stray from this formula and still be considered a *film noir* as long as the style and technique remained true to the *noir* manner. The French critics gave the movies the label of *film noir* (French for black) because they were so dark. The landscape of *noir* was night and the city, and the directors utilized darkness and shadows in a black-and-white format to create a feeling of being engulfed or encroached upon by the darkness. The action always took place at night, and the atmosphere was shot through with tension, both sexual and violent, that loomed and threatened much like the darkness that sought to engulf the screen. Shadows obscured expressions or identities, so that the audience had no more clue of who to trust than did the hapless protagonist. The mood was one of paranoia and despair in a chaotic modern society.

Anyone with a working knowledge of movies recognizes the formula just described. But what of the continuity of the tradition? Often, the plot line is not repeated, but the powerful motifs and techniques are drawn on to create the magnetic, yet disturbing, *noir* style. The symbol of woman as the locus of evil was used to stunning and violent effect by Arthur Penn in 1967's *Bonnie and Clyde*, which is otherwise thought of as a gangster movie remake that spawned another generation of imitations. Faye Dunaway's Bonnie Parker provides us with the *noir* equation of sex equals violence when she fondles the barrel of Clyde's gun the first time he shows it to her.

The seventies showed renewed interest in the form. In 1973 Robert Altman made a film version of the Raymond Chandler novel *The Long Goodbye*, featuring lanky Elliot Gould as the inglorious detective Philip Marlowe. Altman's quirky twists and turns border on satire, especially the theme song, which not only opens the movie but appears incessantly nearly everywhere, including the grocery-store Muzak. The film's modern setting would also tend to alienate it from the genre, but some critics have said it fits because Marlowe tries to function in a modern, corrupt world where even the police know more than he does.

Probably the most famous examples of modern *noir* style are the noted films *Chinatown* (1974) and *Body Heat* (1981). Lawrence Kasden made an auspicious directorial debut with *Body Heat,* a notably steamy film inspired by 1946's *The Postman Always Rings Twice.* In a true labyrinth of suspense and eroticism, femme fatale Kathleen Turner keeps half-witted lawyer William Hurt biting the apple until the very last, when he can never be sure if she is dead or alive.

Roman Polanski's sumptuous and golden *Chinatown* addresses the issue of the femme fatale more closely, not freeing her from blame, but offering an excuse for her fall from grace. After a seemingly endless and insoluble investigation, femme fatale Faye Dunaway is forced to reveal to bumbling private dick Jack Nicholson that she has an illegitimate daughter born of an incestuous relationship with her father. Thematically speaking, after the evil of the male is revealed, it is found to be unacceptable and the woman (Dunaway) must pay with her life. It is typically *noir* that her death is at the hands of the police, who still don't know what is going on.

Often *noir* technique appears in movies. The framed protagonist played by Richard Gere in 1980's *American Gigolo* often appears with shadows cast across him that give the appearance of a cage or cell, a *noir* technique commonly employed by shining light through venetian blinds. Kim Basinger appeared in a similar "cage" in the 1986 film $9^1/_2$ *Weeks,* in which she plays a woman caught up as unwilling partner in an abusive sexual relationship.

Noir themes have become hot again in recent years, and although there have been poor imitations, such as *The Big Easy,* the true *noir* style is to be found in a handful of films that have garnered much attention despite being out of the mainstream of the American film industry. Adventurous and sometimes bizarre films such as *After Hours, Something Wild, Blue Velvet,* and *Angel Heart,* continue to capture the imagination in their exploration of the dark side of American society. In each film, the hapless protagonist is drawn into a world of darkness and violence, far beyond what he is prepared for. Whereas the first three films finish with a return to a safer realm, *Angel Heart* seals the fate of protagonist Mickey Rourke. Far from locating the evil in yet another female, the devil himself, played by Robert De Niro, leads Rourke on a merry chase only to discover that it is he, the hero, who has sold his soul to the devil. Could this be a commentary on America today? If it's true to the *noir* spirit, definitely.

And that's where we find *noir* in film today. Not as genre imitation, but as technique, spirit, and above all, style. It is a uniquely American style—a manneristic indictment of a morally overwhelming modern world, a world in which the lone individual struggles to maintain his own identity and safety.

2 ◇ What Is Good Writing?

Good writing is writing that succeeds in

> saying something worthwhile
> to a specific audience
> for some purpose.

Under such a definition, we have to recognize many kinds of good writing. It can be formal or casual, elegant or plain, straightforward or subtle. We can encounter good writing in an essay anthology, in *The New York Times,* in a business letter, or in articles from *Atlantic, Car and Driver,* or *Rolling Stone.* But the central feature in all good expository writing, whether it is to inform or entertain, is that *it communicates the writer's ideas effectively to the audience for whom it is intended.* That qualifier "for whom it is intended" is crucial when we talk about good writing because good writers don't work in a vacuum. They know that writing is a social act, an interchange between people and that what works well with one group of readers may not work with a different group of readers in a different situation.

CHARACTERISTICS OF GOOD WRITING

But in spite of the changes in style, tone, voice, and arrangement that writers must make when they are writing for different audiences, it is still possible to identify central characteristics of good expository writing; that is, nonfiction, working writing. Such writing must be

- Substantive

- Clear
- Unified
- Economical
- Grammatically acceptable

When your finished product meets these standards, you know that it's readable, and you will get your point across to almost all of your readers.

Writing that is excellent, however will have two other important qualities:

- Vigor
- Authentic voice

I'll say more about all of these characteristics shortly.

All of us intuitively apply these criteria to what we read. We know that we enjoy reading something and learn from it when it says something substantial, when it's clear and well organized, and when the author gets to the point without wasting our time. We also appreciate lively writing that calls up images and reveals something of the author's personality. We respond best to writing that's *readable*.

Of course, none of us should be so arrogant or impatient that we assume any writing we can't understand must be poorly written. Sometimes authors must deal with complex topics that are difficult to explain, and sometimes we have to be willing to read and reread a piece of writing and work at extracting meaning from it. Nevertheless, if intelligent readers who have enough background information and who are willing to work at understanding a nontechnical piece of writing still have trouble with it, it's probably badly written.

THE PROBLEM OF MODELS

Unfortunately, both in and out of college, it's easy to be intimidated by writing that is full of long sentences and baffling vocabulary, particularly if that writing appears in a textbook or has a scholarly sounding name attached to it. Impressed by writing they can't understand, students sometimes assume that obscure and wordy writing reflects a brilliant mind, and they try to imitate it in college papers. Here is an example:

Once politics is defined negatively, as an enterprise for drawing a protective circle around the individual's sphere of self-interested action, then public concerns are by definition distinct from, and secondary to, private concerns. Regardless of democratic forms, when people are taught by philosophy (and the social climate) that they need not govern their actions by calculations of public good, they will come to blame all social shortcomings on the agency of collective considerations, the government.

—George Will, *Statecraft as Soulcraft,*
quoted in *Austin American Statesman,*
15 May, 1983, C-1.

Not totally incomprehensible, but not very readable either, particularly for a book aimed toward a general audience. Part of the difficulty comes from the puzzling phrase "the agency of collective considerations," but the main problem is that the writing is colorless and abstract. The reader can't see anybody doing anything. No people seem to be involved, yet Will is writing to and about human beings and human problems.

Here is another example of obscure writing that might intimidate someone on first reading. Ironically, it comes from a pamphlet inviting people to submit grant proposals for ways to improve writing.

Studies here should concentrate on the links between discourse rules and cognitive achievement through such mediating factors as social and referential understandings and the teacher's differential distribution due to the varying expectations of student abilities.

—The National Institute of Education,
Basic Skills Research Grants Announcement
(Summer 1977): 5.

This kind of deceptive language recalls the Hans Christian Andersen fairy tale "The Emperor's New Clothes." In that story a pair of confidence men dupe the emperor into believing that he is wearing elegant clothes when actually he is naked. None of his courtiers dare tell him that he has nothing on for fear they are the only ones who can't see the clothes that are supposed to be so grand. In the same way, intimidated readers often pretend to understand confusing writing because they are afraid that if they ask "What does it mean?" other people will think they're stupid. To expose that kind of fraud, someone finally has to become impatient enough to say, "What does this mean? I don't understand." Professors or bosses who have trouble understanding your writing are apt to say so rather quickly.

GOOD WRITING HAS SUBSTANTIAL CONTENT

Good writing says something worth reading—it's that simple. The readers for whom it's intended should find in it something that they want or need to know, something interesting, informative, or even surprising. Thus writing that only repeats conventional wisdom or strings together commonplace arguments is not good writing, no matter how smoothly written or grammatically correct it may be.

As a student writing papers in college, you may find such a definition confusing and wonder how you can judge what a professor finds worth reading. How are you supposed to know what he or she will find interesting? And how can you ever expect to surprise a professor? These are good objections, and the only answer to them is that sometimes you don't know and sometimes you have to gamble. But you can make some educated guesses because in many ways professors are rather predictable readers. You will probably come out well in writing for them if you test your papers by asking yourself these questions.

- Have I given my reader solid information, not just generalities?
- Have I set the information in a context and shown its implications?
- Have I put solid thought and effort into my investigation or report?

If you can answer yes to all three questions, you're doing substantial writing, whether it's for a professor or for a more general audience. And it is possible both to interest and to surprise even professors. They will usually find a solid, well-supported argument interesting, and they will be particularly pleased if you can give them new facts or take a fresh approach to an old topic.

GOOD WRITING IS CLEAR

Expository writing is clear when *the readers for whom it is intended* can read along at a steady pace and grasp the meaning if they put out a reasonable amount of effort. The "for whom it is intended" is important, of course; any of us has a hard time understanding material that is outside our field or area of experience because we don't have the required background information or the vocabulary we need. I, for example, have trouble reading *Scientific American;* someone else might have trouble reading *The New York Review of Books.*

Clear writing doesn't have to be simple, although it often is, but it shouldn't be any more difficult than it has to be, given the subject and the purpose. When asked what qualities they value most in writing, people who must read a great deal professionally put clarity at the top of their list (see survey on pp. 194–7). If they have to invest too much effort in figuring out the writer's meaning, they will give up in dismay or annoyance, or if they can't do that, they will curse the writer as they read.

Authors who want to write clearly use dozens of different strategies, some obvious and some subtle. Those tactics, ranging from keeping their audience in mind to making their writing visual, are ones that aspiring writers can learn rather quickly and begin to put into practice almost immediately. So important are they to good writing that much of the rest of the book focuses on these strategies for making your meaning clear.

GOOD WRITING IS UNIFIED

In all good writing one can sense a controlling pattern, a kind of master plan that holds the parts together and makes the reader feel that everything in the essay belongs there and fits into a unified whole. The reader can move from one idea to another easily and surely because the writer has laid down a path, pointed the readers in the right direction, and guided them along so smoothly that they won't go off on a detour or find themselves distracted by irrelevant details. The controlling pattern might tell a story; it might follow a pattern of claim and evidence, like a lawyer presenting a case in court; it might set up a sequence of causes and effects, like a scientist demonstrating a theory; or it might establish a pattern of assertion and example, as this paragraph does.

The careful writer reinforces the controlling pattern with a sequence of signals that nudge the reader along the way, signals like *first, second, finally, then,* and *consequently.* A writer may use other signals to tell readers when to stop for a qualification; those signals are words like *however, nevertheless, in spite of,* and so on. He or she may also regularly repeat keywords to reassure readers that they're on the right track.

Here is the opening paragraph from a tightly unified student paper written for young readers in an earth science class. In it the writer catches the readers' interest immediately and holds it through a pattern of assertion and support and by repeating his key word.

What is a geyser? Where are they found? When people think about geysers they usually picture Yellowstone's Old Faithful shooting water hundreds of feet in the air. But Old Faithful is only one type of geyser. Geysers normally eject hot, cloudy water like Old Faithful, but did you know that they can also shoot out yellow, orange, and green water? Some of these spouting fountains are not large at all but very small, and they trickle out softly on the land forming steamy, crystal-clear pools of hot water. Some stand alone far from other geysers, while others cluster together in large groups that look like geyser cities. All geysers are different, and each one has its own personality. But all geysers do have something in common: they are all hot and gush from beneath the ground.

—Josh Lucas

Here is a tightly written paragraph by a professional writer, held together by its story and by its visual impact. Notice also how the author has framed the paragraph with the arrival and departure of the Vietcong.

The Viet Cong had come a few nights after the advisors had first moved into the Seminary in early May to tell the Americans they were not beyond the guerrillas' reach. A group had sneaked through the banana groves across the road and started shooting at the mess hall in the middle of a movie. The sergeants, some of whom were old enough to have been through World War II or Korea, had been amused at the sight of captains who had never before been under fire running around in undershorts, T-shirts, and steel helmets, waving .45 caliber service pistols, with which it is difficult to hit a man in the daytime. Periodically the guerrillas would repeat the exercise, usually from the concealment of a stand of water palm on the opposite bank of the river. Several guerrillas would fire a string of shots at the generator or water purification plant and withdraw into the night. No damage was ever done beyond some pockmarks on the stucco. The next morning the advisors would see a Viet Cong flag . . . flying from a tree.
—Neil Sheehan, *A Bright Shining Lie*
(New York: Vintage Books, 1988), 47.

GOOD WRITING IS ECONOMICAL

Good writers don't want to waste their reader's time, so they try to cut all excess words from their writing, get rid of what William Zinsser, author of *On Writing Well*, calls "clutter." As he points out,

The reader is someone with an attention span of about sixty seconds—a person assailed by forces competing for the minutes that might otherwise be spent on a magazine or a book. At one time these forces weren't so numerous or so possessive: newspapers, radio, spouse, home, children. Today they also include a "home entertainment center" (TV, VCR, video camera, tapes and CDs), pets, a fitness program, a lawn and a garden and all the gadgets that have been bought to keep them spruce, and that most potent of competitors, sleep. The person snoozing in a chair, holding a magazine or a book, is a person who was being given too much unnecessary trouble by the writer.

—William Zinsser, "Rewriting,"
in *On Writing Well,* 4th ed.
(New York: HarperCollins, 1990), 9.

If you want to hold that reader's attention, you have to work constantly at keeping your writing terse and streamlined. That doesn't mean leaving out pertinent details—notice that Zinsser takes time to list specifically the forces that compete for a reader's attention—but it does mean trimming out many adjectives, eliminating repetitious phrases, and generally trying to do away with words that do not enhance meaning or advance your idea. You need to be particularly careful to squeeze excess words out of your writing when your main purpose is to inform, but you probably need fewer words than you think even when one of your purposes is to entertain.

For example, here is a colorful, effective, and uncluttered opening paragraph for a paper on unusual jobs for women:

Beth Allen has a very special job. Her first role is a full-time wife and mother. But each morning at 8:45, after the breakfast bustle is over and her family has gone for the day, Beth becomes another character. Quickly she tosses her dish towel onto the counter and whips her apron over a chair. She shoves her feet into a pair of floppy yellow shoes and pops on a fuzzy orange wig. Grabbing several large bunches of helium balloons, she checks her purse for the house keys and bounds out the door. Beth the Balloon Clown has just checked in for work.

—Paula Johnson

It may help to remind yourself that most of the terse uncluttered writing you find in the work of authors like Russell Baker, Ellen Goodman, or Carl Sagan didn't start out that way; almost certainly those authors had to work at revising sentences and cutting out extra words. In several places in this book you will find guidelines for ways to trim your writing. Several sections of the book will suggest how a writer works toward clarity and will give some specific guidelines.

GOOD WRITING IS GRAMMATICALLY ACCEPTABLE

For our purposes, I am defining "grammatically acceptable English" as that which observes standard English usage; that is, the kind of English most educated people in our society use and expect others to use in public writing in college as well as business, government, and journalism. (By "public writing" I mean writing that has been made public for other people to see.) Standard English is the kind of language you encounter in books, newspapers, and business documents or hear people use on radio and television or in public speeches. Most of the time, such usage conforms to those grammar rules you learned in elementary or high school.

But only most of the time. Anyone who has absorbed most of the seemingly endless rules that govern standard English and has a sensitive ear knows that many successful and well-educated people do not always speak or write absolutely "correct" English. Perhaps they confuse *lie* and *lay* or forget to use *whom* when they should; perhaps they say "If that *was* to happen," instead of "If that *were* to happen," or write "Everyone should watch their cholesterol." But such mistakes are minor, so common among even well-educated people that others rarely even notice them. Such grammar is *acceptable*—it suits the occasion and does little damage.

Other kinds of grammatical mistakes, however, are unacceptable in public writing. Errors like "He don't qualify for the job" or "Me and her went to school together" jar readers' sensibilities, distracting them from *what* the writing is saying to *how* the writer is saying it. Such conspicuous lapses can seriously damage the writer's credibility. The frustrated reader reacts with negative responses like "This writer is either badly educated or unbelievably sloppy" or "I don't see how the person who wrote this ever got through school." Writers who cause that reaction in their readers damage their case before they even get through presenting it.

But how can you know which mistakes are relatively minor and which do real damage? Well, you can't always know for sure, of course—mistakes that don't bother some readers can offend other, more particular, ones. Nevertheless, a survey I did in 1980 and a follow-up survey I did with a colleague in 1987 have shown quite clearly that there is a hierarchy of errors, and one can determine which are the most damaging and which are comparatively minor. You will find a scale constructed from those surveys and a discussion of the results in Chapter 10.

Writers also need to pay close attention to their spelling and realize that some mistakes are more costly than others. Probably few readers will get too upset is you misspell *personnel* or *harassment,* but many readers will be outraged if you write *thare* for *their* or *no* for *know.* A surprising number of people get irrationally irritated by bad spelling, making quick judgments that the poor speller is incompetent or ignorant. Of course, that's not a fair judgment. Many educated, published writers are not good spellers, at least not when they're writing drafts. They have learned how to correct their spelling. If you know you are a chronically bad speller, you'll need to take whatever steps you must to correct your spelling before you turn in any paper for public consumption. It's worth the extra care; poor spelling simply costs too much. In Chapter 10 I'll give you several suggestions about ways to check and improve your spelling.

THOSE FINAL TOUCHES

Vigor

You sometimes hear an author's writing described as "strong" or "vigorous," and in a tone that makes it obvious that those terms are complimentary. They are terms that are easier to illustrate than to define, but in general they mean that a writer chooses words that show the readers what is happening through active verbs and clear images, that he or she uses specific examples and striking metaphors to get ideas across, that the writing is concrete, direct, and efficient. It moves along like a person walking vigorously and confidently toward a goal. It's a quality that you can almost count on finding in the writing of first-rate journalists and essayists like Stephen Jay Gould, William Raspberry, Nora Ephron, or Anna Quindlen, and in the oral essays of television commentators like Alistair Cooke or Leslie Stahl. Here is an example from Joan Didion:

> We have reached a certain understanding, my migraine and I. It never comes when I am in real trouble. Tell me my house is burned down, my husband has left me, there is gunfighting in the streets and panic in the banks, and I will not respond by getting a headache. It comes instead when I am fighting not an open but a guerilla war with my own life, during weeks of small household confusions, lost laundry, unhappy help, canceled appointments, on days when the telephone rings too much and I get no work done and the wind is coming up. On days like that my friend comes uninvited.
> —Joan Didion, "In Bed," *The White Album* (New York: Simon & Schuster, 1979).

Authentic Voice

In good writing the reader can sense the *presence* of the writer behind what he or she is reading. The writer's character comes through the writing and makes the reader feel that a real person is trying to communicate ideas and information. The writing does not seem fake or canned or put together by formula. The reader feels that he or she is actually engaging with another person's mind. Writing that has an authentic voice gives you the feeling that only the writer could have written that particular piece—it is distinctive and original. For example, here is the opening paragraph of a student paper that projects a strong and authentic voice:

> A water shortage in Texas? The very thought is difficult to imagine in a state where thousands of farmers depend on irrigation. But when a blistering heat wave struck the state in the summer of '80, Texans were flooded with news about yet another rapidly disappearing resource. No, not oil, copper, zinc, or uranium, but a resource much more important to Texas and far too often taken for granted: an unpolluted supply of water.

Writers are certainly more likely to project an authentic voice in their writing when they care about their topic, but you don't have to be passionate about your topic to sound genuine and knowledgeable. You can communicate your authentic voice by referring to your personal experience and special expertise, by using specific examples to support your generalizations, and by trying to make your writing concrete, straightforward, and personal rather than abstract and impersonal.

EXERCISES

1. Rank each of the following four paragraphs on a scale of one to ten (*one* = excellent, *ten* = terrible), using as your criteria the qualities *significance, clarity, unity, economy, acceptable usage,* and *vigor.* Give the reasons for your rankings.

   A. Airbags are thought by many to be a miracle device which would tend to give many drivers a false sense of security against injury. This would tend to make them less alert and therefore less competent drivers. There are today already far too many incompetent drivers on the road, and a false sense of security would tend to make the situation even worse. It is far safer to have a good driver who can avoid accidents than a bad driver who will cause accidents, but has equipment which will hopefully save him from serious injury or death. Another safety problem with airbags is that in tests, for one reason or another, they have been known to inflate when there was no collision. It is impossible to control a car with an inflated airbag in it, so this would likely cause a collision.

   —student paragraph

   B. Ronnie Prado graduated from high school two years ago and went to work for a small construction company. His weekly paycheck of $180 seemed like a lot of money. He bought a new color television set and a

stereo on credit. The monthly payments were only $65—chicken feed. With all the money he had saved during school, he bought a good used truck. Nice apartment, some new clothes—everything fell into place. In November Ronnie had an accident with his truck. He hadn't insured it against collision, so it cost him a month's pay just to get it running again. The new year brought an increase in his rent of $40 a month. His grocery bill had jumped another $20 a month in the past year. Gasoline was half again as much as it was when he bought the truck, and he often had to drive fifteen or twenty miles to a construction site. By March the Friendly Finance Company had repossessed his television and stereo. The rent was ten days past due, he had no money in the bank, and his girlfriend was talking about marriage. His credit rating was shot. So Ronnie sold the truck, married the girl, and now lives with her parents.
—student paragraph

C. One holds the knife as one holds the bow of a cello or a tulip—by the stem. Not palmed or gripped nor grasped, but lightly, with the tips of the fingers. The knife is not for pressing. It is for drawing across the field of skin. Like a slender fish, it waits, at the ready, then go! It darts, followed by a fine wake of red. Even now, after so many times, I still marvel at its power—cold, gleaming, silent. More, I am still struck with a kind of dread that it is I in whose hand the blade travels, that my hand is its vehicle, that yet again the terrible steel-bellied thing and I have conspired for a most unnatural purpose, the laying open of the body of a human being.
—Richard Selzer, "The Knife," *Mortal Lessons* (New York: Simon and Schuster, 1976), 92.

D. The combination of reasonably reliable contraception controlled by women and their increased economic independence has fundamentally and probably forever altered a broad pattern of sociosexual life rooted in our evolutionary history. For all the vast impact of what we have built around us, more significant still is the effect of the industrialization of our bodies—of having gained control of our reproductive inner tissues as we have of our productive outer world. And while the most visible and active expression of this has been feminism and the social changes with which it is associated, there are other underlying family and reproductive patterns that are becoming discernable also, to which *The Redulant Male* and *Making Babies* guides us in rather different but related ways.
—Lionel Tiger, "Is Sex Necessary? Possible? Fun?" in *The New York Times*, 23 June, 1985, 10.

2. How comparatively readable are these examples from advanced writing students' papers?

A. Recently the President of the University proposed to the Board of Regents that student counseling services be discontinued because of a lack of funds. We students, as a body, need to express our concern over this important development. Throughout our lives we have had and will have need for councelling of some sort. Parents raised us as children, guidance councelors listened to us in high school, and friends will help us as we get older. College is a phase in which we have certain needs. Counceling is one of them. We must all become aware of how vital this service is to us here at school.

B. Today in the world there are more than 200 breeds of dogs and these can further be divided into six groups. Dogs perform a variety of services to the community. They have the intelligence and also the ability to bond with humans. It enables them to help us in different tasks. One such group is the "working dogs" which do many of these tasks for man. Dogs are helpful to many individuals in our society and are becoming more than just a household pet.

C. In bicycle racing, it takes much more than physical exertion to place well consistently. At the pro level, all racers have excellent fitness. Those who most often succeed must go beyond that. They must know when to exert. They must know when not to. They must know how to cruise to minimize effort. And they must know how to relax during times of less than full effort. The whole game revolves around who has been best able to conserve his energy, using it only in controlled bursts to keep them in contention or to take advantage of a competitor's weakness.

3. Reread the three student paragraphs in Exercise 2 above. How strong a voice do you think each one projects? Do you find it authentic? Does the writer seem to be talking about something he or she knows and cares about? If so, how is that impression conveyed? If not, what goes wrong?

4. Clip and bring to class a column from the opinion/editorial page of your local or campus newspaper, one that you think is well written and interesting. Some typical writers might be William Raspberry, George Will, Marianne Means, or a local columnist who is well known. Working in a group with two or three other students, each student should read his or her column aloud and point out what he or she likes about it. Compare opinions and discuss what qualities seem to characterize good writing of this kind.

SUGGESTED WRITING ASSIGNMENT

Write an informative and/or persuasive essay on an aspect of some topic that you find interesting and on which you have already done some reading or discussed with someone—perhaps an issue you are studying in another class, such as censorship in art, the high cost of television campaigns, or obesity in children. Approximate length should be four to six double-spaced pages (1,000 to 1,500 words). Select a publication in which you might get such an essay published and write its name under the title of your essay. Some possibilities could be *Parade Magazine, Newsweek,* or *Health Today.* Here are some possible topics:

1. What constitutes sexual harassment in a specific situation, for example between men and women workers on a construction job, between student and instructor, in a professional situation such as doctor/patient or client/therapist. What should be done in such a situation? Why? Possible places to publish: *Cosmopolitan* or *Working Woman.*

2. Using your own high school experience as a source, identify one or two characteristics of a secondary school system that you think can help students do well. Why are those positive characteristics and how do you think they can be fostered in our school system? Possible places to publish: *Reader's Digest* or *Change* (a magazine for educators).

3. Identify an American-made movie or a popular television show you have seen recently and analyze and discuss how it portrays a segment of American society. What influence might the movie or television show have on its viewers? Possible places to publish: *Premiere* or in the media section of *Time.*

3 ◇ What Happens When People Write?

Many people who have trouble writing believe that writing is a mysterious process that the average person cannot master. They assume that anyone who writes well does so because of a magic mixture of talent and inspiration, and that people who are not lucky enough to have those gifts can never become writers. Thus they take an "either you have it or you don't" attitude that discourages them before they even start to write.

Like most myths, this one has a grain of truth in it, but only a grain. Admittedly the best writers are people with talent just as the best musicians or athletes or chemists are people with talent. But that qualification does not mean that only talented people can write well any more than it means that only a few gifted people can become good tennis players. Tennis coaches know differently. From experience, they know any reasonably well-coordinated and healthy person can learn to play a fairly good game of tennis if he or she will learn the principles of the game and work at putting them into practice. They help people become tennis players by showing them the strategies that experts use and by giving them criticism and reinforcement as they practice those strategies. In recent years, as we have learned more about the processes of working writers, many teachers have begun to work with their writing students in the same way.

AN OVERVIEW OF THE WRITING PROCESS

How Professional Writers Work

- Most writers don't wait for inspiration. They write whether they feel like it or not. Usually they write on a schedule, putting in regular hours just as they would on a job.

25

- Professional writers consistently work in the same places with the same tools—pencil, typewriter, or word processor. The physical details of writing are important to them so they take trouble to create a good writing environment for themselves.
- Successful writers work constantly at observing what goes on around them and have a system for gathering and storing material. They collect clippings, keep notebooks, or write in journals.
- Even successful writers need deadlines to make them work, just like everyone else.
- Successful writers make plans before they start to write, but they keep their plans flexible, subject to revision.
- Successful writers usually have some audience in mind and stay aware of that audience as they write and revise.
- Most successful writers work rather slowly; four to six double-spaced pages is considered a good day's work.
- Even successful writers often have trouble getting started; they expect it and don't panic.
- Successful writers seldom know precisely what they are going to write before they start, and they plan on discovering at least part of their content as they work. (See section below on explanatory and exploratory writing.)
- Successful writers stop frequently to reread what they've written and consider such rereading an important part of the writing process.
- Successful writers revise as they write and expect to do two or more drafts of anything they write.
- Like ordinary mortals, successful writers often procrastinate and feel guilty about it; unlike less experienced writers, however, most of them have a good sense of how long they can procrastinate and still avoid disaster.

Explanatory and Exploratory Writing

Several variables affect the method and speed with which writers work—how much time they have, how important their task is, how skilled they are, and so on. The most important variable, however, is the kind of writing they are doing. I am going to focus on two major kinds here: *explanatory* and *exploratory*. To put it briefly, although much too simply, explanatory writing *tends* to be about information; exploratory writing *tends* to be about ideas.

Explanatory writing can take many forms: a movie review, an explanation of new software, an analysis of historical causes, a report on a recent political development, a biographical sketch. These are just a few possibilities. The distinguishing feature of all these examples and other kinds of explanatory writing is that the writer either knows most of what he or she is going to say before starting to write or knows where to find the material needed to get started. A typical explanatory essay might be on some aspect of global warming for an environmental studies course. The material for such a paper already exists—you're not going to create it or discover it within your subconscious. Your job as a writer is to dig out the material, organize it, and shape it into a clearly written, carefully supported essay. Usually you would know who your readers are for an explanatory essay and, from the beginning, shape it for that audience.

Writers usually make plans when they are doing explanatory writing, plans that can range from a page of notes to a full outline. Such plans help them to keep track of their material, put it in some kind of order, and find a pattern for presenting it. For explanatory writing, many writers find that the traditional methods work well; assertion/support, cause and effect, process, compare/contrast, and so on. Much of the writing that students do in college is explanatory, as is much business writing. Many magazine articles and nonfiction books are primarily explanatory writing. It's a crucially important kind of writing, one that we depend on for information and education, one that keeps the machinery of business and government going.

Explanatory writing is not necessarily easy to do nor is it usually formulaic. It takes skill and care to write an accurate, interesting story about the physician who won a Nobel Prize for initiating kidney transplants or an entertaining and informative report on how the movie *Dick Tracy* was made. But the process for explanatory writing is manageable. You identify the task, decide what the purpose and who the audience are, map out a plan for finding and organizing information, then divide the writing itself into doable chunks and start working. Progress may be painful, and you may have to draft and revise several times to clarify points or get the tone just right, but with persistence, you can do it.

Exploratory writing may also take many forms: a reflective personal essay, a profile of a homeless family, an argument in support of funding for multimillion dollar science projects, or a speculative essay about the future of the women's movement. These are only a few possibilities. What distinguishes these examples and exploratory writing in general is that the writer has only a partially formed idea of what he or she is going to write before starting. A typical piece of exploratory writing might be a speculative essay on why movies about the Mafia appeal so much to the American public. You might hit on the idea of writing such a piece after you have seen several mob movies—*Goodfellas*, *Miller's Crossing*, and *Godfather III*—but not really know what you would say or who your audience would be. The material for such a paper doesn't exist; you would have to begin by read-ing, talking to people, and by drawing on the ideas and insights you've gleaned from different sources to reach your own point of view. And you would certainly expect some of your most important ideas—your own conclusions—to come to you as you wrote.

Because you don't know ahead of time exactly what you're going to say in exploratory writing, it's hard to make a detailed plan or outline; however, you can and should take copious notes as you prepare to write. You might be able to put down a tentative thesis sentence, for example, "Americans moviegoers are drawn to movies about the Mafia and mob vi-olence because they appeal to a streak of lawlessness that has always been strong in the American character." Such a sentence could be an anchor to get you started writing, but as a main idea, it could change or even disap-pear as the paper developed.

Many papers you write in college will be exploratory papers, for exam-ple, an interpretive paper in a literature course, an essay on the future of an ethnic community for a cultural anthropology course, or an argumentative paper for a government course proposing changes in our election laws. Many magazine articles and books are also exploratory, for example, an ar-ticle on the roots of violence in American cities or an autobiographical ac-count of being tagged a "slow learner" early in one's school career. Both in and out of college, exploratory writing is as important as explanatory writ-ing because it is the springboard and testing ground for new ideas.

Exploratory writing isn't necessarily harder to do than explanatory writing, but it is harder to plan because it resists any systematic approach. That makes it appeal to some writers, particularly those who have a reflec-tive or speculative turn of mind. They like the freedom of being able just to write to see what is going to develop. But although exploratory writers start out with more freedom, eventually they too have to discipline them-selves to organize their writing into clear, readable form. They also have to realize that exploratory writing usually takes longer and requires more drafts.

When you're doing exploratory writing, anticipate that your process will be messy. You have to tolerate uncertainty longer because ideas keep coming as you write and it's not always clear what you're going to do with them and how—or if—you can fit them into your paper. Exploratory writ-ing is also hard to organize—sometimes you'll have to outline *after* you've written your first draft in order to get the paper under control. Finally, you also have to have confidence in your own instincts; now that you are fo-cusing on ideas and reflections more than on facts, you have to believe that you have something worth writing about and that other people are inter-ested in reading it.

Of course, not all writing can be easily classified as either explanatory or exploratory; sometimes you'll be working with information and ideas in the same paper and move from presenting facts to reflecting about their implications. For example, in an economics course you might report on how much Japan has invested in the United States economy over the last decade and where those investments have been made; then you could speculate about the long-range impact on American business. If you were writing a case study of a teenage mother for a social work class, you would use mostly explanatory writing to document the young woman's background, schooling, and important facts about her present situation; then you could go to exploratory writing to suggest how her options for the future can be improved.

In general, readers respond best to writing that thoughtfully connects facts to reflections, explanations to explorations. So don't hesitate to mix the two kinds of writing if it makes your paper stronger and more interesting. At this point, you might ask "Why do these distinctions matter to me?" I think there are several reasons.

First, it helps to realize that there isn't *a* writing process—there are writing *processes*, and some work better than others in specific situations. Although by temperament and habit you may be the "just give me the facts, ma'am," kind of person who prefers to do explanatory writing, you also need to become proficient at exploratory writing in order to write the speculative, reflective papers that are necessary when you have to write about long-range goals or speculate about philosophical issues. If, on the other hand, by temperament you'd rather ignore outlines and prefer to spin theories instead of report on facts, you also need to become proficient at explanatory writing. In almost any profession, you're going to have to write reports, summarize data, or present results of research.

Second, you'll become a more proficient and relaxed writer if you develop the habit of analyzing before you start, whether you are going to be doing primarily explanatory or exploratory writing. Once you decide, you can consciously switch into certain writing patterns and write more efficiently. For instance, when you're writing reports, case studies, research papers, or analyses, take the time to rough out an outline and make a careful list of the main points you need to make. Schedule time for research and checking facts; details are going to be important. Review some of the routine but useful patterns you could use to develop your paper: cause and effect, definition, process, narration, and so forth. They can work well when you have a fairly clear idea of your purpose and what you're going to say.

If you're starting on a less clearly defined, more open-ended paper—for example, a reflective essay about Picasso's portrayal of women for an art history course—allow yourself to be less organized for a while. Be willing to start without knowing where you're going. Look at some paintings to get your ideas flowing, talk to some other students, and then just start writing, confident that you'll find your content and your direction. Don't worry if you can't get the first paragraph right—it will come later. Your first goal with exploratory writing should be to generate a fairly complete first draft in order to give yourself something to work with. Remember to give yourself plenty of time to revise. You'll need it.

Finally, resist the idea that one kind of writing is better than another. It's not. Sometimes there's a tendency, particularly in liberal arts classes, to believe that people who do theoretical or reflective writing are superior; that exploratory writing is loftier and more admirable than writing in which people present facts and argue for concrete causes. That's not really the case. Imaginative, thoughtful writing about theories and opinions is important and interesting, but informative, factual writing is also critically important, and people who can do it well are invaluable. Anyone who hopes to be an effective, confident writer should cultivate the habits that enable him or her to do both kinds of writing well.

THE STAGES OF WRITING

When professional writers write, they seem to go through the same stages that creative people in other fields do: preparation, incubation, illumination and execution, and verification. In writing, the stages look like this:

- *Preparation*: Gathering material and making plans.
- *Incubation*: Allowing a period for rest and reflection.
- *Illumination and execution*: Drafting, rethinking, and revising material.
- *Editing*: Checking and modifying final draft, proofreading.

Such a brief summary makes writing look like a neater and more linear process than it really is. Writing is often a messy *recursive* process in which writers move back and forth from one stage to the other—planning, drafting, rereading, revising, stopping to reflect, and writing again. They may loop through the steps of the process several times, particularly when they are doing exploratory writing. Nevertheless, writers do work in stages, and it is useful to try to understand what goes on in each stage.

PREPARATION

Preparation for writing divides into two parts: *preliminary* and *immediate*. The preliminary part includes all the writer's experiences, reflections, and activities before he or she begins to write. One way to describe that accumulation would be to call it everything a writer has stored on his or her mental disk. The immediate part of preparation is working with a battery of strategies to access and use the data on the disk.

Stocking the Bank

Before a writer begins to write, his or her mind acts like a computer, gathering and storing a variety of information from books, television, work,

Hypothetical Diagram of the Writing Process: Preparation Stage

Preliminary Unfocused Activity	Travel, reading, movies, television specials, other classes, sports, hobbies, work, etc. Keeping notebook.
	Mental antennae are out receiving signals from whole environment. Subconscious is storing material.

↑   ↓   ↑

Discovery: Stage 1	Identification of writing task: analyzing audience and purpose.
	Brainstorming Narrowing the topic by subdividing it Freewriting Asking questions: Who? What? When? Where? Why? How? General Research/ Serendipity
	Subconscious is storing excess material

↑   ı   ↑

Narrowing focus and increasing intellectual energy

ı   ↓   ı

Discovery: Stage 2	Taking specific notes
	Collecting material through research and interviews. Thinking of useful analogies. Finding supporting material.
	Choosing preliminary method of organization: outlining, list, thesis sentence and tentative title. Write trial opening paragraph.

social gatherings, political activities, personal interactions—everything and anything. Those data go into a bank and lie there waiting to be tapped. No one should assume, however, that once the data bank is stocked it can be ignored until the writer needs it. As you draw on it for ideas and examples, you have to keep replenishing it by continually paying attention to everything that goes on around you as well as what goes on *within* you—insights, analogies, connections. Keep a notebook or cards with you all the time and try to develop an intellectual antenna or radar probe with which you continually sweep your environment and notice everything that is happening. Form the habit of looking for new experiences and new information and try to be a person on whom nothing is lost.

Writing More about Less

Once you know what your specific writing task is going to be and you have chosen a topic or had one assigned, it's a good idea to start by thinking how you are going to limit that topic. As indicated earlier, trying to do too much in a paper is one of the major pitfalls of even experienced writers; therefore, you need strategies for narrowing and focusing your topic. One strategy is just to start writing and generate a quantity of material that you can then sift through to find the portion on which you want to focus. But that's a slow and often inefficient process. A better way to narrow your topic is to "tree it down"; that is, write your topic at the top of the page, then divide and subdivide it into progressively smaller units until you arrive at one that interests you and seems manageable. Then you can divide that again to find specifics that will help you develop your paper.

For example, a student who wanted to write a paper for college women on poor methods of weight control treed her topic down like this (see p. 33 for a copy of her actual worksheet):

POOR METHODS OF WEIGHT CONTROL

Crash diets
   Fasting
   Water diets
   High-protein diets
   Special food diets, e.g., grapefruit
   The Hollywood Diet
   Liquid protein diets
External methods
   Passive exercise
   Body wraps
   Massage

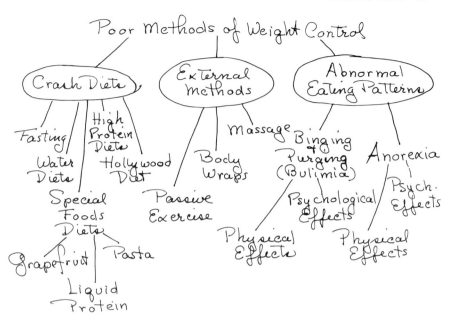

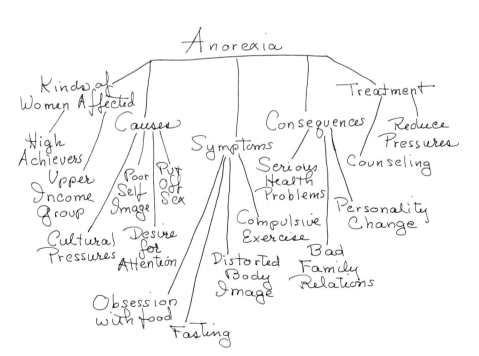

Abnormal eating patterns
    Bingeing and purging (bulimia)
Physical effects
Psychological effects
    Anorexia

She decided to write about anorexia because she had a friend who suffered from it and could use her experiences as an example. Once she focused on anorexia, she treed it down like this and generated a rough outline for her paper:

ANOREXIA

Kinds of women affected
    Upper income/higher social classes
    High achievers/perfectionists
Causes
    Cultural pressures to be thin
    Desire for attention
    Poor self-image/need for approval
    Desire to postpone sexuality
Symptoms
    Obsession with food
    Distorted image of body
    Compulsive exercise
    Fasting to the point of starvation
Consequences
    Serious health impairment, sometimes death
    Drastic personality changes
    Adverse effect on family relationships
Treatment
    Extensive counseling
    Reduce family and social pressures

Here is another example of narrowing a topic. This time the writer wanted to write a paper on computers in education. He started by subdividing like this (see p. 35 for his worksheet):

COMPUTERS IN EDUCATION

College
    Computer science courses
    Tools for science courses
    Drill and practice in language courses

Computers in Education

College   Secondary Schools

Computer   Word   Possible
Science   Tools   Recycling   over emphasis
          for   Promoting   by Media
          Science   Computer   Use in
          Courses   Literacy   Math +
                                       Science
               Drill in   Teaching
               Language   Programming
               Courses

Individual
Micro computers
for Students

Are Computers Being Overemphasized in Our Schools?

Limitations   Limitations   Limitations   Cost
    of   of   of
Computer Use   Current   Faculty
                Software
                            Present   Expensive
Drill   Courses   teachers   to
 +   in   untrained   equip   Bad for
Practice Comp.   schools   disad-
         Sciences   Few   New   vantaged
Writing   Tested   faculty   students
Instructions   Programs   scarce
         Elementary   Software
Writing Programming development   Discrepancies
Skills   behind   among
Center   schedule   schools
     Introducing   Can't furnish
     students   to all students
     to word
     Processing

Registration and record keeping
Word processing
Individual microcomputers for students
Secondary schools
Promoting computer literacy among students
Use in math and science courses
Teaching programming
Possible overemphasis by media and educators

Several of the subtopics looked interesting to him, but he decided to focus on whether the role of computers in schools was being overemphasized by the press and educators. He treed that down like this:

ARE COMPUTERS BEING OVEREMPHASIZED IN OUR SCHOOLS?

Limitations of computer use
Drill and practice in science, math, languages
Elementary programming
Courses in computer science and programming
Writing instructions
Writing-skills centers
Introducing students to word processing
Limitations of current software
Comparatively few tested programs available
Software development far behind promised schedules
Limitations of faculty
Present teachers untrained in computer use
New teachers hard to get
Cost
Expensive to equip schools adequately
Problems of discrepancies in money among districts.
Prohibitively expensive to provide computers for all students
Too much emphasis puts disadvantaged students even further be-
hind

He chose to focus on the cost of computers and their limited applications and to write a paper cautioning administrators not to let themselves be rushed into overemphasizing computers in their schools.

Identifying Your Audience and Purpose

When you think you have your topic narrowed to a manageable size, you're ready to consider two central questions: *Who is my audience?* and

What is my purpose? At this early stage, you may be able to give only pre-liminary answers, but you still need to decide what you want to do with your topic and for whom you're writing. Unless you have some idea, it's going to be hard to focus your paper.

Keeping your audience in mind as you write may be the single most im-portant ability you develop as a writer. Your choices about vocabulary, tone, style, focus, length—everything—depend on who you assume your readers are going to be. Often the chief handicap of writers who work hard but show little improvement is that they don't seem to be able to shape their writing with a specific group of readers in mind. As long as they have only a hazy idea who their readers are, their writing is apt to lack the sharp focus and specific details that characterize good writing.

I'll have much more specific advice about adapting your writing to suit your readers in subsequent chapters.

Discovering Ideas and Accessing Information

As a model topic to illustrate these strategies I will be using a hypothetical proposal to create a university-sponsored day-care center on the campus of an urban university.

BRAINSTORMING

Brainstorming is a quick method of generating a body of material that a writer can use for stimulus. Two principles govern brainstorming: one idea piggybacks on another, and in brainstorming there are no wrong answers.

You can brainstorm by yourself or with other people working on the same project. Often a group is more productive.

The techniques for brainstorming are simple. Using a typewriter, pen-cil, tape recorder, or your computer, concentrate on your topic and start writing down everything that comes into your head, no matter how extrav-agant or irrelevant it may seem. Don't worry about any of the niceties—just write or, if you're in a group, talk and take notes. After fifteen or twenty minutes you should have a wealth of material. You'll have to dis-card or store some of it, but you've begun to generate your paper.

FREEWRITING

Many writers also find *freewriting* a productive strategy for generating ideas. Start by writing out your topic on a piece of paper or your terminal screen; then start writing anything that comes into your head about that topic. Don't try to plan or organize and certainly don't stop to correct any-thing. Think of the process as *harvesting* the fruits of both your conscious

Campus day-care center

Faculty women
Peace of mind
Close to kids
    Save money
for young professors

Students
Lots of women coming
back to school

Universities & businesses have exercise
facilities so why not day care?
  Just as important to employers,
Would pay off
    Lower absenteeism   Increased
    Healthy children   divorce rate
                           single parents —

Other Countries   Women's Lib Angle

Israel ← get   Gives women chance
Sweden   figures   to upgrade skills
France   here
                         Makes up for past
                           discrimination

Objections

Cost?   Good for fathers too—
Unions?   they have to worry about
Family   child care
  interference?
                         What would U. admin-
                         istration probably say?

                         Not U's business —

mind and your subconscious—as you reap what your mind has generated, more will push through to the surface. The important thing is to keep writing and harvesting ideas, so don't stop to worry about details such as finding the right word. If you do, you may interrupt a potentially rich crop of ideas that you are nourishing. If you get stuck, just write down anything that comes to your mind—nonsense words if necessary. Keep your brain moving and soon it will begin to produce again.

You can freewrite for ten or fifteen minutes at a time or you can play around for an hour or more. When I am just beginning on a serious piece of writing, I will often stay at the word processor and try to freewrite as long as I can, perhaps getting up to take short breaks, but staying with it until I think I have exhausted my available resources for the time. Peter Elbow, the teacher who introduced the idea of freewriting in a book called *Writing Without Teachers*, suggests that after a short session of freewriting —perhaps fifteen minutes—the writer should stop to sum up in one sentence the main point of the section just completed. Elbow calls that summary sentence "the center-of-gravity." Then you can start writing again, using that center-of-gravity sentence as the take-off point for your next freewriting session. You can continue this way until you think you have generated enough material.

Freewriting can be a particularly rich discovery strategy because it helps writers to take advantage of those flashes of inspiration that most of us occasionally feel when we are writing. We know that to some extent, we are going to find out what we want to say *as* we write, yet trying to write a complete paper from start to finish by relying on inspiration can produce disastrous results. With freewriting, you can reap the benefits of writing-as-discovery but avoid the risk.

USING COMPUTER INVENTION PROGRAMS

If your college has computers available in its writing lab or skills center, try them out. Many writing labs have what they call *invention* or *discovery* programs available to help writers generate ideas about their topics. In most of these programs you can insert the topic you want to write about and the program will ask you a series of questions to get you thinking about the possibilities of your topic. For instance, on the day-care center topic, it might ask, "Who is interested in a day-care center?" "Who would benefit by a day-care center?" or "What are the arguments against a day-care center?" After each question, write down all the answers that occur to you. Some programs have fifty or more questions—you can skip over any question that isn't relevant—so when you've worked your way through the questions, you should have generated an abundance of material. Print out the answers and you'll have a stock of ideas as resources for your paper.

These programs are entirely mechanical, of course. The computer will ask the same questions whether your topic is peanut butter or the greenhouse effect, and it will help you generate good material only if *you* give serious thought to your answers. But if you approach the questions as the kind of requests for information that a friend might make, an invention program can be a great help in getting you started.

ASKING THE JOURNALIST'S QUESTIONS

Another reliable discovery strategy is to ask the questions that journalists frequently rely on when they are working on an article. Those questions are

Who?
What?
Why?
Where?
When?
How?

Writing out the answers to these questions about your topic can help you put together a framework of assertions that will outline the main points you want to make.

Although a critical reader would quickly realize that this kind of inquiry often yields oversimplified answers, the process can provide the take-off points needed for research or more focused and intensive thinking.

MODEL TOPIC: *Using reporters' questions*

Who: University president and board of regents.
What: Establish a quality day-care center on campus for children of faculty and students.
Why: Increase enrollment, attract better faculty, improve student and faculty productivity.
When: As soon as possible.
Where: Local university.
How: Appoint a director to start the center and appropriate $1.2 million to finance it.

RESEARCHING YOUR TOPIC

If you have a fairly good idea what your topic is going to be and the angle you are going to take on it, one good way to begin generating material is to start doing research. You can begin with the traditional kind of library research such as looking for articles in periodicals or entries in specialized encyclopedias or you can take more direct steps such as interviewing people or visiting institutions or organizations connected to the topic.

For example, if you wanted to write on the model topic of establishing a day-care center on a university campus, you could check to see if anyone has written an article about a center on some campus or if the concept is being discussed. Some good places to look would be in a journal like *The Chronicle of Higher Education* or in a magazine published for university administrators. Your librarians can show you how to find such journals. You could also call other universities in your area to find out if any of them have started day-care centers and, if so, whether you could visit them.

You might also call the department of home economics or the school of social work at your school to find out whether some faculty members are particularly interested in issues about day care; if they are, you could go talk to them. You could also inquire whether any major industries in your city—perhaps IBM or Motorola—furnish on-site day-care centers for their employees. If so, you could interview people connected with such centers to find out how the centers work and what problems they face. Just getting out and doing something connected with your topic will start ideas flowing and help you get started writing.

CULTIVATING SERENDIPITY

In the long run, your most productive discovery strategy may be cultivating *serendipity*, the faculty of finding good things that you aren't really looking for, apparently by accident. But serendipity is more than simple luck; it is a developed ability to stay alert for unexpected opportunities and be aware of what is going on at the fringes of your consciousness so you pick up the chance remark or unexpected event. It is the habit of being places where things happen and talking to people who turn out to know something useful. It is the habit of having your intellectual antennae always tuned to pick up signals. The more mentally active you are, the more interests you have, and the more curious you are, the more likely you are to develop serendipity. And then the happy accidents that seem to happen so often to creative and productive people will begin to happen to you.

Organizing Material

Most writers need to make some plans before they start to write. Writers' plans, however, are as individualistic as authors themselves, and no one should try to prescribe how anyone else should organize his or her writing.

Some writers love outlines, others hate them. For instance, John McPhee, an acclaimed nonfiction writer often published in *The New Yorker*, constructs elaborate and detailed outlines before he starts to write. He makes copious notes, then cuts them up and arranges them on a bulletin board in the form of an outline. He says that as he does so, the ghost of his high school English teacher smiles upon him. On the other hand, Jacques Barzun, another well-regarded author and educator, says in his book *On Writing, Editing, and Publishing,* "For my taste, outlines are useless, fettering, imbecile."[1] Both writers do what works for them, and so should you. There are, however, some useful methods of organization that you might consider after you have generated a substantial amount of material.

OUTLINING ON PAPER OR ON SCREEN

One method is the traditional sentence outline. Writers who like outlines say that they help them classify their material and keep track of the main points they want to make. If you are the kind of person who likes to classify and label, then outlining in sentences may work well for you.

MODEL TOPIC: *Traditional outline*

I. Introduction: the growing number of women faculty and women students at universities raises the issue of day-care facilities on campuses.
   A. Returning women students often cannot afford to come to school full time if they have children.
   B. Women faculty with children cannot teach and do research if they do not have good and cheap care for their children.
II. This situation is harmful to the university.
   A. It loses potential students.
   B. Women students are distracted from their studies.
   C. Women faculty may leave the profession.
      1. They will have to choose between family and career.
      2. They will not get tenure if they do not have time for scholarship.
III. The university could take steps to remedy this situation.
   A. It could provide good child-care facilities at no cost to parents.
   B. It could subsidize off-campus child care for students and faculty.
IV. Conclusion: The university would improve its image and the quality of its faculty and student body by solving the problem of child care on campus.
   A. Industry has benefited from similar plans.
   B. The university would help women to achieve.

---

1. Jacques Barzun, *On Writing, Editing, and Publishing* (Chicago: University of Chicago Press, 1971), 11.

While you may want to write out your points in fairly complete form so the outline gives you a clear guideline, you shouldn't be fettered by strict rules that say you must use complete sentences or that if you have a point *A* you must have a point *B*—after all, the outline is only for you. This is how a sentence outline might look for the day-care topic. Remember too that once on paper an outline is not a blueprint you have to follow. It's an organizing tool that you can adapt as you need to.

If you own a computer, check to see if your word processing program has an outlining component. Such programs can make outlining easy and flexible because they enable you to revise with little effort. With a whisk of the cursor you can add a new point to a category or shift an idea from one subdivision to another; whole categories can be freely moved, expanded, or rearranged. Then, when you have generated as much material as you want in an arrangement you like, you can begin to write on-line, moving through the outline and expanding one section after another until you have produced a draft.

MODEL TOPIC: *Rough outline or list*

Need for Day-Care Center:
    students, esp. returning women
        could bring kids to campus—more efficient, less expensive
    faculty, men and women, esp. young profs.
        most likely to have young kids
        child care major concern—can't teach and do research if no child
            care
        women likely to leave profession

Advantages of on-campus center:
    Convenience
        close to classes and offices
        parents can visit children during day
    Quality
        supervision from home ec. dept.
            qualified apprentices
            child development experts
    Incentive to draw faculty and students
        Univ. would be more competitive, esp. for women
        Shows univ. concern about families and faculty/student welfare
    Research facility for child devel. courses
    Logistics of establishing center
        Use available building—seek grant money to start
        Involve school of social work and home ec.
        Set sliding scale of fees for students/faculty

ROUGH OUTLINES OR LISTS

Some writers, like Jacques Barzun, actually find formal outlines a handicap. They resist anything that limits their freedom to add new ideas and categories that may occur to them as they're working. I am that kind of writer—I resist outlines, particularly with exploratory writing, because I believe they can force me to a conclusion before I am ready for it. Nevertheless, I need to work out some kind of plan as I generate material, and I make a rough outline reminding me of what I *think* I am going to say. Barzun favors what he calls "a memorandum listing haphazardly what belongs to a particular project." That is, he draws up a kind of chart grouping similar points together and listing main ideas in roughly the order he wants to put them down. Here is how such a chart might look for the model topic about an on-campus day-care center.

TITLES AND THESIS SENTENCES

Often choosing a working title for your paper will give you a starting point; a way to focus your writing, point you in the direction you want to take, and remind you of what you are promising your readers.

You may also find it useful to try that old reliable tool, an organizing thesis sentence—it can work particularly well for explanatory papers,

---

MODEL TOPIC: *Possible titles and thesis sentences*

Titles:

The Benefits of a Campus Day-Care Center

Better Child Care for University Students and Faculty

Quality Child Care for a Quality University

Thesis Sentences:

Alternative 1: If the university were to sponsor and subsidize a high-quality, on-campus day-care center for its students and faculty, it would make it possible for more women to enroll in courses, enable them to do better work, and provide an incentive that would help to attract and keep the best young faculty in the country.

Alternative 2: A university-sponsored and subsidized day-care center on campus would benefit the university in several ways: it would provide an incentive for young faculty to come to the university because they would be assured good care for their children; it would allow more women to enroll in courses because they would know that their children were well cared for while they were on campus; it would create goodwill for the university among women's groups and provide a model facility for other organizations to emulate for other local institutions.

---

where you have a fairly good idea of what you want to say before you start. A good thesis sentence can act as a capsule statement of your main points and put them in logical order for you. If you're going to depend on a thesis sentence as your main organizing device, spend the extra effort to work out one that is inclusive and substantial; a skimpy one really isn't worth your time. Remember too that you don't have to include the actual sentence in your paper—it's a tool, not an introduction.

INCUBATION

Allowing Idle Time

Many inexperienced writers don't realize how important it is to allow themselves some idle time when they are writing—or engaging in any creative process, for that matter. After you have done all your preparations to write a paper, you may still have a hard time getting started. You may be pushing too hard and would do better to do something else for a while and let the material you have accumulated just "cook"—or incubate—in your subconscious.

People who study and write about the creative process believe that when scientists, architects, engineers, artists, or other kinds of creative people seem to stop working for certain periods of time, they are not idle at all. Rather they are giving their minds and imaginations a necessary interval for renewal, a time that the subconscious mind must have in order to absorb, sift, and process its data and select what it needs.

We don't really know what happens during this stage. Apparently the creative part of the mind goes on a kind of fishing expedition into the subconscious, but the fishing has to be private and unsystematic. The conscious mind is not in charge here, and the only way it can help is to be receptive to any insight or idea that may surface. After a period of time—it could be hours or days—the subconscious seems to finish the process of sorting, organizing, and making connections, and finds the solution or starting point it has been looking for. When it does, the conscious mind can take over again and use its faculties to get on with the work.

Incubation doesn't happen just once or even a few times during the writing process. Like preparation, it's an ongoing process that can happen several times while you are working on a paper or article. When you begin to see incubation periods as essential to the writing process and learn to trust your subconscious to work for you, you should begin to feel more relaxed about facing even a difficult writing assignment. Take it by stages and have confidence that if you feed your subconscious with materials and nurture it with periods of relaxation, it will come through for you.

Two Important Cautions

But now, having assured you that idleness is not necessarily laziness, I will add two important cautions. First, while you are relaxing from the period of preparation and waiting for the subconscious to do its work, keep some portion of your mind alert and ready to go into action when the moment of insight strikes. You can't know whether the incubation period is going to be a few hours or two or three days, and when the insight or idea surfaces you need to seize it and write it down as soon as possible. If you don't, it can vanish almost as quickly as it came. In fact, it is a good idea to keep notecards or a pad of paper close by all the time you seem not to be thinking about your topic.

Second, don't wait indefinitely for an idea to strike. If after a reasonable length of time your subconscious still stubbornly refuses to produce what you need, put your conscious mind back on the job and try to start writing. Review your notes or your outline and run through in your mind what some of your options might be for getting started. Consciously try some of the techniques for development or just try to get out two or three paragraphs even if you are not very happy with them. The chances are good that the ideas that have been germinating beneath the surface will start to emerge and you can start actually writing your assignment.

ILLUMINATION AND EXECUTION

Creating a Writing Environment

If possible, choose a writing place that is comfortable, familiar, and relatively free from distractions, and do your writing there whenever you can. After a while, the very atmosphere of the place will encourage you to write. Try to write at a specific time and be consistent about it. People who write regularly get so they automatically think about writing at that time of day. Try to select the tools and equipment that seem to work best for you and stick with them. Most people who write regularly have their favorites —yellow pad and pencil for some, typewriter for others—and seem to think they cannot work any other way. In the last few years, many writers have changed over to writing on word processors and wonder how they ever wrote without them.

Many professional writers are compulsive about having just the right equipment and just the right environment for writing. As Jacques Barzun says,

> We know that Mark Twain liked to write lying in or on a bed; we know that Schiller needed the smell of apples rotting in his desk. Some like

cubicles, others vast halls. Writers' requisites, if a Fifth Avenue shop kept them, would astound and demoralize the laity. Historically, they have included silk dressing gowns, cats, horses, pipes, mistresses, particular knickknacks, exotic headgear, currycombs, whips, beverages and drugs, porcelain stoves, and hair shirts.[2]

Such eccentricities may seem like frivolous indulgences or displays of artistic temperament, but at the critical point when you are trying to discipline yourself into starting to write, external physical props may help. When you settle yourself in a familiar writing environment and take up your familiar tools, you give your subconscious mind the signal to start writing. The visual stimulus of the yellow paper or the hum of the typewriter—or maybe now the green characters on the terminal screen—helps to shut out distracting thoughts and put the intellectual processes in motion. Writers who are tempted to procrastinate—and that's almost any of us at times—can help overcome that temptation by creating the best possible circumstances for themselves.

Building Good Writing Habits

As a college student, you already write regularly; as a future professional, you will probably be writing even more. With that in mind, you'll do yourself a favor if you establish writing habits that will make writing easier and more productive. Professional writers all have such routines, and there's nothing mysterious about them. Mainly, they involve being consistent and organized.

- Choose a writing place that is comfortable and relatively free of distractions and do your writing there whenever you can. It doesn't have to be an idyllic setting or even a conventional one—I wrote my master's thesis sitting in a parked car with a portable typewriter on my lap to escape the phone and interruptions from the family. You may have to write at the dining room table or at a computer terminal on campus. The important thing is to get used to writing in a specific place so that when you get there your subconscious says, "Okay, we're going to write now." That message helps you to get to work.
- Set your stage for writing. If you're at home and work best with music in the background, pick out the kind that you find most congenial and turn it on. If you like to eat or chew gum while you work, be sure you have a supply on hand. If you do best if you can look out of window, situate your desk that way. In other words, pamper your-

2. Barzun, *On Writing, Editing, and Publishing*, 12.

self with those little trimmings that create a pleasant environment, and you'll be more likely to want to work.

• Try to choose a time that suits your personal rhythms and ensures you some uninterrupted chunks of time. Try to pick a time when your energy level is high and your mind is running in high gear. I and many other writers I know write best in the morning before we can get sidetracked by the demands of the day. Other writers work best late at night when the house is quiet and they can concentrate better. Again, your subconscious will say, "Oh yes, this is when we write," and be more inclined to stick to the task.

• Find a favorite set of tools and stick with them. Most writers I know now use a word processor and would break the arm of anyone who tried to take it away from them. Unquestionably, a word processor makes writing much easier and quicker than it's ever been before, and if you have access to one, I strongly recommend that you learn to use it. Most word processing programs aren't difficult. But some writers still prefer writing by hand with a yellow pad and pencil or like their old typewriters—if that's what works best for you, by all means stick with it. Again, it's important to develop those consistent patterns that your subconscious associates with writing and to give yourself the subliminal message that says "No excuses—just do it."

But having said all this, I would add a caution. Even though you'll work best if you develop a set of good habits and stick with them, sometimes having everything just right is a luxury you can't afford. Occasionally every writer has to turn to and work under unfavorable circumstances to get a job done on time. I usually write on a word processor, but I have written papers on an airplane with a pencil and legal paper. I'm very much a morning worker, but I have gone back to my desk and written at night even when I didn't want to. So if you have to take a child to the doctor at the time you planned to write or a job interview comes up at the time you hoped to finish your paper, you'll have to throw your routines aside and do the best you can. Rituals and routines can be a great help, but if you depend on them too heavily, you risk making their absence an excuse for not writing.

Overcoming Blocks

But even under the best circumstances, you may still have trouble getting started. For some interesting reasons, such blocks are not surprising.

First, you are having trouble starting to write because you don't have any writing already on the page to go back to for directional signals and guidance. Writing is a powerfully recursive activity in which writers continually read back through what they have already written, looking for clues to help them guide and control what they are going to write. That rereading seems crucial to help writers generate ideas and provide them momentum to keep going. Yet when you are just starting to write, you don't have any writing to look back at. That's why freewriting can be so important. By reading over it, you can often find sentences that will help you get started.

Second, most of us sense that beginnings are very important. As one expert puts it, what we write at the beginning of a paper lays down tracks for us to run on: once we have those tracks down, we can move much more easily, but the direction of the tracks also controls our writing.[3] Because of this we tend to take beginnings too seriously, feeling that they must be good or we'll be in trouble. But there are many good ways to begin a paper; when you're trying to get started, just get *something* down. If you can't think of anything good, lower your standards and put down something terrible. You just need some sentences to start the words flowing—later you can throw the sentences away. What matters is putting down some tracks to run on so you can work up momentum.

What you should not do is wait for inspiration to strike. If you wait until you *feel* like writing, you may never start. As the noted economist John Kenneth Galbraith has put it,

> All writers know that on some golden mornings they are touched by the wand—are on intimate terms with poetry and cosmic truth. I have experienced those moments myself. Their lesson is simple: It's a total illusion. And the danger in the illusion is that you will wait for those moments. Such is the horror of having to face the typewriter that you will spend all your time waiting. I am persuaded that most writers, like most shoemakers, are about as good one day as the next. . . , hangovers apart. The difference is the result of euphoria, alcohol, or imagination. The meaning is that one had better go to his or her typewriter every morning and stay there regardless of the seeming result. It will be much the same.
>
> —John Kenneth Galbraith, "Writing, Typing, and Economics," *Atlantic*, March 1978, 104.

If you are working on a paper over a period of days and have many interruptions, temporary paralysis is apt to set in each time you have to start over. And the longer you are away from your writing, the harder it will be

---

3. James Britton, "Shaping at the Point of Utterance," in *Reinventing the Rhetorical Tradition,* ed. A. Freeman and I. Pringle (Conway, Ark.: L & S Books, 1980).

to get started again. When that problem arises, try going back and rereading what you have already written or even rewrite the last page you did the previous time. Usually that kind of backtracking will get the creative juices flowing again.

FINDING YOUR PACE

Sprinters, Plodders, and Bleeders

Writers work at different paces, and you need to find the rhythms that suit you best. Some writers compose their first draft rapidly, spilling out a veritable torrent of words. They seem to be able to generate material almost as fast as they can think, and they are in a rush to get everything written down before they forget it. They work in spurts, writing several paragraphs very quickly, stopping occasionally to reread and think, but producing a lot of writing at one sitting. I call these writers *sprinters*. Most sprinters think of the first draft as a discovery draft. They don't stop to fuss with words or revise because they plan to write another two or three drafts.

Other writers work at a much slower pace when they are doing a first draft. They write their sentences slowly, stopping frequently to reread and to think. They change words, insert phrases, delete what they have already written, and they spend a great deal of time staring at their typewriters or terminals or chewing their pencils while they plan what they are going to say. They make major changes *as* they write. They also pace, eat, get drinks of water, and worry. I call these writers *plodders*. Plodders may take two or three hours to produce a page or two, but they usually make fewer changes on the second draft. While the plodder doesn't usually regard the completed first draft as the finished product, he or she knows that when it is done, the hardest part of the job is over. Often this kind of draft can be revised fairly quickly because so much thought has already gone into it.

A third kind of writer is the perfectionist. These writers have to do everything right the first time—think out each phrase and each sentence completely before they write it down, and change any word they are not satisfied with. They cannot leave any blanks, and they cannot go on with a new paragraph until they are completely satisfied with the one they have just written. I call this kind of writer *bleeders*. Bleeders suffer more than other writers because they agonize so over decisions, and it takes them forever to produce a piece of writing. When they do finish, however, they don't usually plan to rewrite.

You will have to experiment to find the pace that works best for you, but I recommend that you try to start out as a sprinter. The advantage of "sprinting" is that it gets you started, you get a sense of accomplishment from seeing the paper grow, and you create a text that you can start working on. Even though you may be dissatisfied with what you have produced, writing the second version will be easier. You must, however, count on rewriting. Inspired first drafts seldom do the job.

But if you are not the sprinter type, don't worry about it. Many productive writers are plodders, and some of us just have to work slowly, think out our ideas as we work, and make substantial revisions in the first draft. The progress may seem discouragingly slow, but in the long run plodders may not spend any more time achieving a finished product.

Don't, however, allow yourself to be a bleeder. Bleeders are the kind of writers most likely to develop a writer's block that will keep them from producing at all, and they are the ones most likely to miss their deadlines. Moreover, stopping too long to put one idea into precise form may make you lose the next idea, which can disappear while you are still fussing over the one that triggered it. And finally, at the distance of a day or two, that perfect document may seem much less perfect; then you'll regret the original agony. "Bleeding" has nothing to recommend it.

Postponing Corrections

Whether you are a sprinter or a plodder, put off making corrections in spelling and mechanics until you're ready to write the final copy. Although it is certainly important that you write standard English and that you punctuate your sentences and spell words correctly, don't worry about such matters while you are still composing. When you are actually writing, you have all you can handle just to get your ideas down and organize them into readable form—you shouldn't at the same time be fretting about where to put commas or whether *harass* has one or two *r*'s. You can fix such details later. Writers who begin to focus on mechanics too soon stifle their creative energies; instead of concentrating on expressing their ideas, they spend their time trying to avoid mistakes. That's not productive. Better to write first and edit later.

But the most important reason you should try to keep getting your words on paper or the screen is that *writing is a generative process*. Most writers almost never know exactly what they are going to say when they start writing, even though their writing assignment seems straightforward. Experienced writers count on material coming to them as they write, and so should you. The writing process is *not* linear—you can't expect to move smoothly from one stage to the next, tying up loose ends as you go and finishing by proofreading a completed document. And the more complex and demanding the writing task is, the more complex the process will be.

Maintaining the Creative Tension

When you are engaged in serious writing and want to do the best job that you possibly can, it is important that you try to maintain a kind of *creative tension* as you work. That is, you have to practice a kind of juggling act with yourself so that you can be, simultaneously, a writer and reader of your own work. It's a delicate balance, but a creative one.

One writer and teacher puts it this way:

> The act of writing might be described as a conversation between two workmen muttering to each other at the workbench. The self speaks, the other self listens and responds. The self proposes, the other self considers. The self makes, the other self evaluates. The two selves collaborate: a problem is spotted, discussed, defined; solutions are proposed, rejected, suggested, attempted, tested, discarded, accepted.
> —Donald Murray, "Teaching the Other Self,"
> *College Composition and Communication*
> (May 1982).

Both selves are important in the process as is the tension between the two: the self that is producing text has to learn to listen to the one that steps back from the text and evaluates it.

How much time you spend in this kind of internal dialogue and how much revising you do as a result of it depends mostly on whether you are a sprinter or a plodder. But regardless of which kind of writer you are, once you produce a completed draft of the piece you are working on, you need to give yourself a break from the tension—creative and otherwise—and to get some distance from your work. If you possibly can, put the draft aside at least overnight to allow your mind to clear and give you a fresh outlook on what you have written.

When you begin working on your second draft, give yourself a chance to get the big picture. Try to start out by taking a broad, overall view of what the paper needs rather than working through it one paragraph at a time making corrections and changes as you go. If you try to revise for everything at once, you will have to keep so many concerns in mind at once that you are liable to bog down. Instead, it's a good idea to start out by making a plan for revising and deciding on your priorities. If you don't have time to make all the changes that you would like to make, what are the most important? What does the paper need most? When you have decided that, you can work on your revising in stages and get the most for the time you have to invest.

In Chapter 6, I suggest how you might go about setting such priorities and give specific suggestions for working through different stages of revision. You should probably go ahead and read the chapter now because revising really cannot be separated from the other stages of writing.

EXERCISES

1. List the various writing tasks that people in the following professions must do:

   Engineering
   Nursing
   Banking
   Diplomatic service
   College teaching
   Business management

2. List all the experiences you have had that you might find useful in writing a paper on one of the following topics. Include experiences such as seeing movies and television shows, reading books, or hearing someone speak on the subject.

   What it means to be a premed student.
   The hazards involved in running.
   The great health-club boom.
   The growth of the fast-food industry.

3. Explore a possible topic for a paper—for example, "The Joys of Scuba Diving" or "Mountain Biking"—by asking these questions about the topic and writing out the answers:

   Who? What kind of people are participating?
   What? What is involved in the activity?
   Why? Why do they participate?
   When? When did the activity start, or when does it occur?
   Where? Where does the activity take place?
   How? How is the activity carried out, or how do the people involved act?

4. Write a 100-word summary of the main ideas you would include in a paper on one of these topics:

   Designing a personal exercise program.
   The art of buying at discount.
   Picking the right graduate school.
   Preparing to take the Law School Admission Test.

If you prefer to work from an outline instead of a summary, make an outline for the same topic.

5. Get together a group of three or four people and brainstorm for twenty minutes on one of these topics. Ask one person to be the recorder and write down every idea or suggestion that the group mentions.

Jet lag
Microwave ovens
Junk food
The Sunbelt
Defensive driving
Crash diets

SUGGESTED WRITING ASSIGNMENTS

1. The free magazines put out by airlines publish a wide variety of articles on almost every subject imaginable, for example: the psychology of wearing a tie, the art of tipping, part-time careers, coping with stress, and so on. They frequently feature articles about cities or resorts to which their airlines fly. An enterprising free-lance writer might be able to use a personal interest or hobby as the basis of a salable article for one of these magazines. Some topics are suggested below, but you could get additional ideas by thumbing through a magazine next time you fly. Your article should probably be no longer than 1,000 words unless you and your instructor decide ahead of time that you will need more to do a good job.

   Before you start to write, on a separate sheet write an analysis of your audience and purpose. First, what kind of people do you think read articles in airline magazines? What are they likely to be looking for when they read an article on the topic you have chosen? What questions would they want answered by the article? Second, why would you be writing this article? What would you hope to accomplish with your readers? Remember that articles in airline magazines are more likely to be explanatory than exploratory writing, and they are usually up-beat.

   Remember to give your article a descriptive title that will catch the readers' attention and give them a hint about what to expect.

TOPICS:

   A. The latest innovations in ski equipment.

   B. How to choose a mountain bike for touring in the West.

   C. How to find bargains when you are renting a car.

   D. Off-the-beaten-track vacations.

   E. New careers for women.

2. For the student newspaper on your campus, write a guest editorial on one of the topics given below or on a similar topic based on some controversy that has recently made headlines at your school. The editorial should be no longer than 750 words, because that is the maximum that the paper will print in the guest column, and it should include information—not just passions and opinions—that will help to enlighten your audience and persuade them that your position is valid.

On the first page, specify which portion of the paper's readers you are trying to reach—faculty and administrators make up an important part of the audience for a campus newspaper—and what characteristics they have that will affect how you phrase your argument. Also write out your purpose: what do you hope to accomplish with the editorial?

TOPICS:

   A. The issue of using foreign graduate students with a limited command of English as teaching assistants in some college departments.

   B. A recent faculty proposal to make a three-hour course in American Studies a degree requirement for your university or college.

   C. An administration proposal that starting next year each freshman student will be required to bring a personal computer to school when he or she starts college.

   D. A faculty proposal to require two courses in ethnic studies as a degree requirement for your college or university.

3. Write a review that would be published in your local campus or city paper. Read several reviews in that paper before you start and choose one that you find especially interesting; then clip that review and attach it to the draft of your paper when you hand it in. You could review a book that is currently being talked about on campus, a movie that has recently opened and is controversial, or a new television program that is getting wide attention.
   Before you start to write, analyze your audience. Who do you think reads the kind of review you are going to write? What is their purpose in reading it and what questions do you think they would expect you to answer in the review? Then write out your purpose. What goal are you trying to accomplish with your readers? How do you want them to react?
   Be sure to write an arresting headline for your review.

4 ◇ What Is Your Writing Situation?

When you begin any writing task that's important to you—whether in college or on the job—it's worth the time to stop and assess your particular writing situation. Ask yourself, "What's the big picture here? What are the elements of my situation and how can I approach them?" One good way to take stock of those elements is to ask yourself four questions. Your answers can serve as a framework on which to build your paper.

The four questions are these:

- *Who* is my audience?
- *Why* am I writing?
- *How* do I want to present myself?
- *What* do I want to say?

Although you may not be able to give in-depth answers at the earliest stages of your writing, you should sketch out some preliminary answers, then keep them in mind as you work. The rest of the chapter explains why it's important to do so.

AUDIENCE

Analyzing Your Audience

If someone were to ask me the most important advice that I would give any writer, I would say without hesitation, "Remember your audience! Know who your readers are and what they expect of you."

The advice seems obvious, yet most college writers, graduate students as well as freshmen, have trouble thinking beyond the captive audience of their instructor to a set of real-life readers who make real demands on them. Yet the writing they do after college will be for readers who, whether they are reading for information or entertainment, have definite demands and expectations and will be unhappy if they are not met. That's why it's essential for every writer to learn how to write for different audiences and how to analyze those audiences. To prepare you for such readers, many of your writing assignments in college may call for you to address a specific group of readers. Notice that most writing assignments in this book do just that.

Fortunately, all of us already know a great deal about analyzing audiences, and we do it intuitively in everyday situations. If you were protesting an unauthorized charge on a credit card statement, you would use an entirely different tone and format than you would if you were writing a fund appeal for a local charity. If you were writing a statement for a fellowship application, you would think about who is going to read it and use a different tone and vocabulary than you would use if you were writing a movie review for the college paper.

Yet when we are writing in situations that are not immediate or personal, it can be difficult to keep our readers in mind as well as we should. That's because focusing on audience requires that we *de-center*, try to view issues from other people's points of view and consider how they feel and how they will react. That's a difficult exercise, one that takes practice. The following sets of questions can help as an exercise to raise your audience awareness.

Guideline Questions about Audience

- Attitudes and Beliefs
    - What interests or values do my readers have that I can appeal to? What kinds of arguments are likely to appeal to them?
    - Are they likely to be hostile, sympathetic, skeptical? Can I assume they're open-minded?
    - How will their age, sex, economic, and educational level affect their response?
- Previous Knowledge
    - How much do my readers already know about my topic? How much do I have to explain?
    - What experiences have they had that I can draw on?
    - To what extent should I use or avoid specialized terminology?
- Readers' Expectations
    - What do my readers expect to get from reading?
    - How much and what kind of explanation do they want?

What specific questions will they want answered?
- Possible Pitfalls
    What might make readers react negatively?
    What might make them quit reading?
    About what points do I need to be particularly careful?

Another, less formal way to focus on the needs and expectations of your audience is to keep asking yourself these questions as you write:

- Am I keeping *their* interests and concerns in mind?
- Am I boring them by telling them more than they want to know?
- Am I wasting their time by writing more than I need to?
- Am I intimidating them with unfamiliar terms and references or with language they don't understand?
- Am I threatening them by attacking their beliefs or their self-esteem?
- Am I patronizing them by acting superior?
- Am I disappointing them by not doing what I promised to do in the title or the first paragraph?

Finally, one major point to keep in mind is this: *Always assume your readers are intelligent even though they may be uninformed.*

The Model Topic box that follows shows how a writer might answer these questions before he or she started to write on the benefits of a campus day-care center.

Such an analysis helps you create a mental picture of your readers—it makes them more real to you and gets you thinking from their point of view. Notice, however, that this kind of analysis is easier to do for an explanatory paper like the one modeled here than it would be for an exploratory paper because the writer has a clearer sense of what he or she is going to say. For an exploratory paper, you might want to rough out only a general definition of your readers and wait until after the first draft to refine it to a more specific description. (See the discussion about writer-based prose and reader-based prose in the next chapter and the section on audience adaptation in Chapter 6).

PURPOSE

Analyzing Your Purpose

Once you know who your readers are, think specifically about *why* you are writing. Your first response might be a variation of a comment by the eight-

---

MODEL TOPIC: *Preliminary Audience Analysis for Day-Care Center Paper*

AUDIENCE: *University Administrators and Regents*

ATTITUDES: Administrators care about the college and want to do what will benefit it. Likely to be skeptical about day-care center, but willing to listen if I can show them it's a good idea. Several of them are women so they're especially aware of problem—important to appeal to them.

PREVIOUS KNOWLEDGE: Day-care issues much in news so they should know a good deal about the general problem. Need to know more about how on-campus center would operate. Women and younger men likely to have personal experience.

READERS' EXPECTATIONS: They want an explanation of why college needs a day-care center. Want to know details of how it would be set up. Specific questions: Why superior to other arrangements? What special advantages to college? What facilities would it use? Cost? Quality control? How many would it serve?

POSSIBLE PITFALLS: Be careful not to sound like I'm demanding they do this. Don't go into too many details—focus on the idea and benefits for everyone. Especially need to show why college should take on this new responsibility.

---

eenth-century wit Dr. Johnson, who said, "No man but a blockhead ever wrote except for money." That is, you're writing for a grade. Well, of course—that's a given. But if you're serious about becoming a good writer, you have to move beyond such a limited and simplistic answer and ask yourself what your purpose is within the paper itself. If you're not sure, you'll have trouble focusing your writing. When you finish the paper, you'll have no criteria for judging whether you've satisfied your readers.

For some writing tasks, your purpose may be specified for you. You could be asked to summarize the main points in a lecture or to analyze the rhetoric in a political speech. Often, however, when you choose your own topic you can also choose your own purpose. Then you need to think about the task in detail and decide what you want to do. Using a set of guideline questions can help you.

Guideline Questions about Purpose

• Kind of Writing
   Is this writing going to be primarily explanatory or exploratory? A combination?

What do I hope to do for my readers? Inform? Entertain? Persuade? Explain? Reinforce beliefs? Move to action?

Do I want to combine different kinds of writing? If so, which should dominate?

- Specific Goals

    What specific objectives do I have?

    Should I state them directly in the paper or should I only suggest them?

    What change, if any, do I want to bring about?

- Desired Response

    How do I want my readers to respond? Do I want them to act? To agree? To change their minds? To see matters in a new light? To be moved emotionally?

    Am I most interested in an immediate or long-range response?

- Possible Pitfalls

    Do I have a genuine purpose or am I merely "cheerleading," repeating things my readers already know or agree with?

    Is my purpose hopeless? That is, am I writing an argument to an audience who I know will pay no attention? For instance, advocating stricter gun control to members of the National Rifle Association is pointless.

    Am I writing simply to preach on one of my favorite topics? That is, am I writing simply to let off steam or voice a concern, for no particular reason, with no audience in mind?

MODEL TOPIC: *Preliminary Analysis of Purpose for the Day-Care Center Paper*

AUDIENCE: *College administrators*

KIND OF WRITING: Mostly an explanatory paper. Want *to explain* to the administrators why an on-campus day-care center would benefit college. Persuade them that it's practical and cost-effective.

SPECIFIC GOALS: Present a convincing case based on facts and figures. Appeal to desire to help students and faculty provide good care for their children. State goal directly—no need to hint around.

RESPONSE: Want immediate response from readers. Hope they will agree on the first steps to get center started.

POSSIBLE PITFALLS: Coming on too strong—could alienate audience.

Working through these questions will help you to decide what you want to do in a paper and to generate material you can use. After your first draft, particularly if you are writing an exploratory paper, you may revise your purpose or change your approach, but you'll have a good start.

Finally, finding your focus is an integral part of finding your purpose, but often a writer begins to narrow and define his or her focus more explicitly after having started to write. Therefore, once again a writer needs to maintain a tension between preliminary planning and intuitive discovery. Plan ahead, know your purpose, but unless you are absolutely sure what you are going to write, don't get too committed to that purpose. As you write, you may want to sharpen the focus or change your angle, and you should feel free to do either.

PERSONA

Presenting Yourself

Every time you write for readers, you assume a persona; like an actor in front of an audience, you present yourself to your readers in a way that makes an impression on them. You create an image. You can come across as a passionate advocate for a cause, an established authority, a disillusioned idealist—you can choose from any number of roles. Even if you don't choose a role consciously, some persona is going to come through. Therefore, it's important for you as a writer to develop the habit of thinking about your persona so you can learn to control it.

Controlling Your Persona

A writer can control the degree to which an audience will be aware of his or her presence in the writing. At times your persona should virtually disappear. For instance, if you are writing a technical or scientific report or giving a process analysis, don't intrude yourself into the account. That restriction doesn't mean that you should never use *I*, especially if avoiding the word means that you have to resort to writing "this author" or "the investigator." When you are reporting on your own discoveries *I* is quite appropriate.

In very personal writing in which you are drawing on your own experiences and expressing opinions, you may want to use *I* frequently, use contractions, and generally reduce the distance between yourself and your reader. In more formal writing in which you want to maintain some distance, avoid contractions and establish a serious tone. Whatever style you adopt, keep in mind the role you are playing and try to play it as convincingly as possible.

Remember that the key element of an effective persona is ethical appeal, that intangible quality of a piece of writing that wins readers' attention and earns their respect and trust. Although the strongest ethical appeal comes from having established a reputation for integrity and good work, unknown writers can also convey ethical appeal in several ways: by showing they understand the issues and have done their homework, by using language that is moderate and responsible, and by demonstrating that they are confident. No apologies, please.

The following set of questions will help you think about how you can establish an effective persona when you write.

Guidelines Questions about Persona

- Credibility

  What facts do I need to show that I have done my homework?

  How reasonable are my claims? Have I overstated my case?

  How do I acknowledge that there are other possible points of view?

- Tone

  Is my tone formal or informal? Do I need to adjust it?

  What amount of distance do I want between me and my readers? How do I set that distance?

  What emotional attitude do I project? Do I sound angry, bitter, happy? Is that what I want?

- Voice

  How do I show my genuine concern for what I'm writing?

  How do I project a confident, knowledgeable image?

Bear in mind that usually you won't be able to plan your persona completely ahead of time because it grows from the choices you make as you draft, revise, and polish. Nevertheless, by working through these preliminary questions and checking them again as you revise, you can consciously shape the image you present to your readers.

MESSAGE

As the last step in analyzing your writing situation, decide on the message you want to give your readers—it's not necessarily the same as your purpose. Although you'll probably refine that message as you write and revise,

---

MODEL TOPIC: *Preliminary Analysis of Persona for the Day-Care Paper*

CREDIBILITY: Need to make a reasonable claim that college will benefit from the center, not that it's absolutely necessary. Have figures and examples from similar centers run by other colleges or institutions. Acknowledge possible objections but show they can be overcome.

TONE: Need to be careful about tone . . . keep it respectful and not too informal. Want to sound concerned but not angry. Come across as a practical person.

VOICE: Acknowledge a personal stake in the paper—use example of own problems. Sound reasonable and fully informed, confident that administrators will listen and be interested.

---

it's important to have a good idea what your main point is going to be before you start to write. That's true for exploratory writing as well as explanatory writing because knowing that message gives you an anchor for your paper.

You should be able to state your message succinctly even if it is still rather general at this early stage. For example, here are several ways in which the main idea for the model topic could be stated. Notice that they vary according to the different focuses that different writers might give to such a paper.

- The university can increase student enrollment and attract more qualified young faculty if it establishes a low-cost, high-quality day-care center on campus.
- Establishing a high-quality, moderately priced day-care center on campus would demonstrate the university's commitment to providing educational opportunities for returning women students.
- By establishing a high-quality, subsidized day-care center on campus, the university could raise its academic status by attracting outstanding graduate students and high-caliber young faculty.

Writing down any of these messages as a starting point would help the writer focus and control the paper.

EXERCISES

1. Here is a sample showing how one might go about analyzing the audience for a specific writing situation.

The writing situation: a young person applying to the board of elders of a church for a tuition scholarship to a college affiliated with that church.

Audience analysis: group of mature men and women who want to spend their church's limited resources wisely. They want to be sure that the person who gets the scholarship is an active church member who has a good academic record and can demonstrate that he or she needs financial help to go to college. They would also like to know whether the applicant plans to work while in school and what career plans he or she has.

Write a similar analysis for the audience for these writing situations:

A. A patient complaining to the county medical society about a doctor who performed an unnecessary hysterectomy.

B. A citizen petition to the city council for a zoning change that would prohibit apartment houses in a new subdivision that is being opened.

C. A government pamphlet on nutrition designed especially for low-income families.

D. A fund-raising brochure to raise $100,000 for new instruments for the college band.

2. Here is a sample showing how one might analyze a reader's reasons for reading a particular piece of writing:

An article on buying antique clocks: The readers of this article would read it to find out where to shop for such clocks, how to tell if they were genuine, what features to look for in good antique clocks, and how much they might have to pay for the clock that they might want to buy.

Write a similar analysis of readers' reasons for reading the following:

A. An article on how to buy ski gear.

B. An article on reading levels of students in the city's public schools.

C. A political advertisement for candidate for state judge.

3. Here is an example of the way one might analyze a writer's purpose in a specific writing situation.

An article on white-water canoeing: The writer of this piece would probably want to let readers know what white-water canoeing offers to people interested in outdoor activities, what kinds of skills it requires, where one might go to participate in the sport, and how much it costs.

Make the same kind of analysis of writer's purpose for the following writing situations:

A. An article for parents on the effects of television watching on preschool children.

B. A report on a new brand of microwave oven for a consumer magazine.

C. A brochure on the benefits of exercise, to be distributed to company employees.

4. Here is an example showing how one might analyze the persona he or she wanted to create for a writing situation.

Driver writing to a judge to appeal a six-month suspension of a driver's license: The writer wants to communicate the image of a sober, industrious person who will no longer speed and who must be able to drive in order to keep working.

Analyze the persona a writer might want to create in these writing situations:

A. A lawyer is writing to a school board to explain why they cannot fire a teacher who has worn a bikini in a bathing beauty contest.

B. An official of a drug company is writing an article to explain to physicians the side effects of a new tranquilizer.

C. A student is writing a professor to ask for a letter of recommendation to graduate school.

SUGGESTED WRITING ASSIGNMENTS

As a part of each assignment, write a one-paragraph analysis of your audience (including a statement about where your paper would be published and what your readers would want to know), a one-paragraph analysis of your purpose in writing, and a two- or three-sentence analysis of the persona you want to project in your writing.

TOPIC 1: Assume that you are in charge of publicity for an organization you belong to and have been asked to write a news release to announce *one* of the following events. Remember that when you write a news release, you hope to get a newspaper to publish it free; therefore, one of your audiences is the newspaper editor who decides whether to publish and the other the group of newspaper readers you are hoping to reach. The news release should be around 250 words.

Events from which to choose:

A. A seminar on résumé writing for women reentering the job market.

B. Start of a new group of Adult Children of Alcoholics.

C. A seminar on starting a part-time business while in college.

D. A meeting on tracing family genealogies.

TOPIC 2: Some law schools ask their applicants to submit as part of their application an essay answering this question: "Why do you think the admissions board of our law school should look favorably on your application?" In no more than 600 words, write such an essay. Before you write, make a careful analysis of your audience and the persona you want to present.

5 ◇ Drafting Your Paper

First drafts can vary tremendously, depending on the kind of writing you are doing, on how important the writing is, and, of course, on your temperament and habits as a writer. Some writers can do a good job on a simple writing task in only one draft if they take pains with it and then edit it carefully. For more complex writing assignments, however, I think it helps to consider a first draft a *discovery draft*. Assume that you're writing it to organize your ideas and discover what you want to say; when you do that, you can turn off that self monitor that criticizes as you write and just get something down. Often a first draft is little more than an exploration. You can trim, focus, and develop it later.

WRITER-BASED AND READER-BASED PROSE

Sometimes it helps to think of your first draft as "writer-based" prose,[1] written more for yourself than for a specific group of readers. At this stage it may not be productive to ask, "How is this going to affect my reader?" or worry about a carefully laid out argument. It's more important to keep the ideas flowing.

The idea of writer-based prose can be useful not only when you're discovering your content but also when you are writing the first draft of an argumentative paper on an issue about which you feel strongly. Under those circumstances, you like to use forceful, emotional language that expresses anger or frustration but that you know won't work well with your

1. Linda Flower, "Writer-Based Prose: A Cognitive Basis for Problems in Writing," *College English* 41 (September 1979): 19–37.

readers. In a writer-based draft you can get the anger out of your system and blister your opponents with terms like *disgraceful* and *outrageous*, and not worry about whether you're being biased or irrational. But once you have vented your rage—and in the process thought of supporting arguments—you can go back to your draft and consider how you can revise it into "reader-based" writing that your audience would be likely to pay attention to.

For example, here's how writer-based and reader-based first paragraphs might look for the model topic about a campus day-care center.

> WRITER-BASED: The child care situation on this campus is absurd. Even though in the last five years the number of women in their twenties and thirties who have returned to our college has increased more than 100 percent, more than half of them never graduate, and for a very good reason. Our administration is so short-sighted it has made no attempt to help them deal with the single most important obstacle to their continuing their education: the lack of a low-cost, quality day-care center on or close to campus. Young faculty also need such a center, and it's high time someone did something about starting one.

The paragraph projects a strong voice and the statement is clear and straightforward, but the angry tone is likely to alienate the very administrators the author wants to convince. Now let's see how the author could change the same paragraph into reader-based prose.

> READER-BASED: In the past five years the number of returning women students in their twenties and thirties has more than doubled on this campus. Unfortunately, however, half of these women never graduate, and many of them feel that the major obstacle to their continuing their education is the lack of a quality, low-cost day-care center on or close to campus. If our administration could take the initiative to start such a center, it could help not only these students but also the growing number of young faculty at our college.

This opening paragraph also does a good job of laying out the main idea, but now the author has softened the angry tone that would put the reader on the defensive and instead considered how to appeal to the reader's concern.

When you begin to revise writer-based prose into reader-based prose, you shift from focusing on your own need as an author to express yourself to thinking about the needs of your audience when they read what you have written.

Not all drafts must be writer-based, of course. Often you can be thinking about your readers when you start to write and not let that concern interfere with generating content. But when you have trouble starting a paper or when you're doing exploratory writing, focus on expressing your ideas in writer-based prose at first; you can shift your approach later.

SOME SUGGESTIONS ABOUT OPENINGS

Beginnings are hard—even experienced writers agree on that. First paragraphs are important, and sometimes nothing that comes to mind seems good enough. In that case, my advice is simple: *lower your standards.* Put down your ideas in flat, graceless prose if necessary and go on. Once you have something on paper that you can go back and reread, the next paragraphs will come more easily. For the time being, consider that in your opening paragraph, you're "circling to land" or "warming up for the first pitch." Don't take your preliminary efforts too seriously.

In Chapter 9, I will make specific suggestions about ways to write good openings. Right now I want only to mention some of the patterns professional writers often use to get started.

Illustrations

You might begin with an example that illustrates the main point you are going to make. For instance, if you are writing an article urging your legislature to pass more stringent penalties for drunk driving, you could start our like this:

> Last Sunday morning three teenagers were returning from a regional basketball tournament in Dallas when their car was struck broadside by a drunk driver careening down the wrong side of the highway at 110 miles an hour.

If you were writing an essay urging that American schools increase the length of their school year, you might start out like this:

> In Japan, students go to school 243 days a year. In Germany, they go to school 240 days a year. In the United States, they attend school 180 days a year, a figure that puts them third from the bottom in a list of twenty-seven industrialized nations.

Such openings work well because they focus on specific details that are apt to be interesting to your reader and they give the reader a strong signal about what to expect in the rest of the essay. They also give you a concrete anchor from which to start writing.

Quotations

A quotation relating directly to your topic can become a good opening for a paper. For example, a professional journalist introduces an essay on how air-conditioning has changed American society like this:

> "The greatest contribution to civilization in this century may well be air-conditioning—and America leads the way." So wrote British Scholar-Politician S. F. Markham thirty-two years ago when a modern cooling system was still a luxury.
> —Frank Trippett, "The Great American Cooling Machine," reprinted in *The Riverside Reader,* Vol. II, ed. Joseph Trimmer and Maxine Hairston (Boston: Houghton Mifflin, 1983), 337 (©1979, Time, Inc.).

If you were going to write an article about an athlete's disenchantment with playing college football, you might begin:

> The English wit Oscar Wilde once said, "There are two tragedies in life: one is not getting what you want; the other is getting it."

Starting off with a quotation immediately gives the writing a personal touch and suggests that you are well educated and alert and have good resources to draw on.

Anecdotes

An opening anecdote can work especially well because it catches the readers' attention with a visual image of people doing something and pulls them into the writing by arousing their curiosity. This anecdote about President Harry Truman's mother from an article on famous men and their mothers provides a good example.

> Early in the evening of August 14, 1945, in the living room of her yellow clapboard house in Grandview, Missouri, a small, spry woman of 93, talking to a guest, excused herself to take a long-distance call in another room. "Hello, hello," the guest heard her begin. "Yes, I'm all right. Yes, I've been listening to the radio. . . . I heard the Englishman speak. . . . I'm glad they accepted the surrender terms. Now you come to see me if you can. All right. Goodbye."
> "That was Harry," she said, coming through the door. "Harry's a wonderful man. He has a noble disposition and he's loyal to his friends.

I knew he'd call. He always calls me after something that happens is over."

—David McCullough, "Mama's Boys,"
Psychology Today, March 1983, 32.

Generative Sentences

Another good way to start a paper is with a *generative sentence*, one that generates expectations in the reader's mind. For instance, here are two opening generative sentences.

> The growing trend of doctors choosing to practice only in the nation's largest cities raises some serious questions about the quality of health care available to the American people.

This opening sentence tells the reader what to expect from the essay and promises to generate specific additional information about the issue.

> Highly successful athletes usually have certain distinctive personality traits.

This opening sentence promises the reader to identify the specific traits and discuss them. Both sentences signal to readers that the writer is going to follow one of the most common thought patterns in informative writing: general to specific.

COMMON PATTERNS OF ORGANIZATION

Readers expect to find a pattern of organization when they read, especially when a writer presents an argument. Thus it's useful for writers to be aware of common patterns in argument and other expository writing, because such patterns can provide the organizing framework for a first draft. They are

- Reasoning from evidence
- Claims and warrants
- Definition
- Cause and effect
- Comparison
- Narration
- Process

Reasoning from Evidence

Writing that takes this form is roughly patterned on the so-called scientific method; that is, the writer gathers evidence, examines it, and draws conclusions. Reasoning from evidence is also a common pattern in legal arguments, both in and out of the courtroom. These associations with law and science make this an especially effective pattern for certain purposes and certain audiences. For example, if you need to persuade a group of skeptical readers to accept an idea to which they may not be very receptive, consider this kind of argument. For instance, if you wanted to convince a senator that "down home, good ol' boy" appeals are no longer good campaign strategies, you could cite evidence showing that voters in your state are concentrated in the major urban areas and that more than half of registered voters are now working women.

Writers use this pattern when they invoke the results of surveys to support their claims. For example, in another part of this book I argue that certain kinds of grammatical errors are much more damaging than others; thus it's important for writers to recognize those errors in order to avoid them. As a basis for that argument, I cite evidence from two surveys made among business executives and professional writers. Those surveys provide strong support for my claim, even among strict grammarians.

You can use this writing pattern in two ways: either you can give the evidence first and then generalize from it or you can state your conclusion first and then give the evidence on which you base it. In most cases, I prefer to state the argument first and then present the evidence. With that format you get your readers' attention and prepare them to accept the evidence more readily.

Any writer needs to be careful not to fall into the common fallacy of overgeneralizing from scanty evidence, but usually you can make commonsense judgments about how large the sample needs to be. If you wanted to generalize about students' political beliefs at a college of 3,500 students, you would need to interview at least 200 students. Citing just three examples of dishonest officials as proof of corruption throughout the state would hardly be convincing, but if those three officials were all on the city council of one town, they could indeed demonstrate corruption.

Making sure that your sample is random is probably even more important than its size. You must be careful to choose a sampling method that will give you an accurate cross section of the population you are writing about. One way is to select every tenth person or every fiftieth person from a directory or list. But that list has to be relevant to the kind of information you want. If you were trying to find out how air travelers in your city feel about the local airport facilities, calling every fiftieth name in the phone book would not give you an accurate sample because many people don't travel. Instead you would have to choose a cross section of travelers who passed through the terminal on three different kinds of traveling days —perhaps on a business day, on a Saturday, and on a holiday weekend.

When you want to get a random sample for other kinds of broader-based surveys you have to be sure that your sample includes representative groups chosen according to race, sex, income, education, occupation, and age. In general, the broader and more serious your claim is, the more care-fully you have to plan your sampling strategies if you want to get convinc-ing results.

Two cautions: First, have enough facts to support your case and be sure they're accurate. The force of this kind of reasoning comes from the *weight of facts*. If your evidence is skimpy or skeptical readers spot an error, you'll lose ground. Second, present your evidence clearly, using all the tricks you can to make it readable (see the section on the body lan-guage of your writing, pp. 181–3). Readers quickly tire of facts, figures, and data if they're not skillfully presented.

Claims and Warrants

Another common thought pattern that all of us use frequently is that of *claims and warrants*. That is, we make claims (assertions) and then we give warrants (reasons) to support them. For example, someone might write, "In the 1990s, competition among employers for top women graduates will become so keen that businesses will have to provide high-quality, on-site day-care facilities if they hope to attract the best." Such statements can be classified as *informal logic;* they don't go through all the steps of formal proof, but they make a rational appeal to common sense. Claims and war-rants, like reasoning from evidence, typify the kinds of arguments lawyers use in court.

BASIC TERMS AND PATTERNS

The English logician Stephen Toulmin claims that nearly all arguments, but particularly legal ones, can be broken down into terms of claims and warrants. He has devised a model to describe these arguments; it employs five basic terms.[2]

> *Claim:* The assertion made by the person arguing. Usually it is clearly stated and readily apparent.

> *Data:* The evidence or examples used as supporting material. Data may be given or the arguer may assume that they are common knowledge.

2. Stephen Toulmin, *The Uses of Argument* (London: Cambridge University Press, 1958), 6.

Warrant: The chain of reasoning connecting the claim and the data. Sometimes the warrant is spelled out, but often it is not because the person arguing assumes it is obvious to the audience.

Support: Additional material used to reinforce and make credible either the data or the warrant.

Qualifier: A limitation attached to some part of the argument to keep it from sounding too absolute or sweeping (frequently in the form of such words as *possibly, probably,* or *most likely*).

In their most basic form, arguments built on the Toulmin model use only the first three terms. They move from the data (evidence) to the claim (assertion) and they are supported by a warrant (a reason or explanation).

DATA ──────────────────────────────⟶ CLAIM

                         │
                         │
                         │

                     WARRANT

STANDARD TOULMIN ARGUMENTS

Here are two examples:

DATA: Most young professionals ──────⟶ **CLAIM:** Companies who hope
responding to national survey   to attract top women
said they plan to have both a   graduates will have to offer
career and children. They say   good child-care facilities as
quality day care is very   part of their incentive plans.
important to them.

        WARRANT: Because young women professionals
        consider their children's needs when they
        choose a job, they will tend to select one that
        offers child care.

DATA: Urban commuter traffic ──────⟶ **CLAIM:** For Americans,
jams get worse every year.   personal cars, traditionally a
Auto air-conditioners create   symbol of freedom, are now
pollution. Parking congestion   causing major social and
is increasing in most cities.   economic problems.

        WARRANT: Things that cause environmental
        and economic stress cause major problems.

EXPANDED TOULMIN ARGUMENTS

The above diagrams sketch out the structure of these rather simple arguments. Sometimes, however, a writer wants to make more complex, less clear-cut arguments. When that happens, he or she can add a qualification to any element in the structure. For example:

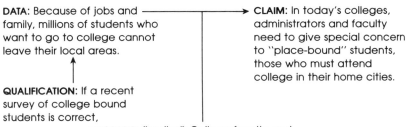

DATA: Because of jobs and family, millions of students who want to go to college cannot leave their local areas.

QUALIFICATION: If a recent survey of college bound students is correct,

CLAIM: In today's colleges, administrators and faculty need to give special concern to "place-bound" students, those who must attend college in their home cities.

WARRANT: (implied) College faculty and administrators want to serve the best interests of their students.

Sometimes writers also realize they must provide additional support for one or more parts of the argument. In such cases, another element appears. For example:

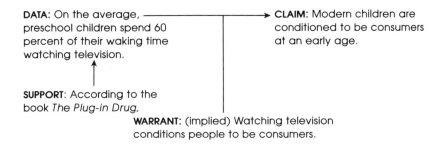

DATA: On the average, preschool children spend 60 percent of their waking time watching television.

SUPPORT: According to the book *The Plug-in Drug,*

CLAIM: Modern children are conditioned to be consumers at an early age.

WARRANT: (implied) Watching television conditions people to be consumers.

Here is an example of an argument in which the author adds both extra support and a qualification.

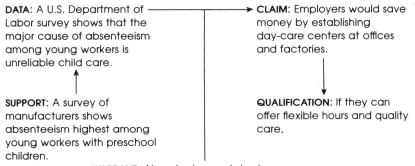

DATA: A U.S. Department of Labor survey shows that the major cause of absenteeism among young workers is unreliable child care.

SUPPORT: A survey of manufacturers shows absenteeism highest among young workers with preschool children.

CLAIM: Employers would save money by establishing day-care centers at offices and factories.

QUALIFICATION: If they can offer flexible hours and quality care,

WARRANT: Absenteeism costs businesses a great deal of money.

ADVANTAGES OF CLAIM/WARRANT ARGUMENTS

Organizing your arguments in this way has several advantages. The first is that readers who prefer rational arguments are apt to respond positively to the data/warrant/claim pattern because they recognize its resemblance to courtroom procedures. They expect someone who makes a *claim* to *support* it with *data* (or evidence), and they expect him or her to give a *warrant* (or explanation) that shows the reasoning behind the claim. Arguments phrased this way and backed with solid data have a legitimate ring to them.

The second advantage of Toulmin arguments is that they're flexible. You can analyze the structure of an argument you're making and decide which part you need to emphasize, given your audience and your writing situation. Consider, for example, the model topic we've been working with. Analyzed for its data / claim / warrant pattern, one version would look like this.

DATA: Forty percent of new Ph.D.s are now women. Forty-two percent of woman college students are now over twenty-five. ⟶ **CLAIM:** A modern university needs on-site day-care facilities to attract women students and faculty.

WARRANT: Young women want to raise families and will tend to favor colleges that provide day-care facilities.

You would choose which part of your argument to emphasize according to its audience. If you're writing to a college governing board made up mostly of older men, you might choose to expand on the warrant, pointing out that large numbers of women in their twenties now expect both to attend college and have families; they feel they shouldn't have to choose between being mothers and being economically secure. If you're writing to a college president who is a woman and who has raised a family, you won't need to expand the warrant. She will already agree with it. In that case, you'll do better to expand on the data, giving lots of facts that emphasize how many women need to have day-care centers on campus.

In other situations, you might recognize that you need to add qualifications to your claim or give additional support for your warrant. Because your situation changes each time you present your argument, it's always important to tailor the terms of your argument with your audience in mind.

A third advantage of the Toulmin method is that it allows you to arrange the parts of an argument in different ways. You might catch the audience's attention by making the claim or major assertion first, then presenting the data to support it. Virginia Woolf uses that approach in the following paragraph:

> [Claim] It is unthinkable that any woman in Shakespeare's day should have had Shakespeare's genius. [Warrant] For genius like Shakespeare's is not born among labouring, uneducated, servile people. [Data] It was not born in England among the Saxons and the Britons. It is not born today among the working classes. [Warrant restated and supported] How then, could it have been born among women whose work began . . . almost before they were out of the nursery, who were forced to it by all the power of law and custom.
> —Virginia Woolf, *A Room of One's Own*
> (New York: Harcourt, Brace & World, 1929), 50.

Woolf could also have begun her argument with the warrant or, by rearranging her sentences slightly, she could have omitted the warrant and let her readers supply it. And perhaps she would have strengthened her argument by beginning with the qualifier, "*Probably* no woman in Shakespeare's time . . ."

You can decide which parts of an argument might be omitted and which parts need to be stressed only after analyzing audience and purpose. These reminders may help you to make such decisions: Remember to

- Make your claim explicit and indicate what your data are.
- Spell out your warrant if your readers are inclined to be skeptical or if they're uninformed on the topic.
- Add a qualifier if you know your claim is debatable.
- Add support for major points the reader might challenge.

Notice too that Toulmin's approach to constructing arguments allows you to combine claim/warrant arguments with inductive arguments just as we do when we argue extemporaneously. We observe individual cases, make a generalization on the basis of those cases (induction), and then we present that generalization as a claim. The paragraph previously cited from Virginia Woolf illustrated the process. She investigated the origins of dozens of people of genius in England and found that none of them were uneducated or had come from the laboring classes. She then generalized that genius is not likely to come from those two groups of people. Using induction again, she examined the conditions in which women lived before the nineteenth century and realized that almost all of them were uneducated and treated like servants. From that data she generalized that they could not have become great writers.

Finally, the Toulmin model for arguments helps you generate material you can use to develop your ideas. These last two examples demonstrate how the Toulmin approach can be used to construct a chain argument in which the claims from one step of the argument can be used as the data for the next step.

Most of us find it easy enough to express our opinions, but sometimes we have trouble when we have to produce evidence (data) to back them or give explanations (warrants) for them. However, if you habitually ask yourself, "What is my warrant for this claim?" or "What supporting data can I find to strengthen my case?" you will find that such questions are tools for discovery. They force you to probe your experience and examine your store of information. Generally that is a thought-provoking process.

If you can train yourself to try the Toulmin approach when you undertake a writing task that requires you to make a claim or argue a thesis, you should find it a time-saving and productive strategy.

Definition

Another natural thought pattern that one can use to organize writing is *definition*. We use definitions when we want to persuade, explain, or evaluate, and often they form the basis of essays or even whole books. The historian Barbara Tuchman, for example, wrote her book *The March of Folly* to define "woodenheadedness" in national affairs. Plato's *Republic* is a definition of justice.

The most common methods of defining are these:

- Attributing characteristics:
  A quality day-care center must have separate rooms for different age groups of children, an area for outside exercise, professionally trained personnel, and carefully chosen toys and playground equipment.
- Analyzing parts (this can overlap with attributing characteristics):
  The student body at today's urban colleges is richly diverse, made up of retired people as well as full-time students, of immigrants from all over the world as well as native-born Americans, and of welfare parents as well as young, affluent students.
- Giving examples:
  Typical urban universities are the University of Illinois at Chicago, Northeastern University in Boston, the four-year colleges in the City University of New York system, and the University of Louisville in Kentucky.

- Stating function:
  The function of the public urban college or university is to make quality education accessible at a reasonable cost to those large numbers of citizens who cannot or do not want to leave their home areas.

Definition is a particularly useful pattern of organization when you write a paper or an argument in which you are *judging* or *evaluating*. You can use it to create a standard or yardstick for the way something ought to be, then apply that standard to an existing institution or situation and show how it should be changed. In a 1990 article in *The New York Times*, educational labor leader Albert Shanker used the French system of child care as a model by which the United States might judge its own system. He listed the French system's characteristics as

- Being available to all children regardless of family income.
- Employing highly trained personnel who are well paid.
- Providing universal preventive health care.
- Offering a variety of care options.

He then went on to argue that by failing to provide comparable care, the United States is cheating its children.

Definition also plays a crucial role when you are *arguing about moral principles* or *ethical issues* because you must base your argument on a definition of what is right or wrong, good or bad. For instance, in the column mentioned above, Shanker is arguing that the United States has a moral obligation to provide good care for all the children in the nation. This kind of approach works well when you can start with a definition of values that your readers will almost have to accept, such as freedom of speech or equal opportunity for all citizens.

Cause and Effect

When we argue from cause and effect, we are using one of the most common of all thought patterns, one that is a basic means of survival and a sophisticated tool for persuasion. Because this thought pattern is so fundamental, it should be one of the first ones you consider when you are going over your options for how you might organize a paper. It works well for many kinds of college papers; for instance, for a nursing course you might write a paper on the effects of diabetes on pregnant women or for a history course in civil rights legislation you might write a paper on the role that

Rosa Parks and the Selma bus incident played in changing local ordinances on segregated facilities.

Cause-and-effect arguments are particularly useful when you want to convince readers who you suspect may not share your values and who are likely to respond only to pragmatic arguments. Rather than argue from the shaky ground of what's moral or right—shaky because your readers may not agree with you—you're much better off to talk about good and bad effects, about what works and what doesn't. The history of child-care legislation in the United States provides a good example of how a cause-and-effect argument can hit its mark when other, less pragmatic approaches fail. In the 1950s and 1960s, proponents of getting state and federal governments involved in better child care were stone-walled because most legislators argued that child care was strictly a family matter and the government shouldn't interfere. The legislators were arguing from a definition of *family* with a built-in bias against mothers of small children working outside the home. By 1990, however, the situation changed greatly because of the vast numbers of working (and voting) mothers, many of them single, and their importance to the national economy. Now such legislators can be convinced to support tax credits for child care because it should have good effects, and in 1990 Congress passed the most sweeping child-care legislation ever proposed.

In constructing an argument, then, look for ways to show your readers that what you propose will have good effects, that it will solve an important problem. In fact, cause-and-effect arguments are often problem-solving arguments and, as such, have wide appeal. But you should keep one caution in mind. Cause-and-effect arguments can quickly go wrong if a writer oversimplifies or suggests that complex problems have simple causes or easy solutions.

Circumstantial Arguments

Sometimes you may want to make a cause-and-effect argument in terms so compelling that your audience will almost have to agree with you. In that situation you can construct a *circumstantial argument,* one in which you claim that the chain of cause and effect is so strong that if *A* occurs, *B* is inevitable. When you want to make this kind of argument, choose language that conveys great urgency. Typical phrases are "Under the circumstances, we have no other choice . . . ," "We are forced to take these steps . . . ," and "Given this situation, we must . . ."

For example, in writing an environmental impact statement, you could point out that if a manufacturer continues to use a local lake for cooling, the water temperature will rise enough to cause an increase in algae and pollute the lake. Or in arguing for an increase in the dues of an association you belong to, you could stress that increased costs for rent, utilities, and paper will bankrupt the organization if it does not get more income. Carefully constructed arguments from circumstance are hard to refute, so if you think your case is a particularly strong one, reach for those phrases that signal a crisis.

Comparison

Another good way to employ common thought patterns in your writing is to draw *comparisons*. In drawing a straight comparison, you simply show likenesses or differences that illustrate and strengthen the points you are making. For example, if you are asking to prepare an analysis of the advantages and disadvantages of instituting "flex-time" as company policy, you could cite the experiences of several other companies that have adopted flex-time. If you were trying to persuade your readers that they should begin an exercise program, you could give figures that compare the blood pressures of exercisers and nonexercisers. Or if you wanted to argue the benefits of a free-market system as compared to controlled systems, you could compare the productivity of farmers in the United States to that of farmers in countries that have state-controlled farm programs.

Hard-fact comparisons like these can be convincing, particularly if you're sure your readers are the kind who want substantial evidence before they make a decision. Straight comparisons also work well when it's important to your readers that they be perceived as meeting standards and staying up to date on everything. For example, college administrators often respond quickly to the suggestion that their programs or faculty might not be as good as those of comparable institutions and will do what they can to keep up with other colleges and universities.

Unfortunately, while hard-fact comparisons can be convincing, often they are also dull. Pages of figures and charts can quickly bore readers and send their minds off somewhere else. So use them sparingly and learn how to present them effectively (see pp. 181–3 on the body language of your writing).

ANALOGIES

For a more striking kind of comparison, turn to analogy. You can use an opening analogy to catch the readers' attention and bring them to a flash of recognition. For example, here is a lovely analogy that immediately draws the reader into the article.

Like Galileo's observation that the earth revolves around the sun, the A. C. Nielsen Company's report of an unexpectedly sharp drop in the national television audience last winter has altered the accepted view of reality. And like the telescope Galileo used, a new instrument —the "people meter"—provided the new information.

The big three networks are fighting the conclusion and trying to force the messenger to recant. But like those who believed the sun circles the earth, they seem fated to find themselves on the wrong side of the revolution.

—Randal Rothenberg, "Black Hole in Television," *The New York Times*, 8 October 1990, D–1.

One mark of a good writer is the ability to draw good analogies that clarify the unfamiliar by linking it to the familiar. Often they bring a visual and dramatic touch to writing. Remember, however, that analogies don't *prove* an argument; they only strengthen it.

A FORTIORI REASONING

Another useful pattern of comparison is the *a fortiori* argument (pronounced ah-for-shee-or-ee). The term means "all the stronger." When we use this kind of reasoning we claim that if a person or institution can do one difficult thing, then it is logical to expect it can do a similar but easier thing—that is, there is all the stronger reason to assume they can. This kind of comparison underlies comments such as "If our university can afford to build a new ten-million-dollar stadium, it should be able to spend a million dollars on minority scholarships."

The all-the-stronger approach to developing an argument relies on the kind of commonsense reasoning that all of us use when we appeal to the readers sense of what is logical and consistent. For instance, "If we can spend billions of dollars to prosecute and imprison drug dealers, why can't we spend a few million to strengthen our drug prevention and rehabilitation facilities?" One must be careful, however, not to let *a fortiori* arguments deteriorate into oversimplification of the issues. Often such arguments become little more than outraged complaints about priorities and they can be hard to develop effectively. Issues of apparently conflicting priorities are usually more complex than they seem. So although they can be good for capturing an audience's attention, it's not a good idea to depend totally on *a fortiori* comparisons.

Narration

Although we usually think of narration as storytelling, writers of nonfiction can also use it in many ways. For instance, it is the basic pattern for case studies, and it works well when a story will vividly illustrate a point. Certainly narration can enliven and strengthen much everyday, working writing. Those short tales that we call *anecdotes* or *incidents* work especially well.

An anecdote is a miniature, self-contained story that usually focuses on a person in order to illustrate a point. For instance, I often tell of my own discouraging experiences in an intensive spoken French course to explain how students with poor writing skills feel when they face a threatening writing assignment.

Incidents are also short but complete accounts that make a point, but usually they focus on an action rather than a personality. For example, in "Marrying Absurd," her ironic essay about the wedding industry in Las Vegas, Joan Didion emphasizes her feelings about the city by giving capsule narratives of two weddings she observed: in one she describes a drunk bride in an orange minidress stumbling out of the chapel and falling into the car; in the other she tells about the father of an obviously pregnant bride making ritual wedding-night jokes to the bridegroom.

Whenever you incorporate narrative into your writing, remember that good narrators use concrete, vivid language to *show* their readers what is happening. They strive for visual elements to add *presence* to their writing. More in Chapter 8 on some ways to achieve those visual effects.

Process

A *process* paper is a "how-to" paper; it could range from a sheet of directions for assembling a doghouse to a book titled "365 Days to a More Beautiful You." Typically, the person doing a process paper leads the reader through a series of steps chronologically, explaining and illustrating, sometimes with diagrams.

Much of the day-to-day writing that goes on in technology, business, and the professions is process writing, and to function effectively in those fields, most people have to master the art of writing clear process papers. In some fields, such as engineering and computer science, achieving clarity is not easy, and executives in those professions often require that their people take special courses in technical or scientific writing. For the most part, however, writers who have trained themselves to write clear and direct expository prose can also become good process writers for nontechnical papers. Many of the suggestions in other chapters for organizing and developing your writing will help you with process writing.

COMBINING METHODS

I think it's useful for every writer to know about and be able to recognize the common patterns of organization. I also think it's useful to know that certain patterns are likely to work well in certain situations. For example, when I feel very strongly about an issue but know the people I am trying to convince don't necessarily share my emotional biases, I deliberately construct a cause-and-effect argument rather than use an argument from definition. That is, I don't try to convince my readers to do something because I think it's morally correct; I try to convince them to do it because the effects will be in their best interest. I also habitually use claim/warrant or reasoning from evidence arguments for skeptical readers who I know place great stress on reason.

Nevertheless, I also know that many experienced writers seldom stop to think about what kinds of argument or patterns they are going to use when they write. Rather they rough out what they're going to say, gather their material, make notes, and start writing. They could probably identify the patterns they're using—an argument from circumstance or an extended definition, for instance—but they're not conscious of those patterns as they work. And they seldom write according to just one pattern, but move from one to another as the topic seems to demand.

So don't feel that you need to pick a pattern for your writing and stick to it as you work; combine them when it seems useful to do so. Know what the patterns are and what their possibilities are, but don't feel enslaved by them. Use them creatively—to help you generate material and to give structure to your writing. Use them pragmatically—to put your argument in its most persuasive light.

EXERCISES

1. Working with two or three other students in a small group discussion, consider what illustrative examples or anecdotes a writer might use as an opener for papers on these topics.

   A. Advantages of starting one's college education at a community college.

   B. The reason some professional athletes command multimillion-dollar salaries.

   C. Why television soap operas are popular on many college campuses.

   D. The purpose of instituting multicultural courses in a college curriculum.

2. Here is an example of a generative sentence that could help you get started writing a paper about the admission process for many prestigious colleges.

   Many prestigious colleges such as Michigan, UCLA, Yale, and Johns Hopkins rely too heavily on objective machine-scored tests that cannot measure motivation, perseverance, or creativity and that may be culturally biased against minority candidates or nonnative speakers.

Construct a similar generative sentence that could provide the basis to start writing on one of these topics.

   A. Your reasons for choosing the profession you plan to enter.

   B. An explanation of hypertext.

   C. The place of high school football or basketball in your home town.

   D. Your beliefs about people wearing furs.

3. Review the sections on claim/warrant arguments and Toulmin logic. Then working with two or three other students, construct a data/warrant/claim argument that might be used for writing about each of these propositions. Try to diagram the layout for each argument.

   A. Computer hackers who disrupt a university computer system should (or should not) be charged with a felony offense.

   B. Professors should (or should not) be allowed to require their own text-books in courses they teach.

   C. Colleges and universities have (or do not have) an obligation to provide health care and counseling services to enrolled students who have alcohol or drug problems.

   D. Multimillion-dollar salaries for entertainment stars are a commentary on the priorities of the American public.

4. Write out cause-and-effect arguments that you could use to support these propositions.

   A. Divorced women as well as men should be liable for child-support payments.

   B. In recent budget negotiations, a committee of your state legislature has proposed cutting the appropriation for research at state universities by 7 percent; write to the committee giving your reasons for agreeing or disagreeing with the proposal.

   C. The Federal Communications Commission should put tighter regulations on the kind of advertising allowed on the children's cartoon programs shown on television at popular hours.

5. Working with two or three other students, create short narratives or anecdotes that could be used to start a paper on one of these topics.

   A. The increasing number of people who eat at least half their meals at fast-food restaurants.

   B. The increasing number of incidents of date rape reported on college campuses.

C. The contrasts between affluence and poverty that one sees in many major cities in areas that have been "gentrified" by developers.

SUGGESTED WRITING ASSIGNMENTS

Before you start your draft, write a preliminary analysis of your audience and purpose, using the guideline questions from the previous chapter (pp. 58–9; p. 60). Put these analyses on a separate sheet to be turned in with your draft.

TOPIC 1: Collect several brochures from various places around your campus and community; some good sources are the offices of campus agencies such as the Student Financial Assistance Office, Student Dean's Office, Student Union, and the University Credit Union. Other possible sources are doctor's offices, banks, grocery stores, and so on. With other students in your class, analyze these brochures to see how they present information.

Now draft a brochure for an agency or institution, giving as much information as you can squeeze into no more than 500 words. The writing should be clear, simple, and lively so the audience can read the brochure quickly and absorb the information easily. Several possible topics are listed below, but you might also get an idea from one of the brochures you examine.

A. A guide to getting around your campus for students in wheelchairs.

B. A guide to student recreation for budget-minded students.

C. A brochure on health services available to women students.

D. A brochure on how to look for on-campus jobs.

E. A guide to popular music spots for students.

TOPIC 2: Draft an argument for or against one of the propositions below, using one or more of the patterns of argument discussed in this chapter. Your audience for this should be your campus newspaper, and your argument should not run over 500 words, the maximum for the "guest opinion" column.

A. Your college should (or should not) require each student to take two courses in cross-cultural studies before he or she can receive a degree. Such courses might be in African-American or Hispanic literature or history, in women's studies, in sociolinguistics, or in Middle Eastern history or art.

B. Your college is proposing to increase student fees for the coming year but has promised that it will consult with students on how those fees will be spent. Argue for your priorities for spending such fees.

C. A student organization called Students Older Than Average (SOTA) is protesting the spring round-up parade on campus that features elaborate floats that are partially subsidized by student activity funds. They argue that they get no benefits from the floats because most of them aren't on campus over weekends. They want the proportion of the activity fund that they contribute, several thousand dollars, to be spent for a campus lounge where commuting students could relax between classes. Argue for or against their proposal.

6 ◇ Revising

Experienced writers who care about doing good work plan on revising almost everything they write. They don't expect to sit down and write a report or an essay and be finished with it in one or two sessions. Rather they see revision as an essential part of any writing task that is not strictly routine, something they plan on as part of their writing schedule. Often, particularly with exploratory writing, they expect to develop a piece of writing through the revision process, depending on it to help them generate ideas as they go and to focus their writing.

When you learn to look at revising this way, a process by which you develop writing rather than one by which you correct it, you may find that it's easier to write. You'll feel more relaxed about your work, knowing that you don't have to get everything right from the beginning. A draft is just a draft, something to work with, not something you're committed to. It can also help to know that experienced writers have some reliable and systematic strategies for revising, and that those strategies can be learned. Understanding and learning those strategies is what this chapter is about.

THE REVISION PROCESS

Different Kinds of Revising

Not all revising is the same, and in order to talk productively about the different kinds of processes involved, it's useful to have some descriptive terms and understand what each involves.

One kind of revising I call *large-scale,* or global, revising. Such changes include

- Shifting or narrowing the focus of your paper.
- Deciding to direct the paper to a different audience.

- Changing your main purpose.
- Cutting substantial amounts in one part of the paper and expanding it in another.
- Reorganizing the paper to shift emphasis.

In other words, changes that significantly affect content. They're substantive, not stylistic.

Small-scale, or local, revising is quite different. This kind of revising involves

- Adding examples and details.
- Combining, rearranging, or changing sentences.
- Revising opening and closing paragraphs.
- Cutting out excess words and phrases; streamlining.
- Finding more effective words and phrases, especially verbs.
- Strengthening transitions.
- Improving the tone.

Changes like these are essentially surface changes. They're important for keeping your reader interested, creating a livelier, more readable style, and for making your paper more concise and effective, but they don't seriously affect content. They certainly can affect how your readers respond to your writing. That's why you'll find lots of advice about just such details in the next three chapters.

From my point of view, a third kind of revising is really what I call *editing;* I'll talk more about it later in a separate short chapter. Editing involves

- Checking for accuracy and consistency; seeing that details are right and that you've followed up on any promises you made.
- Improving the "body language" of your writing by breaking up paragraphs, putting in headings, and breaking long passages into lists or chunks.
- Eliminating obvious repetition.
- Checking spelling and punctuation.
- Proofreading for typographical errors.

Notice that such changes are the kinds of changes an outside reader, that is, an editor, could make on a paper even if he or she know nothing about the content. Unlike the changes writers themselves make when they are doing either large- or small-scale revision, editing changes affect neither the content nor the writing style of the paper. They do, however, drastically affect the rhetorical impact of your paper—that is, the impression it makes on other people. Many readers react so negatively to a carelessly edited or poorly proofread paper that they won't even finish reading it. That's why you can never afford to neglect editing and why you should even get help with it if you think that's necessary.

Nevertheless, editing changes are really *corrections*, not revisions. I think it's important to keep that distinction in mind and to separate the two processes in your mind. You must do your own revising because only you can really know what you want to say and how you want to say it. You also need to know how to do your own editing or correcting, because you can't depend on someone else to clean up your work.

The time to concern yourself with corrections is *after* you have revised, not while you're still shaping the paper for content and style. That's why I've put the suggestions about editing in a separate chapter later in the book.

A PLAN FOR REVISING IN STAGES

I recommend that you begin revising with a plan in mind and try to make yourself stick with it. First, plan to do as little revising as possible when you are writing your initial draft. Inevitably you'll make some changes—I can hardly imagine a writer who doesn't—but keep them to a minimum and push yourself to get out a complete first draft that gets down your main ideas and gives you a document to start working with. Resist getting bogged down in decisions about word choice and sentence structure or even the examples you're going to use.

Next, when you have that initial draft, consider what priority this paper has for you. Is it one of several short papers for a professor who reads papers quickly and marks them as credit or noncredit, or is it a major paper for a professor who insists on solidly argued, carefully written papers and grades accordingly? Is it a piece of writing that could affect your future, such as a personal statement for admission to graduate school or a letter applying for a fellowship? Rank it from one to ten on a scale of importance and plan your revising strategies accordingly. If it ranks near the top of the scale, you'll need to allow yourself time for several drafts, and you should expect to go through all the stages more than once, doing major rewriting and reorganizing as well substantial fine-tuning, polishing, and editing.

Third, make the *major* changes first. When you go through your draft, discipline yourself to look first at your ideas, at how well the paper is focused, and at your organization and support. Consider also whether you've made your purpose clear and if you have a definite audience in mind. At this point it would probably be easier to tinker with words and sentences since you'll see many such things you'll want to change, but resist. Concentrate on the substance first and wait until you have a second draft to make most of your stylistic changes. Whatever you do, don't start out doing a sentence-by-sentence, paragraph-by-paragraph revision. That eats up time and energy and you may never get to the main problems.

In the following section you'll find a specific discussion of what it means to do large-scale revision and an analysis of how the guidelines for large-scale revision were applied to a sample student essay.

First, here is the sample essay, written by a young woman as her final paper in an advanced lower-division writing course at the University of Texas at Austin.

The paper is primarily exploratory. Ann Weid chose country music as her general topic for the semester and had already developed two papers on it so she had accumulated a good deal of information. Although she knew that for her last paper she wanted to write about the place of country music in the rural south and trace its beginnings, she did not have a specific focus when she started nor did she know what material she would use or how she would organize the paper. She counted on its shape developing as she wrote.

SAMPLE STUDENT ESSAY

(NO TITLE YET)

BY ANN MARGARET WEID

AUDIENCE: Readers of *Southern Living* magazine. They live chiefly in the South and are interested in the culture of the South. Many trace their roots to the rural lifestyle.

PURPOSE: I want to give my readers a feel for the place of country music in rural culture, where it came from, and how it still impacts the lives of country people today.

¶1 My earliest memories are of sitting on my father's lap on Sunday mornings listening to Hank Williams sing "Poor Ole Elijah, he never got a kiss." I was raised on the music of Hank Williams and Tex Ritter. My daddy was a great believer in cultural enrichment for the younger generation. This education ranged from the records on Sunday morning to sessions on his lap listening to him read *Tom Sawyer* while he changed his voice to fit the characters.

¶2 In 1977 my parents bought a farm in Fayette County, Texas, where we moved in 1978 from the big city of Houston. One of the first social occasions that I can remember attending in the community was a fireman's feast. The day was filled with homemade kolaches, barbecue, and patriotic speeches. That night there was a street dance. This marked the first of many dances that I was to attend. Through these dances, my cultural identity began to be molded more and more. As was the case with many of the other children my age who were natives of the area, country music began to be ingrained into my cultural awareness. Thus began my long quest for knowledge about the origins of country music and the origin of the local culture. As I investigated, I began to see that the two are hopelessly intertwined.

¶3 Country music traces its roots to rural southern America, specifically the Appalachian and the Allegheny mountain regions of Kentucky. There are more country music performers produced per square mile in that region of the United States than anywhere else in the country. As I began to discover that, I wondered why. This question led me to do more research concerning the history of the area, both geographically and demographically.

¶4 Immigrants—mainly Irish and Scottish—came and settled in Appalachia, drawn by the abundance of unsettled territory that provided fertile ground to grow crops and forests filled with game for meat. Since they were cash-poor, they could not buy the inventions of others so they made everything they needed for the work that they did. Among their needs was included the need for entertainment. Out of this need was born country music as we know it today. One can still hear the Irish and Scottish folk music threading its way through many modern country music songs. One example of this that comes readily to mind is the music of the performer Eddie Rabbit. Randy Travis's work shows, through his choice of instruments and musical styles, those same threads from the origins of country music.

¶5 The hillbilly man whistled his own tunes, sang his own songs, and eventually created his own string instruments with which to entertain himself, his family, and his friends. By exercising his talents out of necessity, he developed them to a level far above that of many who had come from a more advantaged background. This explains the overabundance of musical talent from that region.

¶6 In the 1920s, George Hay, a newspaper reporter from Memphis, Tennessee, was assigned to chronicle life in Appalachia. As part of his assignment, he attended a mountain hoedown, an activity where the mountain people played their stringed instruments, sang, and danced. The excitement and the carefree atmosphere of the hoedown gave him an idea. Eventually, he landed a job as a radio announcer at WSM, the newly established radio station in Nashville, Tennessee. It was at WSM that he put his idea to work. He established the National Barn Dance Program. The program quickly caught on in popularity. It was on December 10, 1927, that the program was renamed. It had been preceded by a program featuring the NBC Symphony Orchestra. In announcing his program, George said, "For the past hour we have been listening to music taken from grand opera, but from now on we will present the Grand Ole Opry." And so the Opry it became.

¶7 Hay's idea was based on a pure-and-simple, "down-home" music that every country resident could relate to. By the late 1920s, the non-professional Opry cast had dropped their dignified coats and ties and donned hilarious hillbilly names for their groups and outlandish costumes to accompany the names. The Possum Hunters, the Fruit Jar Drinkers, and the Gully Jumpers all played to a live audience, which had been brought in to add to the liveliness of the program. Whether it was planned that way or not, the Grand Ole Opry created a demand for personal appearances by the performers. It also created a desire among many of the rural audience to be performers themselves. Thus country music spread over the radio airwaves and across the land to the popularity that it enjoys today. By maintaining that "down-home" style, it has become key to the culture of many rural communities such as the one that I live in.

¶8 Practically every Friday or Saturday night a dance hall is lit up somewhere in Fayette County. The people work hard all week and go to the dance on the weekend to let loose and forget their troubles. Whenever I go, I am struck by the continuity of this institution. Like many of our peers, my husband and I take our babies with us to the dances, packing all their necessities along with a quilt for each to go to sleep while we dance. The ages of the attendees range from a few weeks to seventy-five years and older. The dances are the places where mates are found, children grow up, and old people spend their autumn years in fellowship with others. In this respect, country music is a patch in the quilt of rural culture and rural life is the thread of which the patch is made.

REVISING THE FIRST DRAFT

Ann concentrated on doing only large-scale revising on her initial draft. First, she decided to narrow her purpose significantly. Then she slashed out big chunks of the draft, drastically altered her focus, brought in a major new idea—that country music grew out of hard times—and added material to develop that idea. She reorganized, changed her first paragraphs, but didn't allow herself to get bogged down in stylistic changes. She did keep several paragraphs from the first draft and used them almost verbatim in the second draft.

What follows is an analysis of how one might go through the stages of large-scale revision and how Ann made those kinds of changes in her first revision.

Revising for Focus

In the first draft, particularly for exploratory papers, writers often cover a broad scope, generating more ideas than they can realistically expect to use in their finished paper. As they write, one point reminds them of another, and they put down all their ideas, not sure where they might lead or whether they'll eventually want to use them. Sometimes they'll start off in one direction but, as they write, think of another approach that seems more interesting. The result of this kind of discovery writing is often a broad, but shallow, coverage of their topic.

That's fine. Part of the function of first drafts is to generate material, and it's good to work from abundance, confident that you have more than one subtopic that you could develop. When you reread the draft, you can carve out the most promising material to develop in the second draft.

Notice that Ann has followed this process in her first draft of "The Roots of Country Music." She starts out without a title, but in her statement of purpose (written *before* the draft) she says that she wants to give her readers "a feel for the place of country music in rural culture, where it came from, and how it still impacts the lives of country people." That's a lot to cover in one paper, but she attempts it in the first draft. She starts off well with a personal anecdote and details of the place of country music in her own life and ends up with good visual details in the same vein. In between she writes about the background of country music and how it developed.

In the first draft, then, she really has two main topics, as the small group of students working with her on revision pointed out. She agreed and decided that her main interest was the history of country music so she would focus on that and drop the personal element in her next draft. Not an easy decision because she had put considerable effort into the personal and visual anecdotes in the draft and hated to give them up. She realized, though, that in trying to cover so much the draft lacked focus.

Revising for Audience

In first drafts, particularly for exploratory papers, writers sometimes don't have a clear picture of their readers. They're still "writer centered." With a draft in hand, they can ask questions about their readers. Who cares about the topic? What assumptions can be made about them? What aspect of the topic might be most interesting to them, and what would they want to know? With tentative answers to those questions, they can move toward developing a "reader-centered" second draft.

Ann had already chosen her audience, the readers of *Southern Living* magazine, and was writing with them in mind so her first draft isn't entirely writer centered. She knows those readers are interested in southern culture and history, but on reflection, she realizes they're more interested in the background and history of country music than her personal experiences. That insight was partially responsible for her choosing to focus on those elements of her paper.

Revising for Purpose

Some writers begin a first draft with a clear aim in mind or even on paper in the form of a thesis sentence. That's nice when it happens—it certainly helps one get started. However, more often, writers start with only a strong sense of their general purpose. In that case they have to count on a specific purpose emerging as they write; usually it will. But it's a good idea to have done enough note taking, brainstorming, or freewriting before the first draft so that you at least know what direction you're going in. Otherwise you can waste a lot of time.

If you're writing in response to a specific assignment—perhaps a long paper for a finance course that asks you to identify and discuss three changes in banking regulations that encouraged the savings and loan debacle of the 1980s—be sure you stick closely to the purpose given you. Check your first draft carefully to see that you have.

The biggest change from Ann's first to second draft reflects her shift from a broad, general purpose to the more specific one of tracing the roots of country music. Notice that the idea of country music emerging as a response to hard times, a central motif in the second and third drafts, didn't even appear in first draft but developed as she narrowed her topic and began to expand on it in the second draft. Now she also has a title that reflects the new purpose: "The Roots of Country Music."

Revising for Proportion

Not all large-scale revisions involve substantial cutting and subsequent expansion, but when you drastically alter the focus of a paper, you usually have to cut a major part of the first draft. That can be painful, particularly if you're the kind of writer who spends a long time tinkering with first paragraphs, even for a first draft. But if you are going to pick out the most interesting part of a rambling paper and develop it, you have to be ruthless about getting rid of material that no longer fits. Then it's time to consider how to expand on and add details to the part that is going to be the center of the second draft.

Notice that Ann succeeded in being ruthless about getting rid of two sections of the first draft, sections that she probably enjoyed writing. But they no longer fit into her new purpose and had to go. Now she starts out with the idea of country music as a response to hard times and expands on its origins from the music of nature. She adds details about specific hard times that country people endured and about specific country western songs, giving lyrics to support her points. At the end she draws an analogy between blues and country music and reinforces the theme of hard times. The second draft is now substantially different from the first, better focused and rich in detail.

Revising for Organization

When you've made substantial changes in a draft and shifted your focus, the final thing you need to check on when you're writing the second draft is organization. Does the paper still have a clear pattern and will your reader will be able to stay on track without any trouble? If not, look for gaps or faulty arrangement and see what you need to do to fix them.

Ann reorganized her paper dramatically when she changed her focus, starting with a new opening paragraph introducing the theme of hard times, which is then expanded on in the second paragraph. She still uses most of the narratives about country music and its growth in popularity, but she has moved the material around (easy to do with a word processor) and devised a completely new ending that rounds off the paper nicely.

A SAMPLE REVISED DRAFT

The Roots of Country Music

by Ann Margaret Weid

¶1 Southern sounds were the first sound from which country music evolved—the music of nature. The wind blowing through the trees in the southern mountains, the water laughing as it tripped over the rocks in those unspoiled southern streams, and the birds singing their lonely southern love songs were the first sounds heard by the settlers in the new territory which is now Appalachia. The settlers had brought their own music from their homeland, the British Isles, and it evoked the same sense of freedom that they now heard in this natural music. Their music, which was played chiefly on stringed instruments, shared another familiar characteristic with the natural music of Appalachia—it had the mournful quality that appealed to the listener. It was this mournful quality which enabled the players and the listeners to vent their emotions and derive from the music a sense of peace and relaxation which they needed, for those were hard times.

¶2 Hard times are the lifeblood of the South's music—country music. Country music traces its roots to rural southern America, specifically the Appalachian and Allegheny mountain regions of Kentucky. There are more country music performers produced per square mile in that region of the United States than anywhere else in the country. Maybe it's that the hard times of which the South has seen so much were of such long standing that they required an outlet.

¶3 Immigrants, mainly Irish and Scottish, who came and settled in Appalachia, had seen their share of hard times—the potato famine and domination by the British—and would see many more in their new-found home—the Civil War and its aftermath, the family feuding and the killing that accompanied it. These early southerners were drawn by the abundance of unsettled territory which could provide fertile ground to grow crops and forests filled with game. With this vast new territory came the freedom to live according to their beliefs, a freedom that had been sorely lacking in their homeland.

¶4 These early southerners were rich in freedom, but they were cash-poor. They could not buy the inventions of others so they made everything they needed for all that they did. Among their needs was entertainment. Self-sufficient out of necessity, they whistled their own tunes, sang their own songs, and developed the stringed instruments they had brought from their homeland and added new ones. By exercising their musical talents out of necessity, the mountain people developed them to a level far above that of many who had come from a more advantaged background.

¶5 The stories of hard times and the Celtic melodies can still be heard echoing across the generations in the music of many modern country artists. It shows in their choice of instruments and the musical keys in which the songs are written. And the hard times from which the music was born is still evident in today's music, as well as a nostalgia for better times.

¶6 The nostalgia is evident in lyrics such as those in Randy Travis's song "Forever and Ever Amen." They read, "As long as old men sit and talk about the weather, as long as old women sit and talk about old men." It is also evident in the lyrics of Alabama's ballad "High Cotton": "We were sitting in high cotton. Old times there are not forgotten. Those fertile fields are never far away." Hard times figure in Loretta Lynn's song "Coal Miner's Daughter"—"I was born a coal miner's daughter . . . my daddy worked all day for a poor man's dollar" and in the words of Hank Williams's song "I'll Never Get Out of This World Alive."

¶7 The route that country music took out of Appalachia and across the nation can be traced back to Memphis, Tennessee, in the 1920s. The journey began when George D. Hay, a reporter for a newspaper in Memphis was given an assignment to chronicle life in Appalachia. As part of his assignment, he attended a mountain hoedown where the mountain people played their stringed instruments, sang, and danced. The excitement and the carefree atmosphere in which mountain people seemed to forget their hard times gave him an idea. When he eventually landed a job as a radio announcer for the new radio station in Memphis, he put his idea to work and established the National Barn Dance Program. It quickly caught on in popularity, for hard times were nationwide.

¶8 Hay's idea was based on a simple "down-home" type of music that everyone who had ever had hard times could relate to. By the late 1920s, the nonprofessional cast had dropped their dignified coats and ties and donned hilarious hillbilly names for their groups and outlandish costumes to accompany the names. The Possum Hunters, the Fruit Jar Drinkers, and the Gully Jumpers all played to a live audience, which had been brought in to add to the liveliness of the program. One night as Hay was announcing the program, which was preceded by the NBC Orchestra, he said, "For the past hour we have been listening to music taken from Grand Opera. From now on we will listen to the Grand Ole Opry." Whether it was planned that way or it just happened, the "Opry" created a demand for personal appearances across the country by performers.

¶9 Country music, born of hard times, is to us southern people what blues is to black people. It's soul music which we use to vent our emotions and deal with our hard times. Over the radio waves our southern soul music was spread to everyone in the country to whom hard times were familiar. Since there will probably always be hard times from which to escape, there will probably always be country music to provide that escape. For pity's sake, what do the people in the North do with their hard times?

REVISING THE SECOND DRAFT

When you have a solid second draft in hand, you're ready to start the small-scale revision that deals mainly with surface features—the details of style. They're worth spending time on if you want to turn out a paper that's clear, tightly organized, economical, and smoothly written.

The main procedures you need to concern yourself with at this point are these:

- Cutting and condensing
- Adding color with details
- Rewriting and rearranging sentences
- Improving word choice
- Strengthening transitions

* Revising opening and closing paragraphs
* Improving tone

In the next two chapters, I talk about how to do all of these things and give some specific strategies that will help you turn solid, but mundane, writing into prose that purrs along like a well-tuned car. Thus I won't expand on these points here—read over those chapters and take what you need from them.

You may find it useful, however, to look at Ann's final draft of "The Roots of Country Music" and, after you finish, to check my analysis of the small-scale changes she made to polish and refine her paper.

A SAMPLE FINAL DRAFT

THE ROOTS OF COUNTRY MUSIC

BY ANN MARGARET WEID

AUDIENCE (REVISED): Readers of *Southern Living*, a magazine directed to readers interested in southern culture and life. Because country music is one of the great accomplishments of the South, I think this piece about its history and development would appeal to the readers.

PURPOSE (REVISED): To trace the roots of country music in the United States and show that from the time of the early settlers to the present, country people have used music to help them cope with hard times.

¶1 Hard times are the lifeblood of the South's music—country music. Country music traces its roots to rural southern America, specifically the Appalachian and Allegheny mountain regions of Kentucky, and to the hard times of those early settlers. Those hard times, of which the South has seen so many, were of such long standing that they naturally required an outlet.

¶2 Southern sounds were the first sounds from which country music evolved—the music of nature. The wind blowing through the trees in the southern mountains, the water rippling over the rocks in those clear southern streams, and the birds singing their lonely southern love songs were the first sounds heard by the settlers in the new territory. The settlers had brought their own music from their homeland, the British Isles, and it evoked the same sense of freedom that they now heard in this natural music. This music also shared a mournful quality with the natural music of the South, allowing its players to vent their emotions and derive from the music a sense of peace and relaxation that they needed.

¶3 The people who settled Appalachia were used to hard times. They were immigrants, mainly Irish and Scottish, who had had their share of troubles during the potato famine and the ongoing domination of the British Empire. These early southerners were drawn to the region by the abundance of unsettled territory which could provided fertile ground to grow crops and forests filled with game. With this vast new territory came the freedom to live according to their beliefs, a freedom that had been sorely lacking in their homeland.

¶4 These early southerners were rich in freedom but they were cash-poor. They could not buy the inventions of others so they made everything that they needed. Among those needs, particularly in times of hardship, was the need for entertainment. Self-sufficient out of necessity, they whistled their own tunes, sang their own songs, and not only refined the stringed instruments that they had brought from their homeland but invented new ones. From necessity the mountain people of the South developed their musical talents far beyond those of many who had come from a more advantaged background. The hard times that were part of the culture fed the music.

¶5 The hard times and Celtic imagination can still be heard echoing across the generations, feeding the music of many modern country artists. Their use of stringed instruments originally used in Celtic music and the keys in which their songs are written reveal the unique heritage of that portion of the South.

¶6 For the early southerners, the hard times did not end with their emigration to America. In fact, one could say they had just begun. Part of the careworn history of that region of the country are years of family feuding in which families sometimes lost whole generations to bloodshed over matters of pride. Then, just as that bloody chapter began to close, a more devastating one was being written—the Civil War. Once again, family was pitted against family. But the people of the South stuck together in their fall from glory and grandeur to abject poverty and degradation.

¶7 Whether it was the length of the hardship or the unity of her people, the South developed a music and culture all her own. And this music had an appeal which could reach any person who had seen a share of hard times. The vehicle for the journey of the music of the South out of this region and across the nation was the Grand Ole Opry, and the driver was George D. Hay.

¶8 George Dewey Hay, the "Solemn Ole Judge," began his career as a newspaper reporter for a daily in Memphis, Tennessee, in the 1920s. As part of an assignment to chronicle life in Appalachia, he attended a mountain hoedown, where the mountain people played their stringed instruments, sang, and danced. The excitement and the carefree atmosphere in which mountain people found that they could forget their hard times gave him an idea. When he landed a job as a radio announcer for the new radio station in Memphis, he put his idea to work and established the National Barn Dance program. It quickly caught on for hard times had spread nationwide.

¶9 Hay's idea was based on a simple "down-home" type of music that everyone who had ever had hard times could relate to. By the late 1920s the performers had dropped their dignified coats and ties and donned hilarious hillbilly names for their groups and costumes to match. The Possum Hunters, The Fruit Jar Drinkers, and The Gully Jumpers all played to a live audience which had been brought in to enliven the program. At about the same time, the name was changed. One night as Hay was beginning the program, which had been preceded by the NBC Orchestra, he said, "For the past hour we have been listening to music taken from Grand Opera. From now on, we will listen to the Grand Ole Opry." Whether it was planned or it just happened, the "Opry" created a demand for personal appearances by performers all over the country. Over the radio airwaves country music spread throughout the country.

¶10 Country music, born of hard times, is to us southerners what blues is to the black people. It's soul music which we use to deal with our hard times. Since there will probably always be hard times from which to escape, there will probably always be country music to provide that escape. For pity's sake, what do the people in the North do with their hard times?

Analysis of Small-Scale Changes

First, Ann revised her audience and purpose statements to reflect what she actually does in this final draft.

Then, notice that the paper is much tighter. By changing paragraph 2 from the previous draft into her opening paragraph, Ann immediately introduces her readers to her central idea: country music grew out of southerners' hard times. She repeats the motif several times in the paper and reinforces it in her closing paragraph.

In this draft she eliminates paragraph 6 of the previous draft, the one quoting nostalgic lyrics from contemporary country music songs, because it doesn't tie directly with her central idea. She gets rid of other details from the previous draft, such as the information from paragraph 2 that there are more country musicians per square mile in Appalachia than in any other part of the country.

She streamlines the narrative of the paper, moving smoothly from the account of how the early settlers developed country music through its spread across the South to its current popularity. She adds color with a new metaphor in paragraph 7. She cuts sentences from the first and last paragraphs and makes minor word changes, such as substituting *performers* for *nonprofessionals* and *southerners* for *southern people*. All these are minor changes, of course, but the total effect is a smoother, more polished, and more readable paper.

REVISING IN PEER GROUPS

In many writing classes today students work together in peer groups to help each other with revising. Such groups work well for a number of reasons.

For one thing, they give each writer a chance to write for an audience other than the instructor. When you know who's going to read your paper, you're more likely to take the matter of audience seriously and think ahead about what will interest them and how you can explain your ideas clearly. You also benefit from immediate feedback on drafts, getting responses and constructive advice as you are developing your paper.

When you work with writing groups in class, usually you will find that a community of writers forms rather quickly. That is, both the class and individual groups come together through their writing and through their genuine interest in what each other is doing. After some initial self-consciousness, they look forward to reading each other's work and responding to it, and they take pride in each other's achievements. It's a good experience for any writer.

Working with other writers as they draft and revise can also increase your confidence in your own writing. You're likely to find that other writers struggle to get started and that their first drafts aren't wonderful either. Writing groups can also make you a more confident reader; you'll find out how much you can help other writers and what good papers all of you can turn out when you cooperate.

Guidelines for Working in Writing Groups

Working in groups can be difficult at first. Sometimes students are reluctant to comment on each other's work, protesting, as some of my students have, "Who am I to tell other people what's wrong with their writing?"

My answer is, "Try not to think of this as telling people what's 'wrong.' That's not what groups are for. You're acting as an interested reader who wants to find out what someone else has to tell you. Then you respond by making comments and asking questions. You try to give others the kind of feedback you'd like to have."

Giving others good feedback means avoiding two extremes. You shouldn't just say everything is wonderful for fear of hurting someone's feelings, nor should you be hypercritical, picking on surface errors. Neither kind of response is helpful.

When you start to work in groups, observing certain ground rules will help to get a productive conversation started. Here they are.

• Start by paying attention to *what* other writers are saying, just as you

Response Sheet for Large-Scale Revision

Author's name _____

Paper title _____

Name of person responding to draft _____

1. What strengths does this paper have? What works well?

2. To what extent does the writer seem to be keeping the audience in mind?

   Any suggestions for improvement?

3. What does the writer's purpose seem to be?

   Any suggestions for improvement?

4. How well does the draft focus on a central topic?

   Any suggestions for improvement?

5. What questions might a reader have after reading the draft?

6. What additional examples might improve the paper?

7. What are two suggestions that could be made for the next draft?

8. General comments?

Response Sheet for Small-Scale Revision

Author's name _____

Title of draft_____

Name of person responding to draft _____

1. What is especially interesting or effective about this draft?

2. What good stylistic features are evident?

   Suggestions?

3. What seems to be the central idea of the draft?

4. How well does the draft seem to address its audience?

5. Comment on the opening paragraph.

   Suggestions?

6. Comment on the organization of the draft. How well unified is it?

7. What suggestions, if any, might one make about cutting at some places?

8. At what places, if any, might additional details or examples help?

9. Comment on the conclusion.

10. Questions and general comments.

hope they'll pay attention to what you're saying. In other words, look at content first.

* Remember that a draft conference is not the place to argue with a writer about his or her ideas. Try not to say things like "I think you're wrong." Each writer has the right to his or her own ideas; your role is to help that writer express those ideas clearly and effectively, not to disagree with them.

* When you are commenting on a first draft, focus on large issues, the kind that figure in large-scale revising. Don't waste time on surface problems in parts of the draft that may be cut when the writer revises.

* Establish the rule that no one starts out by apologizing for his or her draft or by making excuses. That's a temptation, of course—all of us are a little nervous when we first show our work to someone else. But by definition, drafts are works in progress, and it only holds up productive discussion to take time for apologies.

If you are in a writing class in which groups meet regularly, your instructor will probably have additional useful suggestions. If you are not in that kind of class, you may want to set up a group as a way to get useful feedback as you're writing—when it is most valuable to you.

Responding to Drafts

In my class I use response sheets for responding to students' drafts instead of writing on the papers themselves. I have found this keeps me focused on large-scale concerns and on the priorities I want to emphasize in the class. Within your group, you may find the response sheet helpful in working with drafts. Fill one out for each draft you receive from other members of your small groups, and use them as the basis for discussion in group conferences. This way, each student leaves his or her draft conference with written and oral comments to draw on in revising.

REVISING UNDER PRESSURE

Sometimes we simply don't have time to write three drafts of a paper or tinker with our sentence structure and word choice enough to turn out really polished work. That's particularly true on the job, where you may be asked for a report or analysis in twenty-four or forty-eight hours; no extensions granted. What happens to revising under such circumstances? Do you resign yourself to turning in a sloppy piece of writing?

No. You really can't afford that, especially on the job. I recommend that you develop habits that will serve you well when the pressure is on. And I also recommend strongly that you learn to write on a word processor so you can revise and edit instantly when you need to.

First, no matter how pressed you are, plan to do two drafts. Get the first one out quickly, stopping occasionally to reread and run a mental check to see that you're covering the essentials. Make a hard copy of the first draft and read it carefully, making notes on it. Then when you write the second draft, do pay attention to spelling and punctuation and get it right. If you're a terrible speller, get someone else to read your revised first draft before you recopy it.

Second, when you are not under pressure and can take time to think about matters of style, work on internalizing some sentence patterns that strengthen and clarify your writing (see especially suggestions in Chapter 8). For instance, avoid passive verbs; start sentences with a person or thing who will be the subject; put people in your writing; avoid long introductory clauses; use short, strong verbs instead of verb phrases. The more conscious you become of these ingredients of good writing, the stronger will be your first drafts.

Third, because you're not going to have time to move from writer-based to reader-based prose, keep your audience in mind constantly. As you write, ask yourself,

- Am I telling my readers what they want to know? Or more than I need to be telling them?
- Am I using language they'll understand?
- Am I using a straightforward, step-by-step pattern that can't lose them?
- Am I answering the questions they would have on the topic?

Fourth, read the first draft to see what you can cut. Getting rid of wordiness is the most visible way to improve your writing.

Finally, be confident that you can write successfully under a tight deadline. There are thousands of writers who turn out amazingly good work under pressure—it is possible. Remember too that the more often you work at careful revision when you have time, the better you will get at revising under pressure.

WHEN TO STOP REVISING

Writing teachers and writing textbooks constantly stress the conventional wisdom that all good writing is rewriting, and mostly they're right. Everything we know about the writing process suggests that writing is generative, that it develops through stages, and that writers improve their work as they work through drafts and try out various options. For most writing tasks, however, one can reach a point of diminishing returns with revising. Even on important work, that point probably comes at the fourth or fifth draft. If you have put substantial efforts into those drafts and made significant changes as you worked, tinkering with words and sentences in the process, I doubt that writing another two or three drafts will make a big difference, at least not in proportion to the amount of effort invested. Not everyone would agree, but such people may be the "bleeders" I described in Chapter 3, compulsive revisers who can't let their work go. For the following reasons, I suggest that you consider carefully before you go on to a fifth or sixth draft.

First, when you have read and reread something a dozen times, you lose your distance from it and can no longer see its flaws. Like the blocked writer in Albert Camus's novel *The Plague*, you could agonize indefinitely about whether you should describe the horse as "brown" or "chestnut." At some point you have to realize that such trivia makes no difference.

Second, you may be blocking your growth as a writer by worrying too much over the problems that one writing assignment presents. Instead of continuing to wrestle with some problem that seems intractable, you would learn more by moving on to a new challenge.

Third, you run the danger of becoming a perfectionist who is not willing to turn loose a piece of writing because it's not exactly right. But nothing is ever "exactly right." That kind of reluctance can become an excuse not to show your writing and thus to shield yourself from criticism. But you cannot improve your writing unless you are willing, finally to expose it to the judgment of others.

Ultimately, you have to do some cost accounting about your revising. What are you willing to invest for what kind of payoff? How much do you care about doing really good work? Are you willing to put in the extra eight or ten hours that it might take to turn a draft that would earn a B into a paper that would get an A? Are you willing to write and rewrite, get feedback, and rewrite again and perhaps again? Is that a good investment for you? Is your writing so important to you that you are willing to make it your top priority?

Writers who face these questions often have second thoughts when they realize how much time and effort they will have to invest to revise solid, competent writing into first-rate writing, and they may decide to settle for less than the best because they have other priorities. That's a legitimate and often sensible decision. It's good to know, however, that most satisfactory writers *can* become good writers. Whether they have the time, energy, and will to do so is another matter. But anyone who decides he or she wants to be an excellent writer is going to have to work at revising. It can pay off handsomely.

7 ◇ Holding Your Reader

One writing teacher compares the task of a writer to that of a tour director escorting a group of sightseers who do not have to pay their fares until they arrive at their destination and get off the bus. The job of both author and tour director requires that they keep their audiences so interested in what is going on that they will stay until the end of the journey. Readers, like tourists, are capricious and impatient, and they will go off and do something else if they get confused, bored, or led off on a detour that seems pointless to them. When you write, you may find it helpful to keep this analogy in mind and from time to time ask yourself, "Are my readers liable to get off the bus here?" And writers, like tour directors, must keep their audiences oriented. If there is any way for readers to get lost, they will!

All writers need to keep this caution in mind as they write (especially their second or third drafts) and to work consciously to help their readers stay on track as they are reading. Once they stray, they are hard to recapture. For that reason, a writer needs to have some specific strategies for holding readers.

But you should also remember that the most important way of holding your readers involves a principle, not a strategy. That principle is that *most readers will stay with you as long as they are learning something.* As long as you can give them information that interests or entertains them, teach them something they didn't know before, you are likely to keep them reading.

CHOOSING A GOOD TITLE

Titles play a crucial part in getting off to a good start with your readers. In fact, your prospective readers will often decide whether or not to read what you write primarily on the information you give them in the title. That's why it's so important that your title be clear, accurate, and, if possible, interesting. It should also perform some very specific functions.

First, a good title should *predict* the contents of the paper accurately enough for the reader to decide if he or she wants to read it. Titles like "The Roots of Country Music" or "How to Get the Most Car Stereo for Your Money" are direct and accurate enough to immediately attract readers who are interested in those subjects. Good titles also influence your course instructors, because they can signal whether you have chosen a manageable topic, and they help prepare your readers to concentrate on what you've written. A title like "Irony in Shakespeare's Histories" is so broad it would immediately trigger an instructor's skeptical instincts; one like "Richard's Manipulation of Women in *Richard III*" would probably make a better impression because it looks more specific and manageable.

An effective title *limits* the topic and *focuses* it for the readers; it helps point them in the right direction. It also prepares them to process the writer's message and thus makes it more likely that they will understand it. On complex issues, the writer can give the reader even more help by adding a more specific subtitle. For example, "Excellence or Elitism: Which Do Ivy League Colleges Promote?" or "The Cycle of Starvation in Africa: What Lies Ahead?"

A good title *identifies* and *categorizes* so that someone who is doing research can immediately tell whether an article relates to his or her topic. That may seem like a remote concern when you're writing for college courses, but it's a good idea to get in the habit of writing a title that won't allow your article to get lost. Some day you may turn something you have written into a publishable article, particularly if you go on to graduate work. So when you choose a title, imagine the cataloger or file clerk who may some day have to classify your paper but doesn't have time to read it. Will he or she be able to decide easily where it should be filed?

You can make your work easy to classify by using key words in your title that serve as "descriptors" for the computer. For example, an article on ways to start a small business while you are in college should have the words *small business* and *college* in it—perhaps "How to Work Your Way Through College by Starting a Small Business." That does everything a good title should do. If, however, you titled such an article "A Profit on Your Own Campus," would-be future readers would have no way to locate the article. In general, it's a good idea to get in the habit of testing your titles with the question, "Could this be misconstrued?" If it can be, you need to change it.

Finally, in most instances you should resist the impulse to give your writing cute, facetious, or deliberately ambiguous titles. They're tempting, particularly if you like jokes, but they're risky. You may mislead your readers or annoy them because they don't share your sense of humor, and, of course, such titles are the ones most likely to be misclassified.

WRITING STRONG LEADS

The lead of any piece of writing is critically important. In those first paragraphs and pages, you can make or break yourself with your reader. One well-known author and editor, William Zinsser, puts it this way:

> The most important sentence in any article is the first one. If it doesn't induce the reader to proceed to the second sentence, your article is dead. And if the second sentence doesn't induce him to continue to the third sentence, it's equally dead. Of such a progression of sentences, each tugging the reader forward until he is safely hooked, a writer constructs that fateful unit: the "lead."
> —William Zinsser, *On Writing Well*, 4th ed.
> (New York: HarperCollins, 1990), 65.

Even if you're not competing for that fickle audience of magazine readers, you still risk losing your readers' attention if you write weak openers. Readers like editors, vice-presidents, or members of admission committees are busy and impatient folks. Asked how long it takes them to make preliminary decisions about the manuscripts, reports, or personal statements that come across their desks, most would respond, "A minute or two. I read the first page or two and usually I can tell if it's worth my time to go on."

Harsh? Yes, indeed. But realistic too. If you want to hold your readers, you have about ninety seconds to convince them that what you are going to say will be interesting or informative or useful to them. "But," you say, that's not really true of professors. They have to read what I write." Well, yes and no. Professors are busy and impatient too, and although they may have to read your papers, they don't have to like them or take much interest in them. If your writing begins with a long dull paragraph or you fail to make your main point clear, you stand to lose your reader—even when it's your instructor. I have known a professor who would draw a line and write, "I stopped reading here," if she couldn't grasp a student's main idea by the middle of the second page.

So openings are crucial, and you need to think carefully about how you handle those first few paragraphs. You don't necessarily have to come up with a startling or gimmicky opening to catch your reader; in fact, in many writing situations, such an opening would be so inappropriate it could do more harm than good. But for any opening, keep this in mind: *Good open-*

ings let the reader know what to expect. In your opening section, you make a promise, or *commitment,* to your reader and raise his or her expectations. (More on this important concept of the writer's commitment in Chapter 9.) Then you must go on to fulfill that promise and meet that commitment, or you will quickly lose your reader.

Writers use many kinds of opening commitments; two of the most common are those that promise *to intrigue* and those that promise *to inform.* The writer who wants to intrigue can do so with an anecdote, a quotation, an analogy, or an allusion of some kind. For instance, for a magazine article about the savings and loan debacle of the late 1980s, an author begins with this elegant first paragraph.

> Ever since the first Florentine loaned his first ducat to his first Medici, it has been one of the most shopworn clichés of the financial industry that the best way to rob a bank is to own one. This maxim, like all maxims, is rooted in a basic truth about human nature: to wit, if criminals are given easy access to large sums of money, they will steal, and under such tempting circumstances, even honest men may be corrupted. To forget this is to invite madness and ruin. In our time, such madness and ruin has visited in the form of the savings and loan scandal.
>
> —L. J. Davis, "Chronicle of a Debacle Foretold: How Deregulation Begat the S&L Scandal," *Harper's Magazine,* September 1990, 50.

Davis has intrigued his readers with a promise to tell them about the circumstances that led to the savings and loan crisis.

The management consultants Thomas Peters and Robert Waterman begin one of the chapters in their book *In Search of Excellence* with this intriguing quotation: " 'The Navy,' says ex-Chief of Naval Operations Elmo Zumwalt, 'assumes that everyone below the rank of commander is immature.' " Having raised their readers' curiosity about how such a statement is related to business management, the authors go on to explain.

Here is a promise-to-inform opening from a *Smithsonian* article on astronomy:

> Ever since the human mind first grasped the immensity and complexity of the Universe, Man has tried to explain how it could have come into being.

The article goes on to explain the Big Bang theory of the origin of the universe and the formation of galaxies.

Which kind of opening is better? There is no easy answer; each time you write you have to decide according to what you perceive as your readers' expectations and according to your purpose in writing. Intriguing openers can capture fickle readers and persuade them to go on reading, but they can also annoy readers if they delay too long in getting to the point. Although the straight informative opening may not seem as interesting, often it is safer, particularly for documents in business or industry, because readers there generally want to go straight to the point. You will have to decide.

WHAT FIRST PARAGRAPHS DO

You make your strongest commitment to your reader in your opening paragraph, giving strong signals and setting the tone for the rest of your paper or article. An opening paragraph should do these things.

* Engage the reader's attention.
* Predict content.
* Give readers a reason to continue reading.
* Set the tone of the writing.

Another way to put it is that the opening paragraph lays down the tracks for both writer and reader. It draws the readers in with a promise, it gives them signals about what lies ahead, it creates a link with the next paragraphs, and it establishes the writer's tone and stance by using certain kinds of language and structure.

Different Kinds of Opening Paragraphs

I can't give you clear-cut formulas for opening paragraphs because different kinds of writing tasks call for different kinds of openings. Sometimes —when you're writing technical reports or case studies for example—you'll have definite specifications about how your opening paragraphs should look and what they should cover. For other kinds of writing, there may be traditional patterns you should follow. If you think that might be the case, ask for specific directions so you won't be penalized for failing to conform with the approved model.

In other, more diverse kinds of writing, however—travel articles, informative essays, book or movie reviews, persuasive articles, to name just a few—you may use many kinds of opening paragraphs, all of them effective in different situations. Choose your introductory paragraph according to your writing situation, taking into account your goal and the kind of audience you envision yourself writing for. Here are several possibilities.

STRAIGHTFORWARD ANNOUNCEMENTS

In many instances, you will do best to begin with a direct, clear, and economical statement. Certainly this guideline applies to writing whose main purpose is to convey factual information to a busy reader; for instance, market reports, case studies, summaries of action, or requests for information. In this kind of writing, the reader wants key information as quickly as possible—no anecdotes or ceremonial preliminaries. For example,

> Set in the heart of Athens, a splendid neoclassical villa holds some of Greece's most extraordinary art and artifacts. The Benaki Museum, founded in 1930 by Hellenophile and collector Anthony Benaki, is one of the world's most captivating treasure houses.
> —Kathleen Burke, "Golden Ornament from Greece," *Smithsonian*, November 1990, 202.

Direct openings that announce your thesis also work well for academic research papers. For instance, here is the opening paragraph of a paper done for a course in international business:

> Lockheed Aircraft and Gulf Oil were recently prosecuted by the federal government for giving bribes to foreign businessmen in order to make their products more attractive to those potential clients. During indictment proceedings both corporations contended that their cash payments were both necessary and common among international businesses. The question then is how common is bribery in foreign nations and whether the United States should prevent our corporations from offering bribes even when doing so is a common and accepted practice.

Straight-to-the-point opening paragraphs also work well when you are writing a request. Although many of us are reluctant to be blunt when we have to ask people for time or money or favors, most readers prefer a straightforward request to a preliminary buildup that wastes their time. When you have a legitimate and reasonable request to make, state it quickly and clearly so you don't waste your readers' time.

OPENING ANECDOTES OR NARRATIVES

In other writing situations, you must find a way to entice your audience with the promise of something interesting to come. When you have only those first two minutes to catch the attention of a reader with no obligation to read what you write, you need to make that opening paragraph particularly provocative. Experienced free-lance writers know a multitude of ways to meet this challenge, but one of the most common is the description or anecdote that lures the reader into the world the author is going to write about. Here are two examples:

> A wiry young climber slips spider-like up an outward-angled rock face, clipping a nylon rope into carabiners attached to bolted anchors as she goes. Though the moves are finger-wrenching, she breezes through them: Earlier in the day, while hanging by top-rope and drilling holes for the bolts needed to secure her in case of a fall, she had scrutinized every fingernail-width handhold and foothold on the face. Now, after dipping her fingers into a brightly colored bed of sweat-absorbing chalk, she lunges for the last hand-hold and pulls herself over the top of the cliff.
>
> —Ed Webster, "To Bolt or Not to Bolt,"
> *Sierra,* November–December 1990, 30.

> "Please don't call me a guru," Dr. Dean Ornish asks. The voice is softly nasal but insistent, and its request ignores the fact the Ornish has posed for both the *Houston Post* and *People* magazine meditating in the lotus position. But Ornish, 37, has no problem with contradictions. These days, he finds himself preaching that a person can reverse coronary disease and find inner peace by opening his heart according to the Ornish plan—"a different type of 'open-heart' procedure, one based on love, knowledge, and compassion rather than just drugs and surgery"—while the demands of celebrity have turned him into a whirling dervish. Curls lapping at his receding hairline, blue eyes doleful, mustache adroop, he spread his message from his Sausalito, California, office, spinning from the VCR . . . to the fax . . . to the copy machine . . . with enviable deftness. Just this brief exposure to Ornish reveals one essential truth: Unlike the people who have committed to the restrictive diet and coronary-care regimen that has made him famous, Dean Ornish intends to have his cake and eat it too.
>
> —Mimi Swartz, "The Ornish Treatment,"
> *Texas Monthly,* March 1991, 104–105.

These are straightforward but vivid openings that catch the readers' attention, give them strong clues about what to expect from the articles, and stimulate enough interest to make them want to go on reading.

QUESTIONS

Questions often serve as excellent openers. They pique the readers' curiosity and focus their attention directly on the issue. You can use one question or several in a paragraph. For example,

> I've always wondered about dog food. Is a Gaines-burger really like a hamburger? Can you fry it? Does dog food "cheese" taste like real

cheese? Does Gravy Train actually make gravy in the dog's bowl, or is that brown liquid just dissolved crumbs? And exactly what *are* by-products?

> —Ann Hodgman, "No Wonder They Call Me
> a Bitch," reprinted in *The Best American*
> *Essays of 1990*, ed. Justin Kaplan, (New York:
> Ticknor & Fields, 1990), 112.
> This essay originally appeared in *Spy*.

Solving the Opening Paragraph Dilemma

Even experienced writers often find themselves caught in the opening paragraph dilemma. One one hand, they're hyperconscious that they must have a strong first paragraph to capture their readers and set them moving in the right direction. On the other hand, they know they can't afford to spend hours experimenting with different approaches and tinkering with first lines, or they'll never get to writing. They're caught between their high standards and their deadlines. That can be an agonizing experience, one you may have been through yourself more than once.

The best solution to this dilemma is to remember the advice on getting started from Chapter 5. In order to get started writing, get down on paper —or on screen—anything that seems at all relevant: a statement of the problem you want to solve, a question you intend to answer, an anecdote that relates to your topic, even one of those tired openings "In this paper I intend to . . . ." Even if you write a first paragraph that is obvious and dull, just getting it on paper will help you push off and get moving. Remind yourself that whatever you write, even though you love it, you may have to discard it later when you're revising. Right now you need to get on with your writing and produce a first draft.

You don't even need to come up with a wonderful first paragraph for your first revision. For that draft you may be narrowing your idea and rearranging some of your supporting points. With the second revision, you can start thinking seriously about crafting a good lead paragraph that draws on the ideas you've generated and reflects a sense of your audience. As you work on your opener, think about the four things it is suppose to do: catch the reader, predict content, stimulate further reading, and set the tone.

TIGHTENING YOUR WRITING

Writing that is highly readable has a quality called *linearity;* that is, the reader can move steadily through it in a straight line without having to stop to puzzle about what the writer means or double back to reread. Achieving this quality in your writing isn't easy, but it's a goal worth striving for if you want to hold your readers. Think how often you have bogged down in dense, difficult writing or found yourself hydroplaning across the surface, only to realize you were going to have to stop and go back. If you could quit reading, you probably did. If you couldn't, you plowed on but groaned and cursed the writer who was making life so difficult for you. None of us want our readers to feel that way about our writing, particularly not readers who are in a position to penalize us for giving them so much trouble.

There are a number of strategies you can use to keep your readers on track. They range from mastering transition devices to improving the body language of your writing.

Hooks and Nudges

Readers can lose their way or get bogged down in writing for a variety of reasons, of course, not all of them the writer's responsibility. But it is the writer's responsibility to provide hooks—*links* that hold writing together by showing connections—and *nudges,* words that give readers a little push from one point to another. You need a stock of such terms at your fingertips to draw on.

Hooks	*Nudges*
also	this
moreover	then
for example	first
in addition	consequently
however	next
in spite of	

For instance, here is a student paragraph with both hooks and nudges italicized.

> Like a rat that avoids electric shock, a child avoids contact with those who *hurt* him. *So* avoiding *punishment,* except as a last resort, is advisable. *Punishment* instills hate and fear and soon becomes an "aversive stimulus." *Also,* because the only real effect of *it* is to suppress a response temporarily, no permanent weakening of the unwanted behavior takes place. *And* as soon as the effect, or the sting of the *spanking,* wears off, the child repeats *it.*

It is important to realize, however, that the best source of unity in writing comes from the *inside,* from the underlying pattern or internal structure of a piece of writing, not from transitional words tacked on from the outside. Words like *moreover* and *nevertheless* should reflect organization, not impose it, and readers are most likely to feel that a piece of writing is tight and coherent if they sense that it follows one of the common thought patterns discussed in the last chapter. For example, here is a student paragraph that is held together by its narrative pattern, not by transitional devices:

> Just before noon under imposing dark storm clouds in the southern suburbs of Beirut, lunch was being served. It was an austere, poorly lit concrete house recently rebuilt from the rubble which still covered much of the suburb of Burj Al Barajinah, then the headquarters of the Shiite Muslim militia. The wife, clothed in the traditional long black robe of the local Shiite women, served coffee, small oranges and unleavened bread to be dipped in a lentil stew. She spoke with her husband and son with a boldness which custom would not permit out of doors. Friends came and went. One stayed for lunch, a tall man in new fatigues who laid his automatic rifle by the couch and began to eat. The young son, three or four by the looks of him, with chubby cheeks and a healthy pink glow showing through his olive skin, was exchanging playful banter with his mother. After the meal and conversation, the father's and soldier's attention turned to the boy. The father stood up, the boy hugged his father's leg playfully. The father kicked the boy to the ground, and as he was falling the playful smile turned to fear and tears of pain. After the boy stopped crying, the father turned to the visitor with a smile of pride and said, "He too will learn to fight."

Directional Signals

Often you need to add words that will act as *directional signals* to help your reader follow the thought pattern you are using. Some words and phrases act as *pointers* that tell the reader to keep moving forward. For example,

> it follows that
> then
> another
> for example
> hence

(Notice that the categories of pointers and nudging words overlap.) Other kinds of pointers show causality.

> as a result
> therefore

consequently
because
since

All of them move the reader forward.

A different kind of transitional words and phrases acts as Slow or Cau-tion signals to readers, warning them to slow down because they are going to run into some qualification or exception to a point that has just been made. Typical signals of this kind are

however
but
nevertheless
in spite of
on the other hand
instead
not only

These words warn readers to expect a contrasting example and prepare them to adjust their thinking to handle that exception. Thus it's important that when you use this kind of word, you really do follow it with a con-trasting example. Otherwise you will confuse your readers and possibly lose them.

Repeating Words

Repeating keywords, phrases, or stylistic patterns in a piece of writing can help to focus your readers' attention on points you want to emphasize. A repeated word can also serve as an effective hook between paragraphs or between sections, providing the link that keeps readers from feeling a gap as they move from one section to another. This student paragraph fur-nishes a good example of using repetition as links within a paragraph. (I have added italics in the following selections.)

Walt Disney's monumental idea for creating an *amusement park* began when he took his young daughters to an *amusement park* in Los Angeles. The girls were entertained while riding on the merry-go-round, but Walt was bored sitting on a bench eating peanuts. He real-ized the need for a place where children and their parents could have fun together. Impetus for his new *park* came from his own hobby, con-structing his own backyard railroad. Trains were his boyhood passion . . . and he began to talk about building a railroad that would link the Burbank studios, then linked this idea to his conception of a new kind of *amusement park*. He realized that transportation and nostalgia were the key factors in making his *park* different. In July 1955, his dream became a reality with the opening of Disneyland.

Here is a passage in which one word, purposefully repeated in a parallel pattern, repeats the writer's central thesis:

> We believe public radio and public television *can* lead the way. Intelligently organized and adequately funded public broadcasting *can* help the creative spirit to flourish. It *can* reveal how we are different and what we share in common. It *can* illuminate the dark corners of the world and the dark corners of the mind. It *can* offer forums to a multitude of voices. It *can* reveal wisdom and understanding—and foolishness too. It *can* delight us. It *can* entertain us. It *can* inform us. Above all, it *can* add to our understanding of our own inner workings and of one another. In the conviction that it *can* be so, we make these recommendations.
>
> —From the report of the Carnegie Commission
> on the Future of Public Broadcasting, in
> *The Chronicle of Higher Education,*
> 5 February 1979, 9.

These writers value repetition as a simple and useful way of keeping their readers on the track.

Using Conjunctions at the Beginning of Sentences

The prejudice that many writers have against beginning a sentence with *and* or *but* seems to have grown out of the notion that because these words are called "conjunctions," they must always appear between two other words. Not necessarily. They are also strong signal words that tell readers what to expect next. For that reason they work particularly well when you want to stress the relationship of a sentence to the previous one. Notice how the following writers have used *and* and *but* for this purpose. (Again, italics have been added.)

> *Harvard Business Review* subscribers . . . recently rated "the ability to communicate" as the prime requisite of a promotable executive. *And,* of all the aspects of communication, the written form is the most trouble-some.
>
> —John S. Fielden, "What Do You Mean I Can't
> Write?" in *The Practical Craft,*
> ed. Keith Sparrow and Donald Cunningham
> (Boston: Houghton Mifflin, 1978), 47. This
> article originally appeared in the *Harvard
> Business Review,* May–June 1964.

If we hear a well-constructed, grammatical sentence, the ideas fall easily and quickly into the slots of our consciousness. *But,* if we hear a conglomerate, ungrammatical hodge-podge, we have to sort it out at an expenditure of time and effort.

> —Everett C. Smith, "Industry Views the Teaching of English," in *The Practical Craft,* ed. K. Sparrow and D. Cunningham (Boston: Houghton Mifflin, 1978). This article originally appeared in *English Journal,* March 1956.

But works especially well as the opening word of a paragraph that you want to highlight because it states an important qualification or contrast to the content of the previous paragraph. Notice the effect in these examples:

. . . For the most part, readers are assumed to be ideal readers, fully prepared to relate to the fiction or poetry on the author's terms. This expectation is as it should be; it is appropriate for what we regard as creative writing.

But a different expectation exists in business and technical writing where readers are busy executives who want the important findings up front, or are privates last-class who need information at a level they can understand, or somewhere in the bewildering range between.

> —Keith Sparrow and Donald Cunningham, "What Are Some Important Writing Strategies," in *The Practical Craft,* ed. K. Sparrow and D. Cunningham (Boston: Houghton Mifflin, 1978), 114.

. . . As my students argue when I correct them . . . : "You got the meaning, didn't you?" Yes, I did, and so do we all get the meaning when a newspaper, a magazine, a set of directions stammers out its message. And I suppose, too, we could travel by ox-cart, or dress in burlap, or drive around with rattling fenders, and still get through a day.

But technical writing in this age can no more afford widespread sloppiness of expression, confusion of meaning, rattle-trap construction than a supersonic missile can afford to be made of the wrong materials, or be put together haphazardly with screws jutting out here and there, or have wiring circuits that may go off any way at all. . . .

> —Morris Freedman, "The Seven Sins of Technical Writing," in *The Practical Craft,* ed. K. Sparrow and D. Cunningham (Boston: Houghton Mifflin, 1978), 82. This article originally appeared in *College Composition and Communication,* February 1958.

These examples, deliberately selected from a collection of articles on business and technical writing, should convince you that it is not a sin, or even a grammatical lapse, to start a sentence with *and* or *but*. If you need additional proof, check the articles in any widely read magazine. You will find an abundance of corroborating evidence.

OTHER AIDS TO THE READER

Frequent Closure Within Sentences

By giving readers links and signals to keep them moving in the right direction, you meet one of an expository writer's main responsibilities: helping his or her audience to process information as quickly and efficiently as possible. You are trying to keep them from having to reread all or part of what you have written in order to get your meaning.

One way to help your readers is not to make them wait too long to discover meaning. If you can construct your sentences out of phrases and clauses that make sense by themselves, your readers can process meaning as they read rather than having to hold all the content in their minds until they get to the end of a sentence. For instance, here is a confusing sentence from a student paper:

> Furthermore, *that the United States has the best medical technology in the world, yet ranks sixteenth among countries in successful births per pregnancy* results because impossible medical costs force many people to go through childbirth at home.

The strung-out twenty-two–word subject in this sentence keeps readers in suspense for so long that they miss the verb, "results," on the first reading. If the writer had rearranged his ideas into manageable units, readers would not get lost. Here is a rewritten version with the units of thought marked off:

> Even though the United States has the best medical technology in the world, / it ranks below fifteen other countries in successful births per pregnancy / because impossible medical costs force many people to have their children at home.

The revised sentence is easier to read than the original because the words are arranged into segments that make sense by themselves. When we read, we make *closure* when we come to the point in a sentence where our minds make sense of a group of words; at that point, we can rest for a split second before going on to process the next segment. In the revised version, we can pause twice; in the original, we cannot pause at all until we get to the end of the sentence.

Because readers can assimilate information more efficiently when it is divided into small units, in most situations you should not let long, complicated sentences predominate. Frequently, just their appearance on the page frightens off readers. But long sentences in themselves do no necessarily cause reading problems; if closure occurs frequently, a sentence of 50 or 60 words or more can be read easily. Marking off the units of closure in this 108-word sentence from Tom Wolfe's *The Right Stuff* shows this:

> A career in flying was like climbing one of those ancient Babylonian pyramids / made up of a dizzy progression of steps and ledges, / a ziggurat, / a pyramid extraordinarily high and steep, / and the idea was to prove at every foot of the way up that pyramid / that you were one of the elected and anointed ones who had *the right stuff* / and could move higher and higher and even / —ultimately, God willing, one day— / that you might be able to join that special few at the very top, / that elite who had the capacity to bring tears to men's eyes, / the very Brotherhood of the Right Stuff itself.
>
> —Tom Wolfe, *The Right Stuff* (New York: Farrar, Straus, & Giroux, 1979), 24.

Chunking to Avoid Reader Overload

Another way of segmenting your writing to make it easier for your readers to follow is called *chunking;* that is, breaking up long units of writing into parts so that they will be easier to process. If you include too much information in one sentence or one paragraph, you risk overloading the mental circuits by which readers process information, and your readers either give up or have to go back to reread the material two or three times to absorb it.

Chunking is the principle behind grouping the digits in telephone numbers and social security numbers. Would you ever remember your sister's telephone number if it were written 2143889697? Or your social security number if it were written 328939775? If, however, the numbers are split into groups, they are fairly to easy to process and remember.

$$214-388-9697 \qquad 328-93-9775$$

When numbers are written like this, you process each unit separately and put it into short-term memory before you come to the next unit—that's the secret of memorization.

You can use chunking in your writing to break up long sentences that are overstuffed with information or paragraphs that include so many items that the reader gets lost. One way to do that is to break long sentences into shorter ones. For instance, here is a sentence so overstuffed that it's almost impossible to follow.

> With the tension in Iraq cutting off substantial oil imports and its announced intention to last out the boycott however long it takes, the worldwide increase in oil prices and the probable effect of armed conflict on new exploration, and the ongoing determination of both auto manufacturers and several branches of government to resist any real efforts to move toward substantial conservation measures, an energy crisis of some magnitude seems imminent.

However, if we cut up the sentence and reorganize it into manageable chunks, it becomes easy to follow.

> For at least three reasons, an energy crisis seems imminent. First, the the tension in Iraq is cutting off imports and its government says it will hold out against the boycott. Second, oil prices have increased worldwide and the prospect of armed conflict discourages new exploration. Three, U.S. auto manufacturers and several branches of government seem determined to resist any real efforts to push oil conservation.

Another excellent way to chunk an overloaded sentence or paragraph is to break the information into lists. For example, here's a sentence so overloaded that a reader would get lost halfway through.

> The factors that keep individuals interested in their jobs are interesting responsibilities, wide range of responsibilities, challenge, stimulation, recognition, impact on the organization, status, relationship with others, being one's own boss, freedom to act, quality of the organization, and compensation.

Impossible! Now let's redo it into list.

> The factors that keep individuals interested in their jobs are these:

interesting responsibilities	status
wide range of responsibilities	relationships with others
challenge	being one's own boss
stimulation	freedom to act
recognition	quality of the organization
impact on the organization	compensation

You have to wonder whatever made the writer try to jam all that together in the first place. Whenever you find that you're loading a sentence or paragraph with more than three or four points of information, consider breaking it out into a list. (Notice how often I have done that in this text.) Such rearrangement can make a great difference in how your reader will respond to your writing.

AVOID ANTAGONIZING YOUR READERS

My last suggestion on ways to hold your readers is psychological rather than editorial: Remember you will lose readers if you make them uncomfortable or angry. Most people are not willing to read or listen to someone who is attacking them or criticizing their beliefs. If you really want your audience to read what you are writing, you need to consider their emotions as well as their strictly intellectual reactions.

Sometimes, to be sure, you are writing for two sets of readers, particularly when you're writing an argument. The opposition—that group of readers whose position you're criticizing—aren't likely to change their minds. You shouldn't worry too much about making them angry—it's probably inevitable. You should, however, take pains not to anger the other group—those readers who are undecided on the issue and whom you hope to influence. It's important to distinguish between these two segments of an audience when you're constructing your argument.

To avoid threatening readers whom you want to influence, keep these principles in mind.

- *Respect your audience.* From the beginning, assume that your readers are intelligent and rational people of goodwill and that they will respond to reason. Rather than attacking their positions, try to discover what common interests or common goals you may have and work from there. Give your readers the same kind of treatment you like to get when you read.
- *Use objective language.* Strong, biased words such as *disgraceful, vicious,* and *intolerable* are likely to trigger defensive reactions from readers who do not already agree with you. Their first response will be to argue rather than to pay attention to your point of view. If, however, you state your ideas in neutral language, they are likely to continue reading to learn more.
- *Learn to write provisionally, not dogmatically.* Learn to use the *subjunctive mood,* a much neglected but extremely useful verb form that allows you to speculate, hypothesize, or wish, and to express a courteous and inquiring attitude in your writing. Although fewer and fewer people seem to bother with using the subjunctive form of verbs in their writing, careful writers should at least know what the sub-

junctive forms are and when they should be used. They are used when one wants to express a point conditionally or to express wishes. For example,

If Castle *were* in charge, he *would handle* the protesters well.

I wish I *were* not *involved* in that proposal.
If that *should* happen, the admiral *would want* us to know.
You *would be* a great help if you *were to join* us.

Occasionally *had* is combined with a subjunctive verb to talk about events that didn't take place. For example,

Had I thought of it, I *would have written.*
Had he *known* what he was getting into, he *would have been appalled.*

The subjunctive form of a verb should be used in clauses beginning with *that* when the main verb expresses desires, orders, or suggestions. For example,

The lawyer requested that her client *be given* a new trial.
We suggest that there *be* a recount of the votes.

If you use these words in phrases like "If I were," "It might be that," and "We could consider," you create an atmosphere of cooperation and courtesy in which your readers can pay attention to what you are proposing because they are not forced to defend themselves.

EXERCISES

1. Working with other students in a small group, discuss these titles chosen from the table of contents of an essay anthology. How useful are they as forecasters of what the reader would find in the essay? As a group, decide which three titles are the most informative. Which three are the least informative.

   The Fear of Being Alone
   Business As Usual
   Bag Man
   The Full Circle: In Praise of the Bicycle

The Truth about Cinderella
The New Illiteracy
Work in an Alienated Society
Lessons of the Street
The Lesson of the Mask
Techno-Politics

2. Working in a group, try to draft titles that are both informative and provocative for papers written on these topics.

   A. Exercise as a major component in a weight-reduction program.

   B. A review of a display of women students' paintings in a local art gallery.

   C. A comparison of child-care policies in France with those in the United States.

3. Working with other students in a group, evaluate these opening paragraphs taken from papers by advanced student writers. What is your response to these leads? Do they make you want to go on and read the papers themselves? What suggestions, if any, would you make to improve them?

   A. Today in the world there are more than 200 breeds of dogs and these can be divided into six groups. Dogs perform a variety of services to the community. They have the intelligence and the ability to bond with humans in a way that enables them to help them with tasks. One group of dogs is the working dogs, which do many tasks for men. Dogs are helpful to many individuals in our society.

   B. Mike Frazier, manager of the 1984 U.S. Olympic Cycling Team said to me in Dallas recently that many riders testing out as superior athletes statistically are consistently beaten by riders of less athletic prowess but superior skills. An interesting statement in light of the great physical exertion the sport requires. For instance, the 1990 Branders Jeans Tour of Texas covers more than 700 miles in eight days, including one rest day. During the 60-mile stage I saw the riders burned, according to Frazier, enough calories for two marathons.

   C. Every year, our highways needlessly slaughter many thousands of people. And every year, people are reminded that wearing their protective safety belts would dramatically increase their chances for survival. And yet people continue to ignore such advice and suffer the consequences. In an attempt to solve this problem, this country has gone as far as to install systems that virtually force occupants of automobiles to wear protective safety belts. What happened? People resisted to such a degree that the legislation was finally repealed. So, obviously, another solution is needed if the population is to reap the benefits of being protected from their cars. Airbags are such a solution.

4. Write an opening paragraph for one of the topics given in the second exercise above. Then get together with two or three other students who have written on the same topic. Discuss the differences in your paragraphs and see if you can combine efforts to write one paragraph that all of you can agree on.

5. Here are two long but fairly readable sentences from professional writers. Mark each of them off into units of closure that reveal how the content is organized.

> Once that fact is recognized, it may be possible to think again about the proper building blocks of a meritocracy—measures that do not seal fate at an early age, that emphasize performance in specific areas, that expand the pool of talent in more than a hit-or-miss way, and whose limits are always visible to us, so that we are not again deluded into thinking we have found a scientific basis for the order of lords, vassals, and serfs.
>
> —James Fallows, "The Tests and the Brightest,"
> *The Atlantic*, February 1980, 48.

> I yield to no one in deploring prejudice against the young, but I found it unsettling to learn that Mr. Schroeder, five years out of the University of Michigan, and four other young men of approximately the same experience constitute the entire legal staff of the FTC's Bureau of Consumer Protection, the body that now proposes to reform one of the nation's venerable technical institutions.
>
> —Samuel C. Florman, "Standards of Value,"
> *Harper's* Magazine, February 1980, 67.

SUGGESTED WRITING ASSIGNMENTS

As a part of each writing assignment, write a detailed analysis of your audience that specifies characteristics they have that you need to keep in mind as you write, problems that such an audience might present, and what the audience would expect to get from your paper. Also analyze your purpose in writing, specifying what you hope to accomplish in the paper. If appropriate, include an accurate and descriptive title for your paper.

TOPIC 1:   Imagine that you write for the entertainment section of a local newspaper or magazine. One of your weekly jobs is to eat at one of the major restaurants in the city and write a 300- to 500-word review of your experience there for the Saturday paper. Although all the better restaurants advertise in the paper or magazine, your editor wants an honest review that will let potential customers know what they can expect if they eat there. You are gradually building a reputation as a fair and reliable judge of restaurants and so you should keep that in mind as you write. Don't forget to mention prices.

TOPIC 2:   The regents of your college or university are having hearings to determine whether they should tear down the low-rent student housing that was built thirty-five years ago from secondhand army surplus buildings. The housing is unsightly and needs repairs; some of the regents have said that they think it is unsafe. If it is torn down, however, the apartments that would replace it would rent for almost twice as much as the present units, and the campus would be without any low-rent housing for at least two years.

Prepare a ten-minute talk (no more than 1,000 words) against tearing down the buildings to be delivered at the meeting that the regents are going to hold. You will be the spokesperson for the married students who now live in the university housing.

TOPIC 3:   Write a letter to the vice-president for marketing of a major firm such as General Foods or Johnson & Johnson trying to persuade him or her that the firm should no longer run a particular television commercial that you find offensive. Specify what you find offensive and why, and try to give the vice-president a good reason for dropping the commercial.

8 ◇ Writing Clearly

If you care about having people read and enjoy what you write, you need to care about writing clearly. Sometimes when you read an essay that is clear and crisply written, it's tempting to think that clarity comes easily; it doesn't. Most writers have to work at achieving a lucid style that is also graceful and pleasant to read—it requires concentration and careful attention to small details.

Often in a first draft, sentences spin out of control, clutter creeps in, dull phrases proliferate, and abstract generalities and passive verbs threaten to smother the whole thing. It's then that the writer's fitness and flexibility comes into play. Just as the person who wants an active, lean and smoothly functioning body has to work at it constantly, so the writer who wants clear, taut, and effective writing has to work at it constantly. And as fitness requires strategies for maintaining the body, so clarity requires strategies for revising writing. In the rest of this chapter I sketch out a number of strategies that I believe help; they are ones that I practice myself as much as possible.

WRITE CONCRETELY AND SPECIFICALLY

Usually your readers will understand your writing more easily if you use concrete and specific language to help clarify and give substance to abstract and general language. *Abstract language* consists of words that refer to intangible qualities, concepts, ideas, or attitudes. We cannot grasp the abstract through our senses; we can only *conceive* of it mentally. Words like *loyalty, intelligence, philosophy, value,* and *evil* are abstract.

Concrete language consists of words that refer to tangible physical objects or qualities that we can know through our senses; we *perceive* the concrete. Words like *bottle, hot, kitten, car,* and *computer* are concrete.

But most words do not fall so neatly into these either/or categories. Instead we have to classify them according to a scale, place them somewhere on what semanticists call the *ladder of abstraction*. It is from that metaphorical ladder that we derive the term *level of abstraction;* we are also referring to that ladder when we talk about *high-level* or *low-level* abstractions. Here is how the ladder works:

8. ideologies
7. religions
6. western religions
5. Christianity
4. Protestantism
3. Baptists
2. Southern Baptist Convention
1. First Baptist Church of Memphis, Tennessee

None of these terms refers to anything tangible—"Church" on Level 1 refers to a community of worshippers, not a building—but "First Baptist Church of Memphis" is much narrower and thus much less abstract than "ideologies."

You should also learn to distinguish between the general and the specific. *General language* consists of words and phrases that refer to large classes of people, institutions, activities, and so on, or to broad areas of study or activity. Words and phrases like *college, housing, the medical profession,* or *the American people* are general.

Specific language consists of words and phrases that refer to individual instances or persons or to particular details and examples. Words like *Queen Elizabeth, chocolate chip ice cream,* and *Masterpiece Theatre* are specific. When someone says "Use specific details," that person is asking for individual, concrete examples.

We also have different levels of generality. For example,

7. mass media
6. television
5. public broadcasting channels
4. educational programs
3. science programs
2. *Nova*
1. "Spaceship Earth"

At the lowest level we have a single, specific program, and at the highest level we have a classification so broad that we have trouble thinking of all that it includes. Someone who says "He talked at a high level of generality" means that the speaker spoke in broad and general terms, giving few specific examples.

At times, all writers have to generalize and use abstract language. If we didn't, we could never get beyond citing examples (specific acts of violence, say, such as the assassination of an ambassador) to arrive at a generalization about the larger problem (terrorism). But if you want to help readers grasp your ideas quickly, learn how to use the personal, the concrete, and the specific to illustrate your points. For example, an astronomy writer who wanted to help his readers understand the abstract idea of black holes used a concrete analogy of watching streams of traffic pour into a domed stadium. A writer who is writing about horror movies can illustrate the general class with the specific film *The Blood of the Lamb.*

You clarify and strengthen your writing in several ways when you work at making it concrete and specific.

First, you add the *weight of facts* to your writing and anchor it to reality. An environmental essay about the risk of accidents at nuclear power plants takes on greater force when you cite the concrete, specific examples of the leak at Three Mile Island in the United States and the meltdown at Chernobyl in the Soviet Union. An article about the growing menace of teenage gang wars needs specific details such as information about the semiautomatic weapons gang members carry in New York and Los Angeles and the number of innocent victims killed in New York in 1990. Such details are easily available from papers like *The New York Times* and others.

Second, concrete examples and specific details make your writing more interesting to your readers because they can learn from it. If you were writing an essay deploring the poor child-care system in the United States, it's easy enough to generalize about the problems, but you could make your readers see your point more clearly by giving specific details about a model European system and quoting from a pamphlet called *A Welcome for Every Child,* published by the French-American Foundation, which describes the French system of universal child care.

Third, specific details and facts enhance your credibility and make potentially skeptical readers pay more attention to your ideas. Most of us who are concerned with social problems can spin out broad generalities about issues such as racial injustice, the need for educational reform, and inadequate financing for early childhood programs, and our readers will agree with us. But an informed audience wants a writer to move quickly past generalities and platitudes and get to specifics. The writer who holds their attention and earns their respect is one who uses specific comparisons, examples, and statistics to make his or her point. Michael J. Barrett does just that when he argues in a November 1990, *Atlantic* article that one of the major reasons for the declining quality of American education is that we have one of the shortest school years in the Western world.

To be sure, being specific and concrete also involves risks. When you give an example to illustrate a general statement, you run the risk of having your readers disagree with that example. For instance, if you claim that we must increase teachers' salaries to improve public school education, you're probably safe, but if you go on to claim that the experienced teacher who makes $30,000 a year is underpaid, a reader may challenge that statement. If you claim that in order to reduce the budget deficit, we must have tax reform, your readers will probably agree. That's a safe generality. If, however, you propose a national sales tax as the best solution, some readers will immediately disagree. But those are the chances you must take if you are going to move beyond generalities to gain your readers' attention and respect.

Make Your Readers See Something

When possible, make your reader see something. More than ever before, the readers you're trying to reach are visually oriented. Most of them have grown up in a television, movie, billboard culture that stresses images, and they respond more fully to a medium that engages their senses as well as their intellect. The strength of the visual appeal undoubtedly accounts for the breakthrough success of the MacIntosh computer in the 1980s. New users took to it instantly and were able to master its programs because it literally showed them what to do by using graphics and images—sketches of desktops and file folders, paint brushes and trash cans, rulers and clocks and calenders—all designed to teach through the eyes and through association with familiar objects.

You can do the same thing in your writing, not by long descriptions, but by bringing in anecdotes, narratives, and allusions that engage your readers' visual imagination. Here are two professional examples; notice how they engage your senses.

> My father was a farmer with no use for fashions. He married and went into business for himself in the spring of 1946, raising laying hens, vegetables, and berries on a seven-and-a-half acre truck farm. Small-scale horticulture was his real interest. For the rest of his life, he devoted as much time and care to his gardens and orchards and beehives as to his row crops. The eggs he sold to the local plant, the berries and vegetables to the local grocers. It was hard labor, done mostly with his hands and a two-wheeled garden tractor, and it afforded a very meager living.
>
> —Paul Gruchow, "Remember the Flowers,"
> *Sierra,* November–December 1990, 83.

It is hardly a secret that the world economy has become one big, evolving, complex international bazaar. Chopsticks are made in Minnesota for export to Japan. Schwinn bicycles are made in Hungary; so are G.E. light bulbs and Levi's jeans. Silos made in North Dakota are cut in half and shipped to Norway as warehouses. Chicken feet—once the refuse of Virginia poultry fanciers—are sent to Hong Kong to be made into soup. In Japan, Mazda manufactures the Ford Probe, partly owned by Ford. It's sold as an American car. "There is no longer such a thing as an 'American economy,' " insists Robert Reich, an economist and Harvard professor.

> —Jon Bowermaster, "Calhoun County Goes
> Global," *The New York Times Magazine,*
> 2 December 1990, 58, 84.

(Notice how quickly you realize Bowermaster has done his homework for this article—the details show it.)

Here is an example of nonvisual writing that is hard to understand because the reader cannot *see* anything happening.

> This pragmatic approach ascribes to managers a marvelous plasticity in adapting themselves and the people in their organizations to technological change and environmental tempests, whatever happens and as often as they occur. This conviction about human malleability is, in fact, the necessary view of innate human nature required by the organizational imperative; thus it is imbedded solidly within every modern organization. This image is based on the belief that the individual is, by nature, nothing and has the potential to be made into anything. Therefore, organizations must be designed to mold individuals, since there is nothing in their nature to prevent their adapting to whatever value premises and organizational contingencies are required.
>
> —William G. Scott and David Hart,
> *Organizational America*
> (Boston: Houghton Mifflin, 1979), 57–58.

At first reading, one's mind hydroplanes right over the surface of the paragraph because there is nothing in it to engage the senses. The reader can't find a concrete anchor anywhere, nor *perceive* anything. The words *plasticity, malleability, value premises,* and *contingencies* do not refer to anything a reader can, at first reading, connect with people or reality. Although the content of the passage isn't particularly difficult, it's hard to process because the reader has to work at a totally abstract level.

Unfortunately, many students who encounter this kind of colorless and abstract writing assume that the harder something is to read, the more important it must be. Sometimes they even think they should be writing that way themselves, so they try to avoid language that is plain and specific and use abstract terms instead (see discussion of models in Chapter 2). They may also be afraid that they will be asked to write that kind of difficult and abstract style in order to get ahead in their professions. Fortunately that fear is seldom justified. My survey of business and profession people proves that. And it is still the case that in any field, most of the individuals at the top prove again and again that they value clear writing and know how to write clearly themselves. For example, here is a paragraph from a book about the beginning of the universe written by Nobel Prize–winning physicist Steven Weinberg:

> In the beginning there was an explosion. Not an explosion like those familiar on earth, starting from a definite center and spreading out to engulf more and more of the circumambient air, but an explosion which occurred simultaneously everywhere, filling all space from the beginning, with every particle of matter rushing apart from every other particle. "All space" in this context may mean either all of an infinite universe, or all of a finite universe which curves back on itself like the surface of a sphere. Neither possibility is easy to comprehend, but this will not get in our way; it matters hardly at all in the early universe whether space is finite or infinite.
> —Steven Weinberg, *The First Three Minutes*
> (New York: Bantam Books, 1977), 2.

One can hardly imagine a concept more difficult to explain, but Weinberg succeeds by using clear language and giving the readers an image they can see.

Downshift from the General to the Specific

Often you will want to begin a paragraph by making a broad statement that is very general and highly abstract. Although that can be a good start, you need to shift quickly to a lower level of generality, using more specific and concrete language to clarify and reinforce the original broad statement. Notice that is what the author of the example above from "Calhoun County Goes Global" has done to illustrate his generalization about a global economy. Here is another example that moves several steps down the ladder of generality.

> The ancestors of the mammals were a transitional form called the mammal-like reptiles. (Level 6)
>> These animals were ferocious, numerous, and enormously successful. (Level 5)
>>> They reached their zenith about 250 million years ago, (Level 4) and during the next 50 million years they were the dominant form of life on land. (Level 4)
>>>> Inspection of their fossilized remains reveals the reason for their success. (Level 3)

The clumsy, sprawling, "push-up" posture of the original
reptile was replaced in this new model by a construction
in which (Level 2)
    the arms were underslung, (Level 1)
    the elbows tucked in, (Level 1)
    and the body raised well off the ground at all times.
    (Level 1)
    These animals had a fast running gait; (Level 1)
    they could outrace any animal in their day. (Level 1)
        —Robert Jastrow, *The Enchanted Loom*
        (New York: Simon & Schuster, 1981), 32.

You see that the author has started out with a general statement and
expanded on it by giving you details that get increasingly specific as he goes
along. We call this process *downshifting,* and it is an important concept for
you to grasp right now because it is one of the major strategies that authors
use to make their writing clear. You will learn more about this useful technique in Chapter 9.

Make Your Sentence Subjects Specific and Concrete

When you can, choose concrete, specific words as the subjects of your
sentences. When you make such choices, you give your readers a concrete
anchor early in the sentence and make the rest of it easier to follow. For
instance, compare these two versions of the same sentence.

ORIGINAL: The affordability of hotels is the major factor that draws
tourists to Baja California.

REVISED: Baja California attracts tourists mainly because of its cheap
hotels.

The second version is easier and quicker to read because it begins with a
concrete place rather than an abstract concept and uses an active verb, "attracts," rather than the uninteresting verb "is."
    Here is another pair:

ORIGINAL: Voluntary employee participation in the plan is requisite for
its success.

REVISED: Employees must participate willingly in the plan if it is to succeed.

Readers understand the second version more quickly because they can immediately identify "employees" as the subject; "voluntary employee partic-

ipation" takes longer to process and isn't as interesting. "Must participate" is also a more interesting and active verb than "is requisite for."

If you choose concrete, specific subjects for your sentences, you will almost automatically select stronger verbs to go with them. Abstractions can't *do* anything; therefore, you almost have to combine them with "is" verbs. For instance, if you begin a sentence with a subject like "desirability," you just about have to write "The desirability of the program is in question," or "Its desirability cannot be determined." Both are dull sentences because the reader cannot visualize either the subject or the verb. Abstract subjects also tend to attract passive verbs (see pp. 145–47).

Use Agent/Action Sentence Patterns Often

You can cut down the number of abstract subjects in your sentence if you try consciously to write *agent/action* sentences; that is, sentences in which your reader can tell immediately *who* is doing *what* and to *whom*. For example, here are two versions of the same sentence:

ORIGINAL: The instinctual response of a child who is criticized is denial of responsibility.

REVISED: Children instinctively deny responsibility when they are criticized.

You understand the revised version more quickly because someone (children) is doing something (denying). You are also likely to identify more with the actor (children) than you are with an abstraction (instinctual response).

Here is another example:

ORIGINAL: Technological expansionism and the growth of mechanization in the United States have led to more consumption of energy and less availability of resources for future generations.

REVISION: As we have expanded our technology in the United States and built more machines, we have consumed more energy and left fewer resources for future generations.

Again, in the first sentence no agents appear so you can't tell who is doing what. It's hard to tell that the phrases "technological expansionism" and "growth of mechanization" refer to somebody doing something. But when you identify the agent in the sentence as "we" and link it with the action verbs "expanded" and "built," the sentence becomes much clearer.

Clarify Your Sentences by Adding People

Whenever you can, *put people in your writing*. I'm convinced this practice can do more to clear up fuzzy writing than any other single strategy. When you bring people into your writing, you get rid of many of the abstract terms that cloud it, you're also more likely to use strong, active verbs, and you usually make it more visual. For instance, notice the difference in these pairs of sentences when people are introduced into the revisions:

> ORIGINAL: One barrier to fundamental change [in the health-care system] is the entrenched perception of national health insurance as an additional expenditure program.

> REVISION: Because most people think of national health insurance as a program to spend more money, it is hard to bring about real change in the health-care system.

The original sentence is stuffed with abstract phrases—"barrier to fundamental change," "entrenched perception," "national health insurance," "additional expenditure program"—held together with one weak little verb: *is*. The reader can't see anything and gets no sense that people are involved. The revision, however, starts right off with "people" as the subject and as a result follows with three active verbs: *think, spend,* and *bring about*. Those are things that people do; abstractions don't *do* anything. Thus the revision is much easier to read and understand.

> ORIGINAL: Programs ought to be encouraged that explore the implications of the work experience for the curricular framework on campus.

> REVISION: We should encourage programs in which teachers find ways to use students' work experience when they design courses.

The original sentence is loaded down with wordy abstractions—"implications of the work experience" and "curricular framework on campus" (whatever that means)—that give no hint people might be involved in this work that's mentioned or that teachers might have something to do with designing courses. It's all impersonal. Because the revised sentence starts with people, it uses stronger verbs and emphasizes the human beings who are involved.

When you put people in your sentences, even if you refer to them only by the pronouns *I, we, you,* and *they,* you help the reader to visualize what is happening and thus remember the content more easily. You are using the same strategy people use when they illustrate points with stories. You can count on your readers responding more quickly to writing that shows people doing something than to writing that refers mainly to concepts and relies on inactive or passive verbs.

If you want to put more people in your writing but still get nervous about using *I* and *you* in your papers, remember that some outstanding writers use *I* regularly. For example, the respected essayist Lewis Thomas uses *I* frequently, the scientist Carl Sagan uses it occasionally in his book *Cosmos*, and you'll find many instances of first and second pronouns in serious books and magazine articles. So it's not necessarily taboo and can sometimes be used to excellent effect. You should, however, think about your particular writing situation and what your readers' reaction is likely to be. If the professor you're writing for seems rather formal and traditional, you might want to check out how he or she feels about using *I* in a paper. If you get a negative response, find ways to write without using *I*. You would probably also want to avoid it if you're trying to sound quite impersonal or distant. But that doesn't mean you can't find other ways to add people in your writing. It's still a good idea.

Avoid Too Many Nominalizations

The kinds of abstract words that are most likely to clog your writing and make it impenetrable can be called "heavy-duty nouns"; that's my term for nominalizations, nouns created by tacking endings on to verbs and nouns. Here are some examples:

capability	immediacy
recognition	modernity
competitiveness	accountability
viability	inclusiveness
enhancement	utilization
marketability	continuation

In general, when you find your writing has filled up with words that end with *-ity, -tion, -ness, -ance, -ment,* and *-ism,* consider how you can thin them out. Some are absolutely necessary, of course, but probably not as many as you think. These clunky words have no life, no character— they're just inert designations and used too often, they are deadly to a writing style. Take a look at a textbook or article you find hard to read, and you'll find it filled with these unlovely, heavy-duty nouns. If you look back at many of the examples of poor writing I've used in this book so far, you will find that most of them are overloaded with nominalizations. Look at the sample sentences under agent/action sentences, for example.

Here are some more clogged up sentences with possible revisions.

ORIGINAL: Establishment of that policy reveals the officers' conviction that the qualities of innovativeness and creativity inevitably conflict with the higher goal of corporate loyalty.

REVISION: The corporate officers who established that policy show they believe that innovative and creative people will not always put loyalty to the corporation first.

ORIGINAL: Electoral participation is essential for political democratization.

REVISION: People must vote if we are to have democracy.

Notice that you will automatically reduce the number of heavy-duty nouns when you write agent/action sentences.

CHOOSING VERBS FOR CLARITY

Verbs are the lifeblood of writing. They affect not only clarity, but also tone, rhythm, and pace. They strongly affect how vigorous and readable your writing will be. Here are suggestions about choosing these important tools.

Use *To Be* Verbs Sparingly

Although the verb *to be* in all its forms (*is, am, were, will be, are,* and so on) is crucial to expressing many ideas, style-conscious writers use it sparingly. It's a verb that connects and describes rather than acts, and frequently it can get lost or overwhelmed by other words, as in the following sentence.

ORIGINAL: Greater deregulation and liberalization of the global marketing system and a subsequent lowering of international trade barriers that have barred competition is the goal of the conferees.

REVISION: The conferees hope to deregulate and liberalize the global marketing system and thus lower the international trade barriers that have barred competition in the past.

The revision is much clearer, isn't it?

Now notice these two versions of a student paragraph; the writer has strengthened the revision by using active verbs.

ORIGINAL: The implications of teenage sexuality are overwhelming. Probably the least tangible one is the loss of self-esteem among the young girls involved. Lisa is an excellent example. She was sexually active at fifteen; at age seventeen she had an abortion, and at twenty-one she is sleeping with several men and is contemptuous of herself.

REVISION: Teenage sexuality has overwhelming implications. Among the less tangible ones, one must count the loss of self-esteem for the young girls involved. Take Lisa, for example. Sexually active at fifteen, at seventeen she had an abortion. Now at twenty-one she sleeps around and despises herself.

In this paragraph by the professional writer Gordon Parks, notice how he carefully chooses active verbs to give a compelling image of the musician Duke Ellington.

For me, and many other black people then, his importance as a human being *transcended* his importance as a musician. We had been *assaulted* by Hollywood grinning darky types all of our lives. It was refreshing to be a part of Duke Ellington's audience. Ellington never *grinned*. He *smiled*. Ellington never *shuffled*. He *strode*. It was "Good afternoon, ladies and gentlemen," never "How y'all doin'?" We wanted to be seen by the whites in the audience. We wanted them to know that this elegant, handsome, and awe-inspiring man playing that ever-so-fine music on that golden stage before that big beautiful black band was black—like us. (emphasis added)

—Gordon Parks, "Jazz," *Esquire,* December 1975, 140.

In many kinds of writing—technical reports or critical analyses, for example—you don't need to work at choosing colorful and active verbs. Sometimes *is* and *are* work perfectly well, and I don't recommend that you try to eliminate them from your writing. But when you want to make your writing more interesting to read and easier to follow, opt for verbs that do something. And when you revise, check to see if you have overused *to be* verbs or started too many sentences with "It is . . ." or "There are . . ."

Choose Economical Verbs

Your writing will be clearer and more effective if you make a habit of choosing one-word, direct verbs rather than strung-out verb phrases that incorporate nouns and adjectives. For example,

Wordy Version	*Economical Version*
be cognizant of	recognize
put the emphasis on	emphasize

Wordy Version	*Economical Version*
is reflective of	reflects
make an attempt to	try
have an understanding of	understand
make a comparison to	compare
grant permission to	allow

Stretched-out verb forms, although not wrong, tend to make writing sound stuffy and formal. One such phrase here and there does little damage, but too many of them clog writing.

Use Passive Verbs Sparingly

A *passive verb* is a verb form that shows the subject receiving rather than doing the action.

> Gun control *is considered* to be one of the major political issues of the 1990s.

> The gang members *were warned* that they *would be prosecuted.*

Cultivate the habit of revising passive verb constructions out of your writing when you want to strengthen and clarify it. In addition to making writing impersonal and often rather stuffy, passive verbs make it harder to read for several reasons.

First, passive verbs slow writing down not only because it takes more words to express a passive construction, but because the reader usually has to wait until the last part of the sentence to find out what is happening. Thus "Action on the issue has been taken by the board" takes longer to read and process than "The board acted on the issue."

Second, when you write sentences with a lot of passive verbs, you are likely to decrease the number of people in the sentence and increase the nominalizations. Notice what happens in this passage, in which I have bracketed the passive verbs and italicized the nominalizations:

> Considering the *magnitude* of the problem, it is surprising that so little work [has been done] on the reasons underlying the lack of adequate day care in the United States. Indeed, the only sustained *examination* into the matter [has been undertaken] by a *coalition* of women's and children's *advocacy* groups. But this inquiry [has been hampered] by the very *assumption* whose validity [has been questioned] frequently: the *assumption* that the welfare of the child [is best served] when he or she [is taken care] of at home by women, however poorly educated or trained.

A reader has trouble understanding the paragraph because the passive verbs muffle meaning and obscure identities. It's hard to tell who is doing what or what the issues are. If we revise the paragraph using active verbs, the meaning becomes clearer.

> Considering the magnitude of the problem, it's surprising that we know so little about why we have such a poor day-care system in this country. Advocates for women and children have undertaken the only sustained examination into the matter, but a dubious assumption hampers their investigation. That assumption is that the best system for child care is having women, however poorly educated or trained, take care of children at home.

Third, passive verbs cause vagueness because they conceal the agent in a sentence. Consider sentences like these:

> In many countries, bribes *are considered* a legitimate business expense.
> Outside agitators *are being blamed* for the trouble.
> The candidate has already *been selected*.

The reader who wants to know facts—*who* considers bribes legitimate? *who* is blaming outside agitators?—becomes impatient with such evasive statements and may react by concluding that the writer is either too lazy to find the facts or that he or she doesn't want to take responsibility for the statements.

Use Passive Verbs Well

Sometimes, however, a writer needs to use passive verbs. The two principle uses are

- To focus the reader's attention on the action rather than on the agent.
- To express action when the agent is unknown.

For instance,

> Pompeii *was buried* by a volcano 2,000 years ago.
> The operation *has been duplicated* in several hospitals.
> Hundreds of subway passengers *were overcome* by smoke.

Writers working on technical or scientific prose often need to use the passive voice to focus their readers' attention on a process or a mechanism rather than on the persons involved. If you are doing such writing, it's a good idea to check a sample passage from a document in that field. If it uses predominantly passive verbs, you may want to follow the same pattern. But even in technical writing, some editors are encouraging writers to use the active voice occasionally.

CHOOSING OTHER WORDS FOR CLARITY

Choose Adjectives and Adverbs Carefully

In general, you should try to convey your meaning with nouns and verbs rather than relying heavily on adjectives and adverbs. Use modifiers sparingly and try to make them as precise and specific as possible.

Careful writers try to avoid adjectives that seem to become attached to other words almost automatically, such as *common* courtesy, *fundamental* difference, *paramount* importance, or *final* destination. Ask yourself if a particular adjective will sharpen your meaning; if not, get rid of it.

Adjectives like *wonderful, terrific, fabulous, incredible,* and *fantastic* are "fuzzy intensifiers." They don't describe anything; they just reflect the writer's attitudes. Such words may work well in casual conversation, but in writing they give the impression that the writer doesn't want to take the time to search for a more precise term. It's also a good idea to prune out those routine intensifying words *very, really,* and *definitely.*

One kind of modifier, the qualifying word or phrase, raises particular problems. Terms that belong in this category are *rather, somewhat, often, probably, partly, in some cases, generally, for the most part,* and so on. There are dozens of such words that signal exceptions, limitations, or caution, and prudent writers use them frequently to temper their writing and avoid sounding dogmatic or simplistic. Asserting that "In the 1980s only people who do well on machine-scored tests are going to get into medical and law schools" makes an extravagant claim that immediately exposes you to challenge. But if you say, "By the 1990s *it may be* that only people who do well on machine-scored tests can get into medical or law school," the qualification changes the statement from a dogmatic pronouncement to an arguable hypothesis.

You can, however, easily carry this kind of caution too far and end up sounding timid and insecure rather than prudent. That can happen when you begin sentences with phrases like, "It is somewhat the case that . . . ," "It rather seems as if . . . ," "It is possible that one could say . . . ," or some equally timid statement. Weak openers like this give the impression of a person raising an arm over the head to fend off a blow. They are not likely to command the attention or respect of the reader.

So you need to strike a balance between brashness and timidity, between sounding dogmatic and sounding insecure. It's a matter of controlling your tone. In most writing situations you can create a confident but courteous tone by making positive statements that you tone down with an occasional mild qualifier.

Add Metaphors for Clarity

Metaphor, along with analogy, serves as an invaluable device for illustrating and clarifying abstract concepts because it helps readers to *see* the writer's meaning. It explains the unfamiliar by drawing from the familiar.

Here is an example from a well-known contemporary author, the Harvard psychologist Robert Coles.

> I slowly began to realize that we doctors had become diggers trying hard to follow treasure maps in hopes of discovering gold, then announcing—to supervisors, to patients, and not least, to one another—that we had found it. We sniffed, we poked and pried, we got aggressively "active" (one older doctor's advice: become more active when the patient "resists"), and through it all we had our eyes on the place where the treasure was always located—childhood. If we didn't know, we knew what it was that we wanted to know—would know, once we'd made our discovery, once we'd found out the nature of the "nuclear neurotic process" (another phrase in wide circulation).
>
> —Robert Coles, *The Call of Stories: Teaching and the Moral Imagination* (Boston: Houghton Mifflin, 1989), 22.

One of the bonuses of using metaphor is that you can simultaneously enrich and condense your writing. For instance, the sociologist David Riesman illustrated his theories of inner-directed and outer-directed personalities by writing that inner-directed people make decisions by consulting internal gyroscopes that have been preset by parents and society; outer-directed people make their decisions by putting out radarlike signals to test the attitudes of people around them. His metaphors both dramatize his ideas by giving them a visual dimension and communicate them more economically than he could have in a detailed, theoretical explanation. In other words, good metaphors are a kind of shorthand.

Avoid Jargon, Gobbledygook, and Doublespeak

When you encounter writing that is not only flat and colorless, but hard to understand because it is wordy, heavy with abstractions and passive verbs, and padded with qualifiers and evasive language, you should suspect that you are encountering jargon. In its original sense, the word *jargon* means the specialized language of a profession or trade; lawyers, for instance, have to talk about *habeas corpus* and *writs of mandamus,* and editors have to talk about *layouts* and *galleys.* In such contexts specialists are justified in using specialized terms. But writers who use intimidating and confusing language when they are writing for an average audience, or use highly specialized and unfamiliar terminology when it is not necessary, are writing another kind of jargon, that confusing and pretentious kind of language that is sometimes also called gobbledygook, doublespeak, or bureaucratese. This kind of jargon is another form of the emperor's-new-clothes language discussed in Chapter 2.

Certain kinds of evasive or puzzling words and phrases tend to crop up in this kind of writing. The most common are euphemisms, such as *career apparel* for *uniforms,* or *quality-control person* for *inspector;* vague words such as *viable, interface,* or *meaningful;* foreign words or phrases such as *modus vivendi* or *comme il faut;* or gimmicky words like *actualize* and *prioritize.* All of these terms can cause problems for readers, who may have to stop and ask themselves, "Now what is a *quality-control person?*" or "What does *interface* mean?" If they don't know what *modus vivendi* means, they either have to stop to look it up or go on without understanding. And a reader who bumps into a term like *prioritize* will usually do a double take. In fact, perhaps the earliest signal a reader gets that he or she may be getting bogged down in jargon is that feeling of the mind glazing over and the words not penetrating. When that happens a reader has to backtrack and start over again.

Almost certainly people *learn* to write jargon; it does not grow out of a genuine need to communicate. Students seldom write it until the last years of high school or until they get to college. People who write it do so, I think, for several reasons. At one extreme they use euphemisms to disguise unpleasantness—*sanitary landfill* for *garbage dump*—or to alter negative connotations—*golden years* for *old age.* At the other extreme writers may use doublespeak to conceal the truth or mislead the reader. No one has described that kind of jargon better than George Orwell in his essay, "Politics and the English Language":

Defenseless villages are bombarded from the air, the inhabitants driven out into the countryside, the huts set on fire with incendiary bullets, and this is called *pacification.* Millions of peasants are robbed of their farms and sent trudging along the roads with no more than they can carry; this is called *rectification of frontiers.* People are imprisoned for years without trial, or shot in the back of the neck or sent to die of scurvy in Arctic prison camps; this is called *elimination of unreliable elements.* Such phraseology is needed if one wants to name things without calling up mental pictures.

—George Orwell, "Politics and the English Language," in *Shooting an Elephant and Other Essays* (New York: Harcourt, Brace & World, 1946), 88.

Students most often use jargon for reasons that fall somewhere between these extremes. They use it because they think it sounds impressive—the emperor's new clothes again; they use it to protect themselves—if the reader is not sure what they mean, he or she can't get too angry about it; or they use it because they're lazy. It is much easier to string together abstract words and fuzzy phrases than it is to write precise, clear prose.

Here is an example of authentic military jargon used as a classroom exercise by a colleague who teaches future officers to write at the U.S. Air Force Academy:

SUBJECT: Pilferage of Dining Hall Common-Use Items

TO: Wing Group, Staff, Squadrons and Tenant Units

1. Every attempt is made to provide quality service to all patrons of the Dining Hall; however, the excessive pilferage of silverware, cups, glasses, plates and dispensers (salt, pepper, and sugar) has degraded service. Due to supply delays these items cannot always be replaced in a timely manner; additionally replacement of these items consumes funds that could be better utilized for improvement. The cost of these items has steadily increased, thereby requiring a greater expenditure of funds for replacements. Reduced fund allocations dictate maximum utilization of all common-use items and the cooperation of all personnel.
2. It is requested that all barracks, offices, work shops, etc. be cleaned out and these times be returned to the Dining Hall.
3. All personnel should be apprised of this subject and the detrimental effect it has on service and morale.

Notice how stiff and flat this writing is, and how wordy. By writing *in a timely manner* instead of *quickly, fund allocations* instead of *funds,* and *utilization* instead of *use,* and by relying heavily on passive verbs, the faceless author projects a pompous, fussy image that will probably make no impression on the people he is trying to reach.

Eliminate Sexist Language

Finally, you need to think about making your writing as clear and accurate as possible by avoiding sexist language, that is, language that suggests sex discrimination or stereotyping. Such language is not only demeaning to one sex—nearly always women—but potentially confusing because it fails to distinguish among individuals and tends to lump them into categories.

CHARACTERISTICS OF SEXIST LANGUAGE

Sexist language has these characteristics:

* It consistently uses the pronoun *he* as a *generic* pronoun—that is, an all-purpose pronoun denoting any individual whose gender is not specified. For example, "The serious runner takes time in choosing his running shoes," or "Everyone should consider his position on this issue."
* It consistently uses the terms *man* and *men* as a generic term to refer to all people ("All men acquire language by a natural process") and it uses the suffix *-man* with nouns that describe occupation or function ("chairman" or "salesman").
* It typically uses masculine pronouns and terminology to refer to people in professions traditionally thought of as male ("If a doctor is sued, you can be sure he is well insured") and feminine pronouns and terminology to refer to people in professions generally thought of as female ("Today's nurse earns less in real wages than her predecessor did twenty years ago").
* It often suggests that certain traits, attitudes, and behavior are typically male (men are rational, independent, ambitious) and other traits, attitudes, and behavior are typically female (women are emotional, passive, and eager to please). The writer may also use clichés that reflect sexist attitudes: "Chattering females," "the weaker sex," or "swaggering males."

There are other, subtler forms of sexist language. One is to refer to prominent men by their title or last name but to prominent women by their full name or married name: for instance, designating the U.S. president as "President Bush" but the ex-British prime minister as "Mrs. Thatcher" or referring to the American male writer as "Hemingway" but the American female writer as "Eudora Welty." Another is to mention specifically the appearance or marital status of women but not of men. For instance, it would be sexist to mention in a report that a woman employee is

"an attractive blond" or "a divorcée" but not indicate whether a man employee is married or divorced or whether he is attractive or homely.

REASONS TO ELIMINATE SEXIST LANGUAGE

Many writers protest that they are not sexist and that the fuss about
masculine pronouns or the generic term *man* is ridiculous. They claim that
their readers know that the term refers to all people, and that they
shouldn't have to worry about such trivial matters. They also claim that in
order to get rid of all allegedly sexist references they will have to write
awkward sentences. They reject "he and she" or "her/his" as ugly constructions. One can sympathize with these complaints. Getting rid of sexist
innuendoes in writing takes attention and effort—it's a nuisance. Nevertheless, our language changes as our society changes, and for several reasons today's writers need to work at eliminating sexism from their writing.

The first reason is to improve clarity and accuracy. Consistently using
he as a pronoun without considering the gender of the referent may mislead your readers. The sentence *A scholarship athlete must be able both to
practice and to keep up his grades* seems to suggest that there are no
women athletes on scholarship. And the writer who always uses *him* to
refer to a lawyer or doctor or scientist gives the impression of not knowing
that one-third of all medical students and one-half of all law students are
women, and that women now get about one-fifth of the advanced degrees
in science.

The second reason is pragmatic and economic. Today more than half of
all college students and more than half of the workers in the United States
are women. Politically, socially, and financially, these women wield substantial power. They make up a large segment of most writers' audiences,
and most of them dislike sexist language and are sensitive about being ster-
eotyped or patronized by writers. If you want to inform or persuade an audience that is made up even partially of women you need to avoid sexist
language.

A third reason is legal. Federal and state laws now stipulate that a person cannot be discriminated against because of sex when he or she applies
for credit, for a job, for a scholarship, a grant, or for admission to a school
or program. Thus the administrators and executives who are in charge of
advertising and administering the guidelines in any of these situations must
be sure that the language of all documents is completely nonsexist. Anyone
who is going to be writing for a corporation, a bureau, an educational institution, or an agency needs to become conscious of sexist language and
how to avoid it.

The last reason, and from my point of view the strongest, is psychological and ethical. *Language shapes thought*—linguists, anthropologists, politi-

cians, and leaders all know that, and the writer who persists in using only masculine pronouns or suggesting that certain occupations and attitudes are male, others female, reinforces stereotypes and sexist attitudes. I think this quotation demonstrates that truth:

> [The typical writer] would have a wife and one, two, or three children. . . . The writer of forty would own his own house—probably with a big mortgage—but there will be less than the usual number of appliances because he has developed a high resistance to salesmanship. . . . If he owns a television set he will explain apologetically that he got it for the children, but now the writer and his wife have taken to watching a few programs. Probably he is dissatisfied with his work and his mode of life. . . . He has begun to take part in local activities. Recently his wife was elected to the school board, and he would like to run for office himself, but he has decided that the office, and even the campaign, would take too much time from his writing.
> —Malcolm Cowley, *The Literary Situation*
> (New York: The Viking Press, 1955), 195.

Only by great effort can the reader of this passage remember that not all writers are men.

You say the Cowley example is dated and people avoid such language now? Unfortunately, that's less true than one might think. True, many people go to considerable lengths to avoid language that stereotypes, but look at this example written thirty-five years after Cowley, and quoted in *The New York Times*.

> Judge Bowman, a former law professor named to the St. Louis-based appeals court in 1983, is considered something of a star of the Reagan judiciary. He was on the short list for the 1987 Supreme Court vacancy originally meant for Robert H. Bork.
>   Those credentials gave a certain weight to his decision in the Missouri case that "whatever the philosophy of the particular judge, and whether *he* views *his* proper role as broad or narrow, *his* decisions—some of them, at least—necessarily resolve issues previously unsettled and thus will declare law."
> —Linda Greenburg, "Elderly Judges Facing
>   Decision Close to Home," *The New York Times*,
>   13 December 1990, B–16.

Such a lapse is especially glaring because it comes from a federal judge, someone whose public pronouncements shape policy and who, of all people, should be aware that there are many women judges, one on the Supreme Court itself. Many readers find this kind of lapse quite offensive—certainly I do.

WAYS TO ELIMINATE SEXIST LANGUAGE

Cleaning sexist innuendoes out of one's writing takes effort and ingenuity, but if you work at it you can finally make writing nonsexist prose as
much of a habit as spelling and punctuating correctly. Here are some suggestions for ways to go about it:

- When you can, use plural nouns to avoid using the pronoun *he* or the
  phrase *he and she* (often this is the simplest remedy): "Painters who
  want to exhibit their work," rather than "A painter who wants to exhibit his work."
- Reword your sentences to eliminate reference to gender: "The average American drives a car three years," rather than "The average
  American drives his car three years."
- When you can, substitute the word *person* or *people* for *man* or
  woman: "A person who wants to get ahead in business" rather than
  "A man who wants to get ahead in business," and "Young people
  who want to become engineers," instead of "Boys who want to become engineers."
- When you can, substitute *one* for *he* or *she* or for specific reference
  to a man or woman: "If one plans ahead, one can retire comfortably
  at 55," instead of "If he plans ahead, a man can retire at 55." Often
  you can use *you* instead of *one*. For example, "If you plan ahead, you
  can retire at 55."
- Occasionally, when the noun to which you want to refer has to be
  singular, write "he or she" or "his or hers"; such phrases are incon-
  spicuous if you do not use them too often. Some writers use he/she
  or him/her.
- Alternate between using *he* and *she* as pronouns. For example, write
  "An officer who makes an arrest must show her badge."
- Instead of identifying people by their sex, identify them by their role
  or function: student, applicant, consumer, voter, patient, parent, and
  so on. For instance, you can write "Consumers are alarmed by rising
  food costs," instead of "Housewives are alarmed by rising food
  costs." Such a sentence is also more accurate since almost 40 per cent
  of shoppers in grocery stores are now men.
- Refer to women by their given and married names such as Julia Walsh
  or Geraldine Ferraro rather than as Mrs. John Walsh or Mrs. Ferraro.
  Avoid reference to women's marital status unless that information is
  important to making your point.
- Be consistent when you are referring to people by their last names. If
  you write Hawthorne or Steinbeck, also write Dickinson or Porter.
- When you can, replace occupational terms ending in *-man* or *-woman*

with another term. For instance, write *firefighter* instead of *fireman, mail carrier* instead of *mailman, salesperson* instead of *salesman* or *saleswoman,* and *janitor* instead of *cleaning woman. Waiter* can refer to either a man or a woman.

• Be careful not to stereotype people by professions or by supposedly sex-linked characteristics. For example, write "Young people who plan to become doctors should realize they will be in college at least ten years," rather than "The young man who wants to become a doctor should realize that he will be in college at least ten years."

• Don't refer to women's physical appearance unless it is relevant to your point or unless you also refer to men's physical appearance in the same context.

In order to develop a style of writing that is free of sexist overtones, you have to do three things. First, you have to become conscious of those overtones; that may be the greatest problem since many of us are so used to the traditional male-centered style that we have trouble spotting its typical characteristics. Second, you have to cultivate the habit of revising and editing to get rid of those characteristics. Gradually you can internalize the conventions for nonsexist writing just as you internalize other guidelines for style. Finally, and probably most important, you have to care about developing a neutral, nondiscriminatory style. Once you believe that it matters, the changes will come almost naturally.

EXERCISES

1. Working with two or three other students, discuss ways to revise these sentences using more concrete and specific language.

   A. Our recommendation would mean elimination of homeless elements on our city streets.

   B. A knowledge and understanding of the law is a necessity for those who want an alteration of it.

   C. The result of the election is an indication that the legislator has an environmentally aware constituency.

   When you are finished, write a clear version of each sentence.

2. Revise these sentences and put in people or a person as the subject of each one.

   A. The load of responsibility on the lender is great.

    B. A stringent self-evaluation is needed to remedy your problem.

    C. The anxiety that accompanies choosing a profession is a major cause of stress.

3. Working with two or three other students, discuss ways in which one could revise these sentences using more vigorous verbs.

    A. There are several advantages that will be achieved by this ruling.

    B. Vitamins are substances the body requires in small amounts.

    C. There are many things to examine when looking for a used car.

When you are finished, write a stronger version of each sentence.

4. Revise these sentences to replace passive verbs with active verbs. Get rid of any nominalizations you think are weakening the sentences.

    A. Uneducated women are faced with serious apprehension when they are forced into the job market for the first time.

    B. Such information should be made available to consumers before they ask for it.

    C. What should be considered is the capability and suitability of the individual for the job.

    D. It is recommended by administrators that accountability be made a major consideration in giving salary bonuses.

    E. The requirements were put into effect by a group of uninformed people before the problem was recognized.

5. Photocopy a magazine article in which the author uses metaphor or allusion and bring it to class. Analyze what the writer's reason for using allusion and metaphor seems to be. Do you think the technique is effective?

6. Working with two or three other students in a group, try to interpret these jargon-laden sentences and then rewrite each one to make it clearer.

    A. The configuration of human and technical talents to be mobilized often transcends the jurisdiction of formal educational institutions.

    B. "Once upon a time, a small person named Little Red Riding Hood initiated plans for the preparation, delivery, and transportation of foodstuffs to her grandmother, a senior citizen residing at a place of residence in a forest of indeterminate dimensions."—Russell Baker

    C. Our investments are generating a negative capability.

D. Nelson prioritized the company's objectives in terms of viability and expense factors.

7. Working with two or three other students in a group, discuss how you might revise the following passages to get rid of sexist language.

A. The artist must follow his own intuition if he is to do lasting work, whether he is a painter or a sculptor. The man who tries to imitate or do what is currently chic will not make his mark on the culture.

B. The nurse who wants to work with the day-to-day patients in a hospital will often find such jobs are filled by nurses' aides because the hospital administrator has been forced to cut his expenses.

C. Policemen and mailmen are often among the best paid public employees in large cities because they work for the civil service.

D. Hemingway, Fitzgerald, Katherine Anne Porter, Steinbeck, and Joan Didion are among the authors who have kept notebooks on their writing habits.

E. If mankind is to survive beyond the twenty-first century, we must stop global warming.

SUGGESTED WRITING ASSIGNMENTS

As a part of each writing assignment write a detailed analysis of your audience and specify the characteristics they would have that you need to keep in mind as you write, the problems such an audience might present, and what the audience would expect to get from reading your paper. Also analyze your purpose in writing, specifying what you hope to accomplish with the paper. If appropriate, include an accurate and descriptive title for your paper.

TOPIC 1: Observe carefully a street, neighborhood, building, or small area in your city and write an objective report on it that might be used for a paper in an urban sociology class or course on city government. Use concrete and specific but neutral language; appeal to the senses as much as possible and avoid using vague adjectives. Think about what kind of information your reader would want to get from the report and what use that information might be put to outside of class. Some possible topics for description might be the following:

A. A school building that needs to be modernized.

B. A vacant lot that could be converted into a playground.

C. A block close to campus that is being invaded by X-rated bookstores and porno movie houses.

D. The county courthouse that was built in the last century.

TOPIC 2: The generous retirement pay of people who have served twenty years or more in the armed services costs U.S. taxpayers a substantial amount of money. For example, a colonel may retire at forty-two and receive more than $1,500 a month retirement pay while holding down another job; a four-star admiral may retire at the age of sixty with a pension of more than $60,000 a year. These benefits also have the advantage of being tied to the cost of living so that they increase as the price index rises.

Assume the persona of someone who defends or opposes these benefits and write an article expressing your views. Think carefully about the consequences of your argument and support your points. Direct your paper to a specific audience.

TOPIC 3: Write a short article for young people from ten to fourteen years old explaining the basic concepts of some subject on which you are well informed or in which you are very interested. Assume that your readers are bright youngsters who read well and who enjoy learning something new. Try to explain your ideas or give your information in terms they will understand, using concrete examples and analogies. Keep your focus narrow enough so that you can treat the subject in no more than 1,000 words.

Here are some suggestions for topics:

A new discovery in geology, astronomy, archeology, or other science.
What it takes to be a dancer, lawyer, journalist, or other professional.
How weather forecasting is done.
How airplanes fly or ducks swim or whales breathe.
How to budget and spend a clothes allowance.
How to buy one's first horse.
Choosing a sport to participate in.
How to take care of a dog in hot weather.

Remember that your audience doesn't have to read your article and will do so only if you keep them interested. It would be a good idea to look at some children's magazines or the column for young people in magazines such as *Sierra* to get a feel for what kind of writing appeals to youngsters and what qualities articles for them are likely to have. *And remember not to preach.*

9 ◇ Crafting Paragraphs

Paragraphs are artificial units of print (or writing) that writers and editors create in order to divide writing into chunks that will make it easier to read and to understand. We don't actually think in paragraphs in the way that we think in sentences—they're not natural to us. That's why all of us sometimes have trouble deciding when to start a new paragraph or deciding just how long an individual paragraph should be. But every writer needs to develop strong paragraphing skills. They're essential to becoming a competent writer who is conscious of the reader's needs and knows how to meet them.

How do you develop those skills? Partly through practice and partly through intuition. The more you write and the more audience conscious you become, the stronger your "feel" for paragraphs will become because decisions about paragraphs are strongly tied to audience. But there are also two basic principles that underlie the concept of paragraphs, and you can improve your paragraphing skills by consciously thinking about and applying those principles. The first principle involves looking at paragraphs from the *outside;* the second principle involves looking at them from the *inside.*

THE OUTSIDE VIEW OF PARAGRAPHING

When writers and editors break writing into paragraphs for outside reasons, they do so because they care about how writing is going to look. They know that a printed page has its own body language, that it gives off signals to its potential readers before those readers ever read a word. Part of that body language comes from paragraph length, and a page with very long paragraphs intimidates many readers. Those long paragraphs, especially if they are combined with small print, narrow margins, and few subheadings, say to the reader "I am hard to read."

For this reason, editors and audience-conscious writers insert frequent paragraph breaks in order to make a page look "reader friendly." It's the principle of "chunking" again (see pp. 125–27). They are doing it to break up the material into manageable segments so that readers won't feel they are getting too much information at one time. If that seems patronizing, think about your own reactions to long paragraphs—don't you find them a little off-putting? I do. I have rejected more than one book when I was browsing in the library or book store because its paragraphs ran to more than a page.

Writers who are the most audience conscious will base many of their paragraphing decisions on what they know about a specific audience. If they are writing for an audience with widely diverse educations and reading skills—say the readers of *Family Circle* or *TV Guide*—they will write shorter paragraphs than they would for a narrower audience whom they assume to be educated and skilled readers—for example, the readers of *Scientific American* or the *Atlantic*. They will also use shorter paragraphs when they are writing for young readers.

Of course, the terms "short paragraph" and "long paragraph" are relative, but in general, you can consider a short paragraph one that runs from three to six sentences of medium length. A paragraph of seven or eight sentences, depending on their length, is medium to long. Any paragraph of more than ten sentences, or one that covers more than half a printed page, is definitely long, and you should consider breaking it up. As you can tell by glancing over this book, I believe strongly in short paragraphs. I see no reason to give my readers more trouble than necessary, and if I can divide a paragraph without compromising its unity, I do.

Guidelines for Breaking Paragraphs

First, don't worry about paragraph length when you're still drafting your paper or even when you're working on the first revision. Paragraphing for appearance is essentially a stylistic matter, and you'll do better to put it off until you're revising at that level.

Remember that no careful writer chops his or her writing into paragraphs arbitrarily just to make it look better. You must observe some principles and guidelines, or you will wind up with divisions that confuse your readers more than they help them. The traditional rule of thumb is that you start a new paragraph whenever you come to a new idea. That's fine for certain kinds of writing. For example, if you're writing a paper that lists several reasons or classifies a number of examples, you can probably build a new paragraph on each point or example. Paragraphing can be easy when your paper falls into such natural divisions.

The problem, however, is that it's not always that easy to tell when you've come to a new idea—and what if it's a very long idea? If you find your paragraph running to ten or twelve long sentences, you need to think about how it will look to your reader. So you need something to go by that's more specific than the rule of thumb above. When you think a paragraph is getting too long and you want to break it, here are some clues that may signal a place where you could break it.

- *Changes in time.* Look for places where sequence shifts or you designate a time by such words as *second, at that time, formerly,* or *the next day.* You can't always make breaks at those places but often you can.
- *Changes in place.* Look for junctures where you've written "In another part of . . . ," "elsewhere," or "the other side," or have used pointer words such as *this* or *that.*
- *Changes in direction.* Look for places where you're indicating contrast or changing focus with signals such as "nevertheless," "in opposition to . . . ," or "on the contrary."
- *Changes of emphasis.* Look for possible breaks where you shift to a new point of view, using terms like "in spite of . . ." "another possibility," or "If that happens . . ."

For instance, here is an example of a long paragraph that could be broken up into more manageable chunks without its unity being affected:

"People say that Arthur [Ashe] lacks the killer instinct." (Ronald Charity is commenting.) "And that is a lot of baloney. Arthur is quietly aggressive—more aggressive than people give him credit for being. You don't get to be that good without a will to win. He'll let you win the first two sets, then he'll blast you off the court." Ronald Charity, who taught Arthur Ashe to play tennis, was himself taught by no one. "I was my own protégé," he says. Charity is approaching forty and is the head of an advertising and public-relations firm in Danville, Virginia, Trim, lithe, in excellent condition, he is still nationally ranked as one of the top ten players in the A.T.A. **|** In 1946, when he began to play tennis, as a seventeen-year-old in Richmond, there were—male and female, all ages—about twenty Negroes in the city who played the game and none of them played it well. Charity, as a college freshman, thought tennis looked interesting, and when, in a bookstore, he saw Lloyd Budge's *Tennis Made Easy* he bought a copy and began to teach himself to play. When he had absorbed what Budge had to say, he bought Alice Marble's *The Road to Wimbledon,* and, finally, William T. Tilden's *How to Play Better Tennis.* "It just happened that I could pull off a page and project into my imagination how it should be done," he says. **|** Blacks in Richmond could play tennis only at the Negro Y.W.C.A., where Charity developed his game, and, a little later, four hard-surface courts were built at Brook Field, a Negro playground about two miles from the heart of the city. Arthur Ashe, a Special Police Officer in charge of discipline at several Negro playgrounds, lived in a frame house in the middle of Brook Field. When Arthur Ashe, Jr. was six years old, he spent a great deal of time watching Ronald Charity play tennis, and would never forget what he felt as he watched him. "I thought he was the best in the world. He had long, fluid, graceful strokes. I could see no kinks in his game."

> —John McPhee, "Levels of the Game,"
> reprinted in *The John McPhee Reader,*
> ed. William Howarth (New York:
> Vintage Books, 1978), 178–179.

Notice that the first place I broke this paragraph (indicated by a slash) comes at a shift in time—the narrative moves from the present back to 1946. The second place where it could be broken comes at a change in space—the narrative moves from talking about tennis books to the tennis courts at the Y.W.C.A.

Avoiding One-Sentence Paragraphs

Unfortunately, some mass-market writers let their enthusiasm for short paragraphs carry them to the extreme of habitually writing a series of one- and two-sentence paragraphs that are really not paragraphs at all. They are only separated sentences. For example,

> Once upon a time there was a little girl in a small town in South Dakota who dreamed of speaking French.
> So when she grew up and went off to college, a prestigious school in the East, she was ready for her dream to come true.
> "I had a miserable French teacher—I was disappointed," recalled Ann Clark, the chef behind Austin's La Bonne Cuisine School of French cooking. "So I dropped out of school and a girlfriend and I went to France."
> There the two worked as *au pair* girls, live-in housekeepers earning some money and gaining an entry to the ethos of France that had seemed so inviting.
> > —Carolyn Bobo, "France Makes Rich Life for
> > Cook," *Austin American-Statesman,*
> > 21 December 1978, G–1.

Although writers for newspapers probably write these one-sentence paragraphs because the narrow columns of a newspaper make a paragraph of normal length look long and intimidating, this kind of paragraphing chops a piece of writing into arbitrary divisions that are hard to follow. The reader senses no pattern or unity to the writing.

You shouldn't assume, however, that you can never write one-sentence paragraphs. Sometimes they serve well to introduce a major point, or they can make a kind of announcement to which the writer wants to draw attention.

Here are two examples from professional writers. In the first, the author uses the one-sentence paragraph to dramatize a major point in her narrative of an accident.

> Hobo ran ahead, then back, brushing snow crystals and fur against my leg. I put a hand on my skin to warm it and dragged nylon ski pants over the road behind me. Mom said to have them along in case the bus broke down, but she knew I would not wear them, could not bear the plastic sounds they made between my thighs.
>
> No light was on in our home.
>
> —Natalie Kusz, "Vital Signs," reprinted in
> *The Best American Essays, 1990,*
> ed. Justin Kaplan,
> (New York: Ticknor and Fields, 1990), 155.
> This essay originally appeared in
> *The Three Penny Review,* 1989.

In this example in a book about writing, the author starts a chapter with two one-sentence paragraphs.

> So much for early warnings about the bloated monsters that lie in ambush for the writer trying to put together a clear English sentence.
>
> "But," you may say, "if I eliminate everything you think is clutter and strip every sentence to its barest bones, will there be anything left for me?"
>
> The question is a fair one and the fear entirely natural. Simplicity carried to its extreme might seem to point to a style where the sentences are little more sophisticated than "Dick likes Jane" and "See Spot run."
>
> —William Zinsser, *On Writing Well,* 4th ed.
> (New York: HarperCollins, 1990), 20.

So you see a one-sentence paragraph can be effective. If you use one, however, be sure you are doing it consciously and for a definite purpose. They are attention getters, and most of the time you will do better to avoid them, sticking with the principle that a paragraph is a group of sentences that pertain to and develop a single idea.

THE INSIDE VIEW OF PARAGRAPHING

Looked at from the inside, the essential quality of a paragraph should be *unity*. A paragraph is supposed to have a central idea, and everything in the paragraph relates to and develops that idea. The reader finds no surprises, and every sentence fits with the others. Moreover, the sentences follow each other in logical order so that one could not move the sentences around at random: each one needs to be in its particular place to advance the internal development of the paragraph.

How does one go about developing these unified paragraphs? People who write a lot probably develop their paragraphs mostly by intuition. They put down a first sentence and if it seems to work, the second sentence evolves from it. And so they continue, developing their points with examples and explanations, expanding on the idea they started with. If you were to ask them to explain how they write their paragraphs, they probably couldn't tell you. The fact remains, however, that much of the time professional writers are producing paragraphs that fit certain patterns that follow natural thought processes. Apprentice writers can learn something about good paragraph development by studying those patterns and analyzing how they are developed.

Commitment/Response Paragraphs

One important pattern for paragraphs is that of commitment and response. That is, the first sentence of the paragraph makes a *commitment* to the reader, makes a statement that sets up certain expectations and leads the reader to expect that they will be fulfilled. In some cases, the commitment sentence could be called a topic sentence. Whatever you label it, it works by making a promise to the reader, a promise that is developed by the rest of the paragraph.

Commitments in a paragraph can take many forms, as the following examples show. (I have italicized the commitment sentence in each one.)

First, the commitment in a paragraph can be a *generative sentence,* one that suggests more details will follow. For example,

> *The shows [Miss Saigon, Cats, Les Misérables] are more than money-making machines.* The public likes them, and sometimes the critics do too. It is Mackintosh's genius, many people say, that through his years of trial and error in the business he has developed a knack for

knowing what the public will flock to see. Mackintosh himself agrees. "My own tastes happen to be in tune with what the public wants," he says. "I think that's the reason my batting average is so high, not because I've discovered some brilliant formula."

> —Marvyn Rothstein, "The Musical Is Money to
> His Ears," *The New York Times Magazine,*
> 9 December 1990, 84.

The writer makes a strong commitment in the first sentence, "The shows are more than money-making machines" and uses the rest of the paragraph to explain that statement.

The commitment in a paragraph can also take the form of a *question that will be answered.* (Notice this is the pattern I have used in the second paragraph in this section.) Here is another example:

> *How do I capture a city and a time?* It began in the back of a camouflaged RAF lorry that smelled of oil. I clung to the side as the driver swung the lorry fast around the curved Cotswold road from Bourton-on-the-Water to the railway station. All I had left of the uniform I had worn for ten months as an aircraft woman second class in the Women's Auxilary Air Force of the RAF was a pair of issue shoes, heavy black masculine clodhoppers. I carried the suitcase I had kept hidden full of civilian clothes to wear on leave, a civilian ration book, some clothing coupons, and my discharge papers (my ticket). I was dressed in the suit I had worn to to into the WAAF at the recruiting station in Kingsway. That was the beginning of the time in London, and it ended, eighteen months later, not in London, but at a dinner party in New York the evening after I came home from the war.

> —Mary Lee Settle, "London–1944," reprinted
> in *The Best American Essays, 1988,*
> ed. Elizabeth Hardwick (New York:
> Ticknor and Fields, 1988.) 1.
> The essay first appeared in the
> *Virginia Quarterly Review,* 1986.

Writers can also make an opening commitment by *beginning a narrative* in the first sentence and signaling to the reader that the rest of the story will follow. For example:

> *One morning I arrived early at work and went into the bank lobby where the Negro porter was mopping.* I stood at a counter and picked up the Memphis *Commercial Appeal* and began my free reading of the press. I came finally to the editorial page and saw an article dealing with one H. L. Mencken. I knew by hearsay that he was the editor of the *American Mercury,* but aside from that I knew nothing about him. The

article was a furious denunciation with one hot, short sentence:
Mencken is a fool.

> —Richard Wright, "The Library Card," in *Black Boy*
> (New York: Harper & Row, 1937), 214.

Another good way to make an opening commitment in a paragraph is
by *using a quotation*. For example,

> *"You want to fly with the eagles, you got to pay the price*," Dick An-
> deregg told me on the phone. Anderegg is an Air Force major in his
> middle thirties, a fighter pilot so proficient that until recently he was an
> instructor at the Air Force's Fighter Weapons School at Nellis Air Force
> Base, near Las Vegas. Now he works at the Pentagon, as an aide (or
> "action officer," in the current phrase) to a general, and it was in that
> capacity that he became my chaperone for a time early this fall.
>
> > —James Fallows, "I Flew with the Eagles,"
> > *Atlantic,* November 1981, 70.

And don't forget the important technique of *downshifting*, already
mentioned in the last chapter. It is a particularly useful strategy for opening
your paragraph with a commitment and then developing it with statements
on a lower level of generality. For example,

> *The most primary source of all its unpublished material*: private let-
> ters and diaries or the reports, orders, and messages in government ar-
> chives. There is an immediacy and intimacy about them that reveals
> character and makes circumstances come alive. I remember Secretary
> of State Robert Lansing's desk diary, which I used when I was working
> on *The Zimmerman Telegram*. The man himself seemed to step right
> out from his tiny neat handwriting and his precise notations of every
> visitor and each subject discussed. Each day's record opened and
> closed with the Secretary's time of arrival and departure from the office. He
> even entered the time of his lunch hour, which invariably listed
> sixty minutes: "Left at 1:10; returned at 2:10." Once, when he was
> forced to record his morning arrival at 10:15, he added, with a worried
> eye on posterity, "Car broke down."
>
> > —Barbara Tuchman, "In Search of History,"
> > in *Practicing History* (New York: Alfred
> > A. Knopf, 1981), 11.

So writers can choose several different ways to build their paragraphs
around a commitment/response pattern. The important point to remember is that the sentences that follow the opening commitment must
not frustrate or confuse the reader by failing to follow through.

Other Paragraph Patterns

It helps to familiarize yourself with other paragraph patterns that can work well in different writing situations. Some of the most useful are those that reflect common patterns of organization covered in Chapter 5: *induction or reasoning from evidence, claims and warrants, definition, cause and effect, comparison, narration,* and *process.* Here are some examples. You will probably notice that many of them are also *commitment-and-response* paragraphs and many use *generative sentences.*

INDUCTION OR REASONING FROM EVIDENCE

This is a useful pattern when you want to present your reader with a collection of data or impressions that you will then use to develop your idea. For instance,

> Outside the Ryoanji temple, the newest Japanese surfaces shine. The taxi drivers bustle, sweeping huge feather dusters over their cars, flicking specks from the bright metal. The ritual, a writer once remarked, makes them look like the chambermaids in the first act of a French farce. But it is utterly Japanese, a set piece: the drivers handle their dusters like samurai. The scene is a sort of cartoon of the busy, fastidious superego that is supposed to preside in the Japanese psyche. The drivers even wear white gloves. There is probably not a dirty taxicab in Japan.
> —Lance Morrow, "All the Hazards and Threats of Success," *Time,* 1 August 1983, 20.

CLAIM AND WARRANT

This pattern works well when you are setting up an argument and want your readers to know immediately that you are going to give evidence for it. For example,

> You can tell a great deal about a country by observing its waiters. There is the obsequiousness of the London waiter, who thanks you every time he performs a service; there is the professionalism, and sometimes arrogance, of the Paris waiter, for whom the job is often a lifelong metier; and there is the hysterical bustling of a waiter in the Plaka district of Athens, a city perched between the First and the Third Worlds. Finally, there is the take-it-or-leave-it independence of the American waiter, who announces in his every gesture that he is as good as his customer. America is, among other things, a way of carrying a tray of food.
> —Michael Harrington, "Does America Still Exist?" *Harper's,* March 1984, 48.

DEFINITION

This is a useful pattern when you want to explain a term or a concept that is important to your thesis. For instance,

> Poliomyelitis is a disease caused by a viral agent that invades the body by way of the gastrointestinal tract, where it multiplies and, on rare occasions, travels via blood and/or nervous pathways to the central nervous system, where it attacks the motor neurons of the spinal cord and part of the brain. Motor neurons are destroyed. Muscle groups are weakened or destroyed. A healthy fifteen-year-old boy of 160 pounds might lose seventy or eighty pounds in a week.
> —Charles L. Mee, Jr., "The Summer Before Salk,"
> *Esquire*, December 1983, 40.

CAUSE AND EFFECT

This is another pattern that is useful when you are presenting an argument and need to show how you have arrived at your conclusions. For example,

> The influx of backlanders into Fortaleza [Brazil], equivalent to the sudden arrival of more than two million refugees in New York City, has resulted in chaos. The area around the train station, the João Tomé bus station, and the cathedral is overrun with beggars, cripples, and families that huddle at night on dirty sidewalks. Slums have sprung up on the fringes of the city, barely pubescent girls have turned to prostitution, and crime—particularly the theft of anything that can be sold or bartered for food—has increased.
> —Edwin McDowell, "Famine in the Backlands,"
> *Atlantic*, March 1984, 22.

COMPARISON

This pattern works well when you want to develop a point by showing likeness or differences. For instance,

> The "two cultures" controversy of several decades back has quieted down some, but it is still with us, still unsettled because of the polarized views set out by C. P. Snow at one extreme and by F. R. Leavis at the other; these remain as the two sides of the argument. At one edge, the humanists are set up as knowing, and wanting to know, very little about science and even less about the human meaning of contemporary science; they are, so it goes, antiscientific in their prejudice. On the other side, the scientists are served up as a bright but illiterate lot, well-read in nothing except science, even, as Leavis said of

Snow, incapable of writing good novels. The humanities are presented in the dispute as though made up of imagined unverifiable notions about human behavior, unsubstantiated stories cooked up by poets and novelists, while the sciences deal parsimoniously with lean facts, hard data, incontrovertible theories, truths established beyond doubt, the unambiguous facts of life.

> —Lewis Thomas, "On Matters of Doubt," in
> *Late Night Thoughts on Listening to Mahler's*
> *Ninth Symphony* (New York: Viking, 1983), 156.

In developing an idea by comparison and contrast, it also works well to compare by alternating paragraphs. For instance,

> Ross [Lockridge] was an oak of prudence and industry. He rarely drank and he never smoked. He excelled at everything he did. He had married his hometown sweetheart, was proudly faithful to her and produced four fine children. After a sampling of success on both coasts, he had gone home to the Indiana of his parents and childhood friends.

> Tom Heggen had a taste for the low life. He had been divorced, had no children and shared bachelor quarters in New York with an ex-actor and screenwriter, Dorothy Parker's estranged husband, Alan Campbell. Tom was a drinker and a pill addict. He turned up regularly at the fashionable restaurant "21," usually bringing along a new girl, a dancer or an actress.

> —John Leggett, *Ross and Tom* (New York:
> Simon & Schuster, 1974).

NARRATION

A miniature story is frequently a good way to illustrate a point that you have already made or one that you want to make. It also has the virtue of adding a visual element or a personal element to your writing. For instance,

> The legend, at least, is clear: Once upon a time, a few Celtic warlords were roving over the wide Atlantic, extending themselves and their boats northward from Europe. When they spied a green headland, it occurred to them to race for the beach—the first one to touch land, it was understood, would acquire the whole place for himself and his descendents. But as one slower boat slipped slightly but inexorably behind in the churning surf, its captain, the brave O'Neill, decided on a rash act. Deliberately wielding his battleax, he chopped off his own left hand and hurled it ashore, thus claiming the territory forever.

> —Michael Olmert, "Hail to Heraldry, A Most
> Intricate and Revealing Art," *Smithsonian,*
> May 1984, 86.

PROCESS

This kind of paragraph is particularly useful when you have been generalizing about a theory and need to explain specifically how it works. For instance,

> When I write, I like to have an interval before me when I am not likely to be interrupted. For me, this means usually the early morning, before others are awake. I get pen and paper, take a glance out the window (often it is dark out there), and wait. It is like fishing. But I do not wait very long, for there is always a nibble—and this is where receptivity comes in. To get started I will accept anything that occurs to me. Something always occurs, of course, to any of us. We can't keep from thinking. Maybe I have to settle for an immediate impression: it's cold, or hot, or dark, or bright, or in between! Or—well, the possibilities are endless. If I put something down, that thing will help the next thing come, and I'm off. If I let the process go on, things will occur to me that were not at all in my mind when I started. These things, odd or trivial as they may be, are somehow connected. And if I let them string out, surprising things will happen.
>
> —William Stafford, "A Way of Writing," *Field,* Spring 1970.

OPENING AND CLOSING PARAGRAPHS

Crafting Opening Paragraphs

I have discussed opening paragraphs at some length in Chapter 7; you may want to review that if you're having trouble with your opening paragraphs. Here I'll just repeat two key points of advice and give two additional examples of good introductory paragraphs.

First, when you're writing something important, and particularly if it's something you hope to get published, take time to draft a strong, attention-getting opening paragraph that meets the aims I mention in Chapter 7. A strong opener can help you win your reader's confidence at the outset; a poor one will get you off to a stumbling start from which it may be hard to recover.

That said, though, don't let anxiety about crafting the right opening paragraph bog down your writing. Probably the best openers are actually written on the third or fourth draft, when those ideas that have been incubating for a while suddenly come together in an introduction. So if you can't think of just the right way to start, don't worry. It will come to you.

Just for inspiration, here are a pair of examples from two outstanding professional writers.

The first is the opening paragraph from an early chapter of the award-winning book about the Vietnam War, *A Bright Shining Lie.*

He didn't seem like a man anyone could keep down when he strode through the swinging doors of Col. Daniel Boone Porter's office in Saigon ten years earlier, shortly before noon on March 23, 1962. Porter soon had the feeling that if the commanding general were to tell this junior lieutenant . . . that he was surrendering direction of the war to him, John Vann would say, "Fine, General," and take charge. In light of the figure he was to become, it was a small irony that he almost hadn't made it to Vietnam. The plane that he should have taken to Saigon in March 1962, with ninety-three other officers and men, had disappeared over the Pacific. He had missed the flight because, in his eagerness to go to war, he had forgotten to have his passport renewed. A clerk had noticed that the passport had expired, and he had been instructed to step out of the boarding line. Shortly after the plane vanished, the Red Cross had telephoned Mary Jane to inform her that her husband had been lost in the Pacific. Mary Jane had said that he was all right, that he had telephoned and was taking a later flight. She must be mistaken, the Red Cross worker had persisted. Her husband was missing. Passenger rosters didn't lie.

—Neil Sheehan, *A Bright Shining Lie* (New York:
Vintage Books, Random House, 1989), 37.

Notice how Sheehan sets up John Paul Vann, the focus of the book, as a confident young man with a future and uses an attention-getting anecdote to mark him as a man who was also lucky.

The second example is the introduction of an article celebrating the survival of the pioneer spirit in a remote area of Nebraska.

"See that dip behind the hills?" Margaret Hawkins asks, pointing to a saddle-shaped depression in the low, hummocky knolls on her cattle ranch in Arthur County, Nebraska. The new grass on the hills is a patchy, pale green carpet on this day in early May. "The story is that Paul Bunyan made that low spot when he sat down to rest on his way through here." The rangeland that rolls toward the horizon in a succession of long-shouldered mounds doesn't appear to have changed much since Bunyan passed by. Man's mark is minimal here—fences, an occasional windmill, power poles in the hazy distance. Air travelers gaze idly through the clouds at this emptiness and turn back to their magazines. This is the Sand Hills region of western Nebraska, smack in the heart of the Great Plains—cow country, tough and dry and stingy and a long, lonely way from mainstream America.

—Donald Dale Johnson, " 'You Survive Because
Everyone Cares, Everyone Has Walked in Your
Shoes,' " *Smithsonian,* November 1990, 41.

Notice how Johnson makes his setting vivid, by presenting it through the voice and eyes of a native of the region; he then sets the mood for his article by picturing the long vistas of an empty, lonesome country.

Wrestling with Closing Paragraphs

Conclusions are hard. Any writer will tell you that. It's not easy to exit gracefully and leave your readers satisfied, yet not fall into clichés or obvious comments at the end. You hope to leave your readers with a sense of closure, a feeling that questions have been answered and problems resolved—or at least fully explored. To accomplish that in the last paragraph or two can challenge any writer, and many of us continue to struggle with conclusions, no matter how long we've been writing.

For some writing tasks, endings are almost prescribed, and you can find models that will help you. For example, for technical and business reports, case studies, or proposals, the writer is expected to summarize his or her findings and, if appropriate, make recommendations. Such endings are straightforward and not too hard to write.

In other kinds of writing, such as an argument or an analysis, the writer often needs to restate main ideas or arguments at the end of the paper in order to refresh the reader about points that have been made earlier. This is particularly true of papers that run to fifteen or twenty pages. In such cases, it is a good idea to tell the reader you are recapping your argument. Phrases like *finally, I must conclude . . .* , or *in the final analysis* work well in such cases. The structure for this kind of conclusion resembles the summation a lawyer makes for a jury: make the claim, summarize the evidence, and recommend a stance or outcome.

For that wide range of other kinds of nonfiction—theater or music reviews, exploratory personal essays, cause-and-effect analyses, or essays on social issues, for instance—it's less easy to find a pattern. I have looked at dozens of such essays and find an amazing variety of good ways to wind up an essay. It's not easy to generalize. I can, however, make three broad suggestions that you might find useful.

- *Close by summarizing the main points you have made.* This is what the philosopher and medical writer Norman Cousins does in this concluding paragraph to a chapter he has written on the importance of physicians' reassuring their patients.

> Yes, I know that my optimism can be carried too far—but I also know no one is smart enough to fix its limits; and that it is far better to pursue a remote and even unlikely goal than to deprive oneself of the forward motion that goals provide. My life has been an education

in these essentials, and I could no more turn away from them than I could deny my own existence. Sharing the convictions that come out of these essentials, of course, is not without risk. Some people may interpret the effort as overwrought do-goodism; but the risk is worth taking nonetheless, for every once in a while it happens that hope can rekindle one's spirits, create remarkable new energies, and set a stage for genuine growth. At least nothing I have learned is less theoretical than the way the entire world seems to open up when courage and determination are connected to truly important aims.

> —Norman Cousins, *Head First* (New York: Penguin Books, 1989), 68–96.

- *Finish with a recommendation that grows out of the argument you've been making.* This is what Mike Rose does in this last, rather long paragraph that concludes his book on his experiences in working with the educationally underprivileged in this country.

    We are in the midst of an extraordinary social experiment: the attempt to provide education for all members of a vast pluralistic democracy. To have any prayer of success, we'll need many conceptual blessings: A philosophy of language and literacy that affirms the diverse sources of linguistic competence and deepens our understanding of the ways class and culture blind us to the richness of those sources. A perspective on failure that opens the logic of error. An orientation toward the interaction of poverty and ability that undercuts simple polarities, that enables us to see simultaneously the constraints poverty places on the play of mind. . . . We'll need a pedagogy that encourages us to step back and consider the threat of the standard classroom and that shows us, having stepped back, how to step forward to invite a student across the boundaries of that powerful room. Finally, we'll need a revised store of images of educational excellence, one closer to egalitarian ideals—ones that embody the reward and turmoil of education in a democracy, that celebrate the plural, messy human reality of it. At heart, we'll need a guiding set of principles that do not encourage us to retreat from, but move us closer to, an understanding of the rich mix of speech and ritual and story that is America.

    > —Mike Rose, *Lives on the Boundary* (New York: Free Press, 1989), 238.

- *Tie the last paragraph to the first paragraph.* You can give your readers a sense of closure and wrap up your essay by plucking an image or reference from your opening paragraph and including it in your final paragraph. In this article about diving off Australia's Great Barrier Reef the author does just that.

OPENING PARAGRAPH: At first I thought (maybe even hoped) that I'd emerge from the waters of Australia's Great Barrier Reef feeling like Lloyd Bridges, the swaggering hero of the old TV series *Sea Hunt*. I'd have met and triumphed over another teeth-gritting physical challenge, and I'd have the scars to prove it. Instead I returned feeling a lot more like Alice after her traipse through Wonderland: awed, slightly dazed, and not at all sure that anyone would take me seriously once I told them what I'd seen.

CLOSING PARAGRAPH: Emerging from the metaphorical rabbit hole just off the Queensland coast, I found, like Alice, that I "had got so much into the way of expecting nothing but out-of-the-way things to happen that it seemed quite dull and stupid for life to go in the common way."
— Reed McManus, "Dive?" He Said," *Sierra*.
November–December 1990, 71, 80.

EXERCISES

1. Read over these two paragraphs to see where you think you could break them without seriously interrupting the train of thought.

   A. Bradley is one of the few basketball players who have ever been appreciatively cheered by a disinterested away-from-home crowd while warming up. This curious event occurred last March, just before Princeton eliminated the Virginia Military Institute, the year's Southern Conference champion, from the NCAA championships. The game was played in Philadelphia and was the last of a tripleheader. The people there were worn out because most of them were emotionally committed to either Villanova or Temple—two local teams that had just been involved in enervating battles with Providence and Connecticut, respectively, scrambling for a chance at the rest of the country. A group of Princeton boys shooting basketballs miscellaneously in preparation for still another game hardly promised to be a high point of the evening, but Bradley, whose routine in the warmup time is a gradual crescendo of activity, is more interesting to watch before a game than most players are in play. In Philadelphia that night, what he did was, for him, anything but unusual. As he does before all games he began by shooting set shots close to the basket, gradually moving back until he was shooting long sets from twenty feet out, and nearly all of them dropped into the net with an almost mechanical rhythm of accuracy. Then he began a series of expandingly difficult jump shots, and one jumper after another went cleanly through the basket with so few exceptions that the crowd began to murmur. Then he started to perform whirling reverse moves before another cadence of almost steadily accurate jump shots, and the murmur increased. Then he began to sweep hook shots into the air. He moved in a semicircle around the court. First with his right hand, then with his left, he tried seven of these long, graceful shots—the most difficult ones in the orthodoxy of basketball—and ambidextrously made them all. The game had not even begun, but the presumably unimpressible Philadelphians were applauding like an audience at an opera.

—John McPhee, "A Sense of Where You Are," in the *John McPhee Reader,* 2nd ed., ed. William Howarth (New York: Vintage Books, 1978), 2–3.

B. In outline it was a good plan, but it quite failed to take into account the mentality of buzzards. As soon as they were wired to the tree they all began to try and fly away. The wires prevented that, of course, but did not prevent them from falling off the limbs, where they dangled upside down, wings flopping, nether parts exposed. It is hard to imagine anything less likely to beguile a moviegoing audience than a tree full of dangling buzzards. Everyone agreed it was unaesthetic. The buzzards were righted, but they tried again, and with each try their humiliation deepened. Finally they abandoned their efforts to fly away and resigned themselves to life on their tree. Their resignation was so complete that when the scene was readied and the time came for them to fly, they refused. They had had enough of ignominy; better to remain on the limb indefinitely. Buzzards are not without patience. Profanity, firecrackers, and even a shotgun full of rock salt failed to move them. I'm told that, in desperation, a bird man was flown in from L.A. to teach the sulky bastards how to fly. The whole experience left everyone touchy. A day or so later, looking at the pictures again, I noticed a further provocative detail. The dead heifer that figured so prominently in the scene was quite clearly a steer. When I pointed this out to the still photographers they just shrugged. A steer was close enough; after all they were both essentially cows. "In essence, it's a cow," one said moodily. No one wanted those buzzards back again.

—Larry McMurtry, "Here's HUD in Your Eye," in *In a Narrow Grave* (New York: Simon & Schuster, 1968), 10–11.

2. What commitment do you think the writer made to the reader in these opening sentences from the paragraphs of professional writers?

"Some of us who live in arid parts of the world think about water with a reverence others might find excessive."—Joan Didion

"The weeks after graduation were filled with heady activities."—Maya Angelou

"There are, it seems, three principal states of mind in human beings: waking, sleeping, and dreaming."—Carl Sagan

3. Working with two or three other students, discuss what kind of paragraph you could write to complete each of these opening sentences. Then choose

the one that you find most interesting and draft a paragraph together to be shared with the rest of the class.

A. The young woman who walked in and took her place at the front of the calculus class the first day of the semester looked less like a professor than anyone might imagine.

B. Violence has become an almost ordinary fact of life in the lives of a distressing number of young children.

C. The average American squanders energy in ways that he or she has probably never even thought about.

SUGGESTED WRITING ASSIGNMENTS

As a part of each writing assignment write a detailed analysis of your audience and specify the characteristics they would have that you need to keep in mind as you write, the problems that such an audience might present, and what the audience would expect to get from reading your paper. Also analyze your purpose in writing, specifying what you hope to accomplish in the paper. If appropriate, include an accurate and descriptive title for your paper.

TOPIC 1: An organization to which you belong is going to have its annual convention in your city, and you have been asked to serve as local arrangements chairman. Among other things, that means that you must write a letter of invitation to the convention that will go out with announcements of the convention. In that letter you want to convince people that they would enjoy visiting your city and to give them information that would help them to make up their minds about coming to the convention. You do not need to mention hotel rates since that information would be in the announcement. You would want to point out what special events might be going on in the city at convention time, major points of interest such as art museums or zoos, shopping areas close to the hotel, well-known restaurants, and so on. If you want to keep your letter to one page, you could add a separate sheet with specific information. Probably your letter should not run to more than 350 or 400 words. Remember that the opening paragraph is particularly important.

TOPIC 2: You are a married person with a young child and you and your spouse want to move into an apartment nearer your job. In looking for apartments, however, you have discovered that landlords in the neighborhood you want to live in do not allow children. Write a letter to the city council pointing out that such exclusion by landlords is grossly discriminatory and may be unconstitutional. Ask for an interpretation of current city law and suggest that an ordinance against such discrimination needs to be passed if it does not already exist.

TOPIC 3: As part of your duties at the county social services bureau you have the assignment of writing informative pamphlets that will be available to any clients who come into the office. Your supervisor is particularly eager to have a pamphlet that outlines the options open to young unmarried women who have problem pregnancies, because women who would not want to ask for such a pamphlet would probably pick one up if it were displayed. She asks you to write the pamphlet, specifying that it must use direct but neutral language and be simple enough for young people to understand. The brochure should not be more than 600 words.

10 ◇ Editing

Let me emphasize a central truth right from the beginning: *Editing is important*—in college, on the job, in any writing that you hope will be read and understood. For better or worse, readers form their most basic and immediate impressions of writers from careful or careless editing. A carelessly edited, poorly proofread paper says worlds about you to your readers—it suggests that you don't value their opinion enough to take time to get the details right and make the paper easy to read. It also suggests that you may not know the conventions of standard English, as my usage survey of professionals shows (see pp. 194–97). While no one expects your writing to be perfect in every detail, readers do expect it to be neat, readable, and largely correct. You can't afford less, particularly when you are writing a business or professional document.

Consider that editing your paper is like tidying up all those little loose ends after you have completed a major project such as rebuilding an antique car or remodeling your kitchen. The most important part of your job is done, but you still have to attend to a dozen little details if the final product is going to look as good as you want it to. With the car it might be tasks like polishing the hood ornament, cleaning spattered paint from the chrome wheels, and putting an authentic insignia on the radiator. For the redone kitchen it might be installing the hardware on the cabinets, scraping excess putty from around the newly installed sink, and cleaning paint smears off the tile floor. In both cases, until the finishing touches are in place, you're not ready to unveil your work.

You're doing the same kind of thing when you edit a paper: getting it ready to go on public display. You need to check sentence length and variety and perhaps make some last minute adjustments, look to see if you want to make word substitutions, perhaps redo some of the body language of your paper by splitting up paragraphs and inserting headings and subheadings, check and recheck for possible mistakes in usage and spelling, and, finally and very important, *proofread.*

Again, I urge you to learn to write using a word processor. Revising and editing on screen is so easy that it takes much of the drudgery out of what used to be an arduous task. When you know you won't have to retype a paper if you make changes in it, you can think of the final clean-up job as a strategy for success. That way, you'll be willing and ready to take care of those details that make so much difference in the presentation of your paper.

CHECK THE RHYTHM OF YOUR PROSE

One of the keys to becoming your own best editor is to learn to be sensitive to the cadences and tempo of your writing, and to learn how and why certain word choices and patterns affect the rhythm of prose. You must also develop an ear for the way your writing sounds. Is it monotonous, singsongy, clogged with hard-to-say phrases and sentences that make the reader run out of breath? Or does it flow smoothly and help the reader to move along easily? Probably the best way to develop that ear and smooth out the rhythms of late drafts is to read them aloud to yourself. If they sound plodding or draggy or choppy, revise with these rules of thumb in mind.

Adjust Sentence Length and Variety

A series of long sentences slows down writing and forces the reader to plod along slowly in order to process information. Also, unless they are very skillfully constructed, long sentences distance the reader from the writer and weigh down the tone of a paper. On the other hand, an unbroken sequence of short sentences usually creates a choppy effect—they can sound like a parody of Hemingway's style.

To avoid either extreme, when you're editing watch to see that you don't have too many of either kind clumped together. If you do, try occasionally to break up the monotony by inserting a short, crisp sentence among several long ones or by combining two or three short sentences into a longer one with a clause or two. When you read passages from nonfiction writers that you like, notice how skillfully the authors manipulate sentence length, even now and then using a minor sentence or fragment when it will work well (see pp. 184–86).

Adapt Word Choice

Long words—three or four syllables or more—also slow down your writing and affect its tone. Of course, a long word isn't necessarily a difficult word, and you shouldn't choose words primarily on whether they're long or short. Choose the one that best conveys your meaning. But if you have a choice between a long word and a short one that means almost the same thing—for example, *difficult* or *hard,* or *capacious* or *roomy*—make your choice partly on the basis of the kind of pace you want to set for your writing and on the kind of tone you want to convey.

Reconsider the Body Language of Your Writing

It is difficult to make final decisions about how you want your writing to look until you've finished almost all of your revising. But when you are reasonably well satisfied with content, you need to think about strategies that will make your writing look attractive in its finished version. The three principal ones are *dividing, highlighting,* and *forecasting.*

DIVIDING

You make your most important decisions about dividing when you paragraph, and when you are working on the second revision, it's time to think about how your paragraphs look and how you can improve them. Look over your printed manuscript to see if it has long unbroken stretches of type running half a page or more. If so, look for places you can break up those stretches. While you don't want to sacrifice the unity of a tightly constructed paragraph just for the sake of appearance, you may be able to detect a natural break that wasn't apparent before (see pp. 160–62).

You can also break up overstuffed paragraphs by presenting information in list form rather than packed into consecutive sentences. For example, here is an information-packed sentence that looks so overloaded one immediately assumes that it is going to be hard to read:

> The following individuals will be honored at Harvard Commencement this year: J.P. Jones, president of the International Foundation for Human Potential; Mary Hardin Coulthard, winner of the Howson Economics Fellowship; Daniel Moorhead, professor emeritus of biology at Oxford University; and Maxwell Cannon, director of the Harvard Fund for Excellence.

A reader trying to absorb the information in this sentence could do so more easily if it were broken up like this:

> The following individuals will be honored at Harvard Commencement this year:
> J.P. Jones, president of the International Foundation for Human Potential;

Mary Hardin Coulthard, winner of the Howson Economics Fellowship;

Daniel Moorhead, professor emeritus of biology at Oxford University;

Maxwell Cannon, director of the Harvard Fund for Excellence.

HIGHLIGHTING

When you are revising your writing to make it look more attractive, you may decide that you want to draw attention to specific points or set off particular words and phrases so that they will catch the readers' attention. Here are some ways you can emphasize parts of your paper even if your only tools are your typewriter, a pen, and a ruler:

* Indent and use what printers call "bullets" (like the one at the beginning of this sentence). You can make them either with the asterisk sign on the typewriter or by putting it in dots with a pen. For example,

Though the democratic forecasts for the traditional cohort of high school graduates is unfavorable, there are other statistics that suggest collegiate opportunities never before possible for millions of Americans. Recent data establish that:

* 40 million people regard themselves at any moment in time as undergoing some form of career transition;
* 65 million Americans lack basic competency skills;
* 15 million American lack college degrees;
* 12 million professionals require regular in-service education;
* Over $17 billion in educational benefits is available, of which only a tiny fraction is being used;
* New positions are developing for science teachers and pedagogical personnel who are able to educate the handicapped.

> —Robert Neilsen and Irwin Polishook, "Academic Morbidity," *The Chronicle of Higher Education,* 21 April 1980, 9.

You can also add diagrams, simple drawings, or charts that help to give a visual dimension to the information you are presenting. You can set words off with markers at each end like this—<Specifications>; by underlining them—Specifications; or by printing them in boldface—**Specifications.** You can also draw boxes around words or phrases to set them off.

If you want your writing to look especially attractive, concentrate on centering it carefully and leave wide margins all around. And, of course, be sure to double-space! In general, plan on leaving enough white space on a page so that your writing doesn't look crowded. Hold your finished copy at arm's length. Would you want to read it? If you don't think it looks inviting, try using wider margins and a few highlighting devices to catch the reader's eye.

FORECASTING

You can also make your writing easier to read by continually giving your readers signals that forecast what is going to come, thus focusing their attention and shaping their expectations. Remember that titles are particularly important as forecasters (see pp. 111–13).

Other forecasting signals can take the form of headings or subheadings that mark divisions, or they can be single words or phrases. These signals are especially useful when you are writing informative material such as brochures or pamphlets. For that kind of writing, you need to make your writing as visually directive as possible.

For example, a person writing a brochure for college students on how to recognize and cope with stress might use these forecasting signals to mark off divisions and help his or her readers:

What Causes Stress?
What Are the Effects of Stress?
How Can a Person Manage Stress?

CHECK FOR ERRORS IN USAGE

This text makes no attempt to be a handbook of usage or a catalog of rules. What follows is only a quick review of ways to avoid certain usage problems that can be especially troublesome for readers.

Avoid Sentence Fragments

Today editors and writers are more tolerant than they used to be about sentence fragments, that old bugaboo of traditional grammarians. In years past amateur writers have thought—and with good cause—that they must never violate that well-known rule "Always write in complete sentences." A complete sentence was defined as one that had a subject and verb and expressed a complete thought.

In many writing situations, writers would still do well to abide by the familiar rule. My survey of professional people's response to lapses from standard usage (see pp. 194–97) revealed that more than 65 percent of them said that they would object strongly to finding these sentence fragments in writing that came across their desks:

> He went through a long battle. A fight against unscrupulous opponents.

> The small towns are dying. One of the problems being that young people are leaving.

Forty-four percent said they would object strongly to the following sentence fragment, and 32 percent said they would object a little:

> Cheap labor and low costs. These are two benefits enjoyed by Taiwan firms.

I think one must conclude from this evidence that most people in decision-making positions want the writing they see to conform to the rules for sentences that they learned in school.

MINOR SENTENCES OR FORMAL FRAGMENTS

But any person who notices sentence structure as he or she reads contemporary writing will recognize dozens of groups of words that are punctuated as sentences but don't fit the definition just given. They occur not only in advertising, where they are used for their eye-catching, emphatic effect, but in expository prose at both ends of the literary spectrum. For example,

> It's fashionable to knock TV news. Always has been. Thirty years ago, the news on television was amateurish. Not much different from newsreels. Superficial. Today, it's slick. Too many Adonises and Venuses posing as reporters. It's also too controversial. Or not controversial enough. Too liberal. Too conservative. Too heavy on foreign news. Too heavy on local news. Just headlines.
> —Edward Bliss, Jr., "There Is Good Journalism on TV," *TV Guide,* 15 July 1978, 39.

> That quality of elusiveness [about gangs] has deepened fears among New Yorkers shocked by a series of attacks that became known as wilding in the wake of the attack last year on a jogger in Central Park.
> A litany of incidents this year has involved youths in roving groups. The Halloween night killing. An attack by 10 or 12 bat-wielding youths on two Canadian students visiting the city in September after the tourists stopped to help an elderly woman who had fallen. The slaying of a

tourist from Utah on a subway platform as he tried to protect his mother from gang members who wanted money to go dancing.

> —Felicia Lee, "Loose Knit Type of Youth Gangs
> Troubling Police," *The New York Times,*
> 13 December 1990, B–3.

Obviously both these passages work, and work well. They communicate their ideas clearly, economically, and forcefully, yet they employ almost no traditional sentences.

The puzzled student writer might well ask why these writers feel free to use sentence fragments. The answer, I think, is that the so-called fragments that these writers use are not really incomplete groups of words; rather they are what one team of modern grammarians calls "minor sentences" or "formal fragments." This new definition recognizes that when we can read a group of words and make sense out of it, we mentally process it as a sentence whether or not it has all those elements that a sentence is traditionally supposed to have. Or to put it another way, readers can sometimes reach closure at the end of a group of words even if that group does not have a subject or verb; when that happens, that group can be marked off with a period and called a "minor sentence." It is a legitimate division of writing.

TRUE SENTENCE FRAGMENTS

Groups of words that really are sentence fragments—that is, incomplete pieces of a coherent whole—are those that *don't* work by themselves. There may be several reasons why they leave the reader in suspense. They may begin an idea and not carry it through, they may express only part of an idea and thus confuse the reader, or they may form a phrase or clause that does not make sense by itself and yet is not attached to anything else.

Here are some typical examples:

> There are few assertions in the article and little evidence to support them. *An example being, "It is unclear whether these intruders had anything to do with the crime."*

The italicized words here need to be attached to a base; although they are punctuated as a sentence, they make no sense by themselves.

> Unlike doctors, lawyers are ready to practice when they get their degrees. *Although it is often necessary to take an expensive course in order to pass the bar exam.*

The italicized portion should be joined with the sentence; otherwise the "although" raises expectations that the writer does not meet.

> To understand how all knowledge is related. That is the goal of a liberal education.

The writer would get a more economical sentence by starting out, "The goal of a liberal education is . . ."

> Harrison lived out a legend in his own time. *A man who came from nowhere and created a billion-dollar business empire.*

The italicized portion here is really an appositive and doesn't work well standing by itself.

Probably the best guideline to keep in mind about writing sentence fragments is that if you are in doubt, don't use them. And if you do use them, be sure you are constructing minor sentences that convey a finished idea, not broken-off sentences that puzzle or annoy your audience. If you punctuate a group of words as a sentence, but realize it leaves your reader in suspense or seems not to fit with anything, then attach it to a sentence or rewrite it.

Also, when you make decisions about using minor sentences or word groups that are technically sentence fragments, think carefully about your audience and your purpose. Not only professionals, but also professors, particularly English professors, usually prefer that you write straightforward, traditional sentences that will convey your meaning efficiently and not raise any distracting usage problems. Many other audiences, such as a supervisor reading a report or an evaluation committee reading a proposal, feel the same way because, as with most educated readers, their school background has conditioned them to react against sentence fragments. The thoughtful writer knows and respects those attitudes. So if you want to be sure that a serious piece of explanatory or persuasive writing gets a careful, unprejudiced reading from a serious audience, avoid writing fragments.

If, however, you are writing descriptive prose in which you want to communicate impressions or if you are writing an informal, breezy article for a general audience, you may find that putting in an occasional minor sentence or fragment will help to create the tone and tempo that you want. If so, don't be afraid to try using them. Often they are appropriate and effective. But do know what you are doing, and in a writing class, be prepared to defend your choices.

Avoid Comma Splices

Sometimes you may join two groups of words that could be read as sentences with a comma instead of with a conjunction that would show the relationship between those word groups. When you do, you produce a *comma splice* (sometimes also called a *comma fault* or a *comma blunder*). That is, you join independent clauses with a punctuation mark that is so weak it cannot properly indicate the strong pause that should come in such a sentence. Here is an example of a weakly punctuated sentence:

> The first part of the book gave Jim no problem, it was the second part that stumped him.

Notice that the reader does not get a strong sense of separation between the two parts of the sentence. The emphasis would come through more clearly if it were written like this:

> The first part of the book gave Jim no problem, but the second part stumped him.

or this:

> Although the first part of the book gave Jim no problem, the second part stumped him.

Either revision correctly deemphasizes the first part of the sentence and puts the stress on the second. In the original, the parts of the sentence appear to be equal.

For two reasons you should usually avoid comma splices. First, independent commas that "tack" clauses together indicate that you are unsure or unconcerned about the relationship between the parts of the sentences. Second, commas that join independent clauses invite misinterpretation. A comma is such a weak interrupter that the reader is liable to slip right over it.

However, if you want to join several short independent clauses with commas to increase the tempo of your writing, you can probably do so without creating any problems. For example,

> It's not smart, it's not practical, it's not legal.

Avoid Fused or Run-On Sentences

Sentences in which two independent clauses have been run together without any punctuation are confusing to readers. For example,

The success of horror movies is not surprising some people have always enjoyed being frightened.

Without punctuation, a reader at first makes "some people" the object of "is surprising" and then has to go back and reprocess the sentence. Also, without punctuation the reader at first misses the cause and effect relationship of the clauses. This sentence could be revised to:

The success of horror movies is not surprising because some people have always enjoyed being frightened.

Avoid Dangling Modifiers

Modifying phrases that don't fit with the word or phrase that they seem to be attached to can cause problems for readers. Usually those misfit phrases, which we call dangling modifiers, come at the beginning of a sentence as an introductory phrase.

After leaving Cheyenne, the cost of living became a problem.

The reader expects to find out who left Cheyenne and is frustrated.
Here is another example.

On coming back to college, child care isn't easy to arrange.

The reader stumbles over the junction after "college" and has to reread to get the meaning of the sentence. This kind of error is easy to fix once you have seen it. The first sentence could be rewritten as

After he left Cheyenne, Jack found the cost of living a problem.

The second could be rearranged as

Coming back to college, married women often have trouble arranging child care.

Notice that you increase your chances of beginning a sentence with a dangling modifier when you use abstract sentence subjects. If the author of these two sentences had put in a personal sentence subject in the first place, the mistakes wouldn't have occurred.

Make Structures Parallel

Practiced writers use parallel structures frequently in order to unify and tighten their writing. That is, they incorporate two or more points in a sentence by using a series of phrases or clauses that have identical structure. For instance,

> Country Western fans love Willie Nelson, jazz fans love Oscar Peterson, and ballad fans love Judy Collins.

> Stein hit Hollywood determined to live high, hang loose, stay single, and make money.

Sentences like these work by establishing a pattern that helps the reader to anticipate what is coming. It is like seeing groups of similar figures on a test sheet: circles together, triangles together, squares together, and so on. But when people see a figure that doesn't fit—a circle among the triangles, for instance—they find the exception jarring to their sense of unity. The same thing happens when readers find phrases or clauses that don't fit the pattern of the rest of the sentence. Here is an example of faulty parallelism:

> My purpose was to show what services are available, how many people use them, and *having the audience feel the services are significant.*

The reader does a double take after the second comma because the third point is not handled in the same way as the first two.

Avoid Faulty Predication

Every complete sentence must have at least two parts: a subject and verb. The verb, along with all of the parts that go with the verb to make a statement, is called the *predicate* of the sentence. Thus the portion of the sentence that completes the assertion that began with the subject of the sentence is called the *predication of a sentence*. Sometimes, however, people writing sentences try to pair up subjects and verbs, or objects and verbs, that just don't work well together. We call the problem caused by such mismatched combinations *faulty predication*. Most cases of faulty predication seem to fall into one of three categories:

1. Mismatched subject + active verb:

> The rape center will accompany the victim to court.

> Research grants want to get the best qualified applicants.

In each of these sentences the writer has predicated an action that the subject could not carry out; a "rape center" cannot "accompany" someone, and a "research grant" cannot "want." Notice that if the writers had used personal subjects instead of abstract ones for these sentences, they probably would have avoided the mistake. If you start your main clause with a personal subject, you are much less apt to join that subject with a mismatched verb.

2. Subject + linking verb + mismatched complement:

The main trait a person needs is success.

The activities available for young people are swimming pools and tennis courts.

Energy and transportation are problems for our generation.

When people write sentences like these, they seem to have forgotten that the verb *to be* and other linking verbs act as a kind of equal sign (=) in sentences in which the complement of the sentence is a noun. Thus when they use a linking verb after a subject, they should be sure that the noun complement they put after it can logically be equated with the subject. In none of the sentences above could the reader make that equation. "Success" is not a "trait," "activity" cannot be a "swimming pool," and "energy" cannot be equated with "problem."

Again, if the writers of these sentences had started out with personal subjects, they probably would not have gotten into these tangles. These sentences could be rewritten:

A person needs to be successful.

Young people can use the swimming pools and tennis courts.

Our generation faces problems with energy and transportation.

Writers who use the construction, "[Something] is when . . ." are getting tangled in the same kind of mistake:

The worst problem is when motorists ignore these signals.

Community property is when husband and wife share all earnings.

Although a reader is not likely to misunderstand these sentences, they really are substandard usage. The writers are actually saying "problem = when" and "property = when." The best way to avoid this difficulty is simply to make it a rule not to use the construction *is when.*

3. Subject + verb + mismatched object:

These theories intimidate the efforts of amateur players.
The company fired positions which had been there only six months.

In these sentences, the writers have not thought about the limitations they put on themselves when they used the verbs "intimidate" and "fired." Both verbs have to apply to people (or at least creatures). You cannot "intimidate" an "effort" or "fire" a "position." Again, notice that if they had used concrete instead of abstract words as objects, they probably would not have gotten into the problem.

One of your concerns when you read your first draft should be checking your verbs to see that you have matched them with logical subjects and complements. And although there are no rules to follow to avoid getting yourself tangled in predication knots, I can suggest one guideline for avoiding problems: Use personal and concrete subjects whenever you can, and connect your verbs to specific and concrete terms. If you do this and write agent/action sentences (see p. 140) you will eliminate most predication errors.

CHECK FOR SPELLING ERRORS

As I pointed out in Chapter 2, if you have come this far in your education and are still a poor speller, it's unlikely you're going to get much better at this point by memorizing rules. As far as we can tell, only a couple of rules are helpful and even they have many exceptions. So your best strategies at this point are first, *recognize that you're a poor speller,* and second, *develop a set of habits to overcome your handicap.* For that is what it is—a handicap, and in many writing situations, a fairly serious one. Some readers react so negatively to bad spelling that they decide the writer is incompetent before they have read more than a page or two. Many businesspeople are almost fanatics about correct spelling because they worry, with reason, about how customers and clients will react to poor spelling in a document that bears their company's name.

In spite of these dire warnings, don't shy away from using a word because you're not sure how to spell it. Your style suffers and your ideas might too. Hang on to your good ideas and stylish sentences—you can find ways to correct your spelling. Here are some suggestions.

- *When you read through your third draft, circle any words about which you're in doubt or you know are tricky;* for instance, *villain, harass,* and *rhythm.* If you know you frequently confuse *except* and *accept* or *allusion* and *illusion,* always mark those. Then when you proofread, look up any word you've marked. If you typically have trouble with those cussed words that end with *-ible* or *-able* but sound exactly alike, mark those too.
- *Get the dictionary habit.* Teachers have probably been admonishing

you to do so for years, and they're right. Any person who wants to write well should keep a dictionary close at hand and cultivate the habit of consulting it often. As well as verifying spelling, it offers a wealth of information about the nuances of words and about their appropriate use.

* *For convenience, buy a word list as well as a dictionary.* It is an inexpensive, pocket-size book that lists words most commonly misspelled and is much easier to carry with you and consult than a dictionary would be. When you're looking in either a dictionary or word list, consider alternatives to vowel sounds. Words that sound as if they begin with *e* may begin with *i* or *u*; words that sound as if they begin with *u* may be found under *a*.

* *Use ingenuity in locating terms.* The yellow pages of the telephone book can show you how to spell *psychiatrist* or *prosthesis* or *business* or *stationery*. The index of a textbook will give spellings of special terms like *fiduciary* or *eleemosynary*. A thesaurus can give you the spelling of *impresario* if you know it means a director or manager.

* *Keep a notebook or card file* of words you consistently have trouble with; make a practice of adding to it as you edit. In time you'll have a collection of the words that you typically misspell and be able to look them up quickly, and eventually, to memorize many of them. Develop some memory tricks—mnemonic devices—that help. For instance, "remember the *gum* in argument"; "stationary" as an *a*djective has an *a* in the ending"; "villains are *vain*"; or "*Emma* is in a dilemma."

* *Memorize keywords or names* you're going to use in a paper so you won't have to look them up repeatedly. If you're using terms like *syllogism,* and *bourgeoisie, liaison* or names like *Shakespeare* or *Kuhn* in a paper, put them on a Post-It note and stick it up over your desk while you're writing.

* *Watch especially for contractions that sound like other words*—for instance, *we're, they're,* and *you're.* For me, the last is particularly troublesome. I couldn't begin to count the times I've written *your* instead of *you're* and had to go back and change it.

   Watch for other homonyms—words that sound alike but have different meanings. It's all too easy to write *site* instead of *cite, past* instead of *passed,* or *no* instead of *know.* And if you have trouble with *their, there,* and *they're,* circle those words to look up.

* *DON'T count on a computerized spell checker to catch your errors.* By design, a spell checker ignores a number of potential problem spots. It doesn't know or care about the difference between *except*

and *accept;* in its dictionary both are perfectly good words and the fact that you're using them incorrectly doesn't register. Nor does it care if you write, "He had to *bare* with the *boar."* Because it doesn't understand syntax and both words are in its dictionary, it thinks the sentence is perfectly fine. A spell checker will not check for consistency; it will accept both *judgment* and *judgement,* for example. Use a spell checker to catch typographical errors, but don't count on it to do your proofreading. It won't.

• *Get a second reader,* more if possible. Find a friend who is a good speller and ask him or her to read your paper and mark problem words. Ask your instructor to underline any problem words in your second draft. If you are working in revision groups in your class, ask your fellow students to point out misspelled words in your second draft.

However, before you turn to your second reader for help, try your own resources. You can't always count on having someone else around in those final proofreading stages, and you need to develop survival strategies. Gradually you really will become a better speller, or at least you will develop an acute sense for when you need to look things up.

PROOFREAD

Proofreading is painful—that's just all there is to it—but it's absolutely necessary. You're now going "to press" with your writing in order to present it to your reading "public." Because it will become public discourse that represents you, the final checkup and cleanup are crucial.

Writers go about this chore in different ways—some recommend reading what you've written backwards so you can check word by word for typographical errors or misspellings, on the theory that you're reading for technical correctness, not for meaning. I don't agree with that because I think you have to read for both at the same time. Some recommend reading and touching each word with a pencil as you go; others recommend reading aloud slowly. My own method is to start at the top of the computer screen and force myself to read slowly, line by line, and pay attention to each word and sentence as I go. Try any of these methods that seems practical for you. The main points you should keep in mind are these.

First, read your paper through to see that you have corrected what you know are your most common writing problems. Maybe you habitually confuse *its* and *it's.* If so, check for the correct form every time you see it. One of my bad habits is a tendency to "double"; that is, use a pair of words that mean the same thing when one would do. I can almost always prune out weak adjectives, and I overuse *of course, perhaps, kind of,* and *a lot* so I watch for those.

Second, look for typical usage problems. Do the subject and verb in a long sentence agree? When you use *it* is it clear what it refers to? Have you remembered the apostrophe in the possessives? Are there sentence fragments just hanging there? Do your plural pronouns have plural antecedents? And single ones single antecedents?

Third, check punctuation. Have you put apostrophes in possessives and contractions? Do you have commas interrupting the flow of a sentence when they shouldn't or have you left out the comma before the conjunction in a compound sentence? Do you have semicolons to separate independent clauses joined by *however* or *nevertheless*? Are all proper nouns capitalized, especially *English*?

Fourth, have words been left out? Or do you have words left in that you intended to delete? If you revise on a computer, sometimes you'll find leftover words that you thought you had gotten rid of. Look for them. Look particularly at the endings of words. That's where an extra letter or the wrong letter can confuse meaning or make your writing sound nonstandard.

Fifth, check those pesky details. Are all parentheses and quotation marks closed? Are all titles of books, plays, or movies underlined? Are long quotations indented? Are notes, if any, written in good documentation form?

SET PRIORITIES ABOUT ERRORS

What Businesspeople Think about Grammar and Usage

I have long felt that in matters of grammar and usage, not all errors are created equal. Some lapses are so serious that they set off bells in readers' heads, signaling "This writer is careless and/or poorly educated." For example, anyone who writes, "I seen him when I was in New York," has, with most readers, damaged his or her persona rather badly. Other lapses are so minor that they pass almost unnoticed except by the most meticulous readers. For example, the person who writes, "We have a truly unique opportunity," or "The data is confusing in places," has done virtually no damage with 99.5 percent of his or her readers.

I have felt this distinction intuitively, as I'm sure many others have, but we have had no documentation for it. I have also felt that student writers would benefit if I could get some proof that indeed some errors are more damaging than others and thus it was worth their while to take pains to avoid those errors. Therefore, in September 1979, I sent a questionnaire to

101 professional people, asking them how they would respond to lapses from standard English usage and mechanics in each of sixty-three sentences if those sentences appeared in a business document that came across their desks. The 84 people who responded to the questionnaire represented a broad range of professionals: engineers, judges, bankers, attorneys, architects, public relations executives, corporation and college presidents, tax analysts, investment counselors, and a U.S. Congressman, to name just a few. They ranged in age from thirty to seventy, but most were in their late forties and early fifties. Twenty-two were women, and 62 were men. No English teachers were included in the survey.

Each of the sixty-three sentences on the questionnaire contained one error in usage or mechanics, and the respondents were asked to mark one of these responses for every sentence: Does Not Bother Me, Bothers Me a Little, Bothers Me a Lot. The last question asked for an open-ended comment about the most annoying feature they encountered in writing they had to read.

After tabulating all the responses to the sentences and reading all the comments, I came to these conclusions about how professional people react to writing that they encounter in the course of their work:

• Women take a more conservative attitude about standard English usage than men do. On every item, the percentage of women marking "Bothers Me a Lot" was much higher than the percentage of men.

• The defects in writing that professional people complained of most were *lack of clarity, wordiness,* and *failure to get to the point.* They also complained strongly about poor grammar, faulty punctuation, and bad spelling.

• The middle-aged, educated, and successful men and women who occupy positions of responsibility in the business and professional world are sensitive to the way people write. Even allowing for the strong possibility that they were more than normally conservative in responding to a questionnaire from an English teacher, most professionals seem to believe that writers should observe the conventions of standard English usage.

Responses to the individual items on the survey indicate, however, that these professional people clearly consider some lapses in usage and mechanics much more serious than others. Here is the way they ranked items on the questionnaire:

• **Extremely serious lapses from the standard:**
  Incorrect verb forms ("he brung," "we was," "he don't").

Double negatives.

Sentence fragments.

Subjects in the objective case ("Him and Jones are going").

Fused sentences ("He loved his job he never took holidays").

Failure to capitalize proper names, especially those referring to people and places.

A comma between the verb and complement of the sentence ("Cox cannot predict, that street crime will diminish").

• **Serious lapses from the standard:**

Faulty parallelism.

Subject-verb disagreement.

Adjectives used to modify verbs ("He treats his men bad").

Not marking interrupters such as *however* with commas.

Subjective pronouns used for objects ("The army sent my husband and I to Japan").

Confusion of the verbs *sit* and *set*.

• **Moderately serious lapses:**

Tense shifting.

Dangling modifiers.

Failure to use quotation marks around quoted material.

Plural modifier with a singular noun ("*These* kind").

Omitting commas in a series.

Faulty predication ("The policy intimidates applications").

Ambiguous use of *which*.

Objective form of a pronoun used as a subjective complement ("That is her across the street").

Confusion of the verbs *affect* and *effect*.

• **Lapses that seem to matter very little:**

Failure to distinguish between *whoever* and *whomever*.

Omitting commas to set off interrupting phrases such as appositives.

Joining independent clauses with a comma; that is, a comma splice.

Confusion of *its* and *it's*.

Failure to use the possessive form before a gerund ("The company objects to *us* hiring new salespeople").

Failure to distinguish between *among* and *between*.

• **Lapses that do not seem to matter.**

A qualifying word used before *unique* ("That is the *most* unique plan we have seen").

They used to refer to a singular pronoun ("Everyone knows *they* will have to go").

Omitting a comma after an introductory clause.

Singular verb form used with *data* ("The data *is* significant").

Linking verb followed by *when* ("The problem is when patients refuse to cooperate").

Using the pronoun *that* to refer to people.

Using a colon after a linking verb ("The causes of the decline are: inflation, apathy, and unemployment").

11 ◇ Writing Research Papers

The task of writing a substantial research paper should hold no particular terror for people who can handle other kinds of writing assignments at school or on the job. The ways in which one chooses topics, gathers material, generates ideas, and works out a plan of organization are much the same for research papers as they are for term papers, grant proposals, or extensive case studies. In fact, all these kinds of working writing mingle and overlap; in important ways they are more alike than they are different.

There is, however, an approach especially suited to research papers, whether they are for a course, a magazine, a company, an agency, or an organization, and this approach includes the following steps:

* *Topic selection*
  Formulating a research question.
  Identifying the audience.
  Defining the purpose.
* *Research*
  Setting up search strategies.
  Reading, collecting data, taking notes.
* *Writing*
  Organizing your material.
  Mastering the conventions of format and documentation.

TOPIC SELECTION

Formulating a Research Question

On-the-job research projects generally give very specific instructions about deadlines, the type of information needed, and sometimes even the uses to which that information will be put. If you are writing a research paper for a class, on the other hand, you may be assigned a specific topic, a general topic, or a selection of topics to choose from. Or you might be given free rein to decide for yourself what your topic will be. Regardless of the circumstances surrounding your research assignment, your first step must be to formulate a question (or questions) that you hope to be able to answer by consulting outside sources.

You are probably already familiar with this initial step if you have read or conducted empirical research studies in the sciences or social sciences. Such studies begin with a research question formulated as a *hypothesis*—a speculative statement of fact. For example,

- Microwave radiation affects the reproductive behavior of rodents.
- The absence of a father figure in the home adversely affects children's academic performance.
- Radiation from visual display terminals is responsible for some human birth defects.

Although the hypotheses that initiate these types of research study are phrased as statements of fact, they are actually *questions* in the mind of the researcher. The medical researcher, in other words, is not convinced that microwave radiation affects the reproductive behavior of rodents, but is actually conducting the study in order to answer the question, *Does* microwave radiation affect the reproductive behavior of rodents? Similarly, the psychologist or social studies researcher conducts an investigation to discover the answer to a question—*Does* a father's absence from the home adversely affect children's performance at school?

The research that you do in your college courses or on the job will follow the same principles, although the types of questions you ask and the methods you use to collect the appropriate data to answer them will differ according to the field for which you are writing. Strict scientific method demands that questions for scientific study be the kind with yes-or-no answers, even though the research that follows may reveal that the issues involved are not simply black or white. The answer resulting from research may in fact be a qualified yes or no. For example, "*In certain cases, under certain conditions,* VDT radiation is *probably* a contributing factor in producing human birth defects."

Outside of formal scientific/experimental research, however, you need not limit your questions to the yes-or-no variety. You may, for instance, want to find out the answers to questions such as "Why has the women's movement failed to gain the support of minority members and working class women?" "What means of financial assistance are available to college graduates wishing to continue an education in petroleum engineering?" or "How does the American public perceive the war in the Persian Gulf in relation to the Vietnam War?"

Regardless of the particular discipline for which you are writing, however, you must avoid the temptation to begin your research with questions that are based on unproven assumptions or which lead to obvious or foregone conclusions. The question "Why is it imperative for the United States to remain involved in the governmental affairs of Latin American countries?" for instance, is *not* an appropriate topic for academic research because it presupposes the validity of an arguable assumption—that it is imperative for the United States to remain involved in Latin American affairs. Similarly, the question "Why has the women's movement failed to gain the support of minority members and working class women?" would be inappropriate if it were not possible to demonstrate beyond a reasonable doubt that women in these two categories do not, in fact, support the women's movement.

Finally, questions with obvious answers do not make suitable research topics because they lead to papers that are uninformative—and therefore uninteresting—to both reader and writer. To a large extent the information- and interest-value of a research topic depends on the audience for which it is intended. A question such as "How do vaccines work?" would not yield a very interesting paper for a group of immunologists, to whom the information, however complicated and thorough, would be old hat. The very same question, however, might produce a paper that was extremely interesting and worthwhile to a group of parents who wanted to know more about the vaccinations their children were receiving. It is, therefore, very important that you know who your audience is before you begin focusing your research.

Identifying the Audience

The audience for a research paper that you write in college and the audience for a research paper that you write on the job are different, and you need to keep those differences in mind when you plan your paper. In both cases, however, you need to begin by considering what your readers want to get from the paper.

If you are writing a research report for a business or organization, you will probably have a very specific assignment. Your readers want answers to specific questions, and they assume that you know how to gather the information necessary for finding those answers. Furthermore, they expect you to be able to organize and document that information and present it in a clear, concise, and readable fashion. They are far more interested in what you have been able to find out than in how you went about your research. Nevertheless, they expect thorough documentation because it helps them judge the reliability of your sources and enables them to follow up on your research if they need to. Brevity and conciseness are usually important in research writing done for businesses and organizations. And because research projects of this sort are often expensive, you should not waste your time or your readers' with unnecessary comments or the detailed proofs and background information that you might feel a professor expects in academic research writing.

When you write research papers for your college courses, you are usually writing primarily for the professor who gave you the assignment. While most professors hope to learn something from their students' research papers, the research assignment in college courses usually has several other important purposes as well. In addition to reading for content, professors read in order to evaluate their students' knowledge of their subject matter, their ability to find and synthesize information from various sources and to present it in a clear and organized fashion, and their mastery of the formal conventions of research writing in their field. Often, research assignments in college courses are far less specific than those in businesses and agencies because they are meant to provide an opportunity for you to demonstrate your ability to independently pursue questions stemming from material you've studied in your courses. You must, therefore, consider yourself as a part of the audience for your research writing, because it must be your curiosity and interest that motivate this type of independent inquiry. Formulating your own research questions based on a combination of your own interests and the important issues introduced in class becomes a matter of finding your position within the readership of your discipline.

Defining the Purpose

Research writing is by nature data-based; it presents answers to previously unanswered questions, and its overriding purpose is, therefore, informative. Because questions that motivate your research are ones to which you do not have answers at the outset of your investigation, the activity of conducting research is necessarily impartial. Your purpose is to discover the truth by objectively examining evidence and testimonies available to you and to present your findings as clearly and honestly as you are able.

Sometimes, however, your professor may want not only your findings, but the inferences you can draw from those findings as well. You might, for example, be expected to find out all you can about the recreational facilities in a certain area in order to make recommendations about how those facilities should be expanded or improved to meet the recreational needs of the area's inhabitants. Such an assignment requires more than the objective collection of data; it also demands that you interpret those data, make value judgments, and arrive at conclusions. In cases like this you could employ the reasoning from evidence method (Chapter 5) by first describing the data you have found and then moving to a conclusion about it, or you could use the Toulmin method of reasoning (Chapter 5) by making your claim, giving your data, and explaining the warrant between them.

Finally, research can be used to persuade as well as inform. The research itself must still be an objective endeavor, of course, not a selective search for only those sources that support a predetermined conclusion. The very process of doing research on your topic, however, may convince you of the factual or moral superiority of one particular way of conceptualizing your topic. If this is the case, you may very well want to present your findings in such a way that your readers become similarly convinced.

In your investigations into the recreational facilities topic, for instance, your findings may lead you to believe that the area under study already offers adequate recreational opportunities to its inhabitants, and in fact, a great many residents are not taking advantage of the facilities currently available. You have come to believe that instead of spending money on additional playgrounds, picnic areas, and sports arenas, the area needs to advertise its present recreational facilities more effectively. In your paper, then, you would want to show your audience the evidence you have uncovered to support this position, and persuade them that your conclusions are financially sound, practically feasible, and supported by observable facts. Part of the persuasiveness of your paper would come from your objective and thorough examination and conscientious documentation of the available evidence.

If your conclusion is a controversial position, an inductive presentation is often more effective than one in which you make your claim first because it enables you to lead the readers to a position they do not hold initially. If the readers for your research report on recreational facilities initially favor a plan for creating new parks and playgrounds, you would probably want to present and document your research findings first, so that your readers, after being presented with the evidence, would be likely to arrive independently at the same conclusions you have.

Of course, persuasive discourse requires a closer relationship between writer and reader than do other types; you are addressing a specific set of readers and asking them to adopt a particular point of view or course of action. Consequently, although persuasive research papers are still data based, they are usually characterized by a more personal tone than that of a strictly informative research paper.

RESEARCH

Setting Up a Search Strategy

Only when you have defined your research question and identified your audience and purpose are you ready to begin your research. You need to start it early because doing careful research is usually time consuming. Often the process of collecting data proves to be longer and more extensive than you originally think it will be, because some of the sources you consult may direct you to still other sources of information, which you were not previously aware of.

You may find it helpful to make a sort of research outline that lets you know what sources you need to consult and the order in which you need to work through those sources. If you need to send away for information or arrange to set up interviews or conduct surveys, you should take care of these time consuming research tasks first so that you will have time to think about your information before you write your paper. Another rule of thumb for scheduling your research tasks is to begin with those sources that you believe will provide the most direct and specific information. This way, if your research takes longer than you expected it to, you won't find yourself having to begin writing your paper without having consulted your most valuable sources.

Finally, it's a good idea to set a deadline when you must stop researching and begin writing. Once you are well into your research project, you may discover new leads on sources that you were not previously aware of. However tantalizing these leads are, you may not be able to follow up on them, simply because you are running out of time. If this is the case, you might plan to extend your research project further at a later date and mention in your conclusion or in an informational note the potential value of these sources for further study.

Collecting Data: Primary and Secondary Sources

The researcher's next step, of course, is to collect data to either prove or disprove the validity of the hypothesis—or to answer the research question.

In much of the research you do for college classes or on the job, you will be concerned with two types of information sources—*primary* and *secondary* sources. Roughly speaking, the difference between them is the difference between firsthand and secondhand information. Primary sources are those that deal most directly and contemporaneously with your topic; often they are indistinguishable from your topic itself. Secondary sources, on the other hand, generally help you to interpret your primary sources.

In a research paper for a history course, for instance, your primary sources might be newspaper articles or government documents published during the historical period about which you are writing. Your secondary sources, on the other hand, might be books or articles written by historians who have also consulted those same primary sources in their analyses of the same historical period or event. In a research paper for a literature course, your primary sources would be the literary texts that you are interpreting or criticizing, or the letters and journals of the author whose works you are investigating. Secondary sources would include books, articles, lectures, and reviews by literary critics on the subject of your paper. In a scientific research paper, your own observations and experiments might be your primary sources, whereas the reports of other scientific investigators on a similar topic might constitute secondary sources.

If you are asked to do "original research," you must to some extent concern yourself with primary sources, since secondary sources are really someone else's research on the same or a related subject.

Searching Outside the Library

Although a great deal of academic research takes place in the library, this is by no means the only place where you can collect data for college research papers. In fact, there are times when nonlibrary sources can provide more direct, specific, and up-to-date information.

Suppose, for instance, that you were trying to find out what the possible side effects might be of the feline leukemia vaccine. Because the vaccine is a very recent medical development, you might have a hard time finding published information about it in books or even journals and newspapers. You might, however, have access to some experts on the subject—namely veterinarians or faculty members from a school of veterinary medicine, who could answer some of your questions in personal interviews. These individuals would make a much better choice as first sources to consult than would library materials. In addition to the information they could provide in interviews, experts of this sort can often provide you with leads on other useful sources—for example, brochures from pharmaceutical companies or professional reports about the use of the vaccine.

Other potentially helpful nonlibrary sources include television and radio broadcasts, pamphlets published by local community or special-interest organizations, and city and local government record offices. You might even have a topic that calls for you to perform your own empirical research, either by conducting polls and surveys or by scientific experimentation.

If you feel that collecting data through empirical research is in order for your research paper, you must be aware that there are certain ground rules to follow in designing questionnaires and conducting surveys. You will need to minimize the influence that the questions themselves might have on your subjects, and be aware of the extent to which you can generalize from your sample to a larger population. Your professor may be able to give you some guidelines on these and related matters or to direct you to other people or printed sources that can give you the information you need. Researchers in the sciences and social sciences should be familiar with this sort of research technique and may be willing to assist you.

Using the Library

Another type of research—one that is important in all disciplines from the sciences to the fine arts—is library research. Scientists conducting experiments to determine the effects of microwave radiation on the reproductive behavior of rodents, for instance, will consult articles and research reports on the same and related subjects in order to decide how to set up their experiments so as not to duplicate what has already been done. They will also consult the literature in their specialized field to help them interpret their findings or to lend support to their conclusions. And finally, they will use this literature in order to place their own research within the broader range of radiation studies and thus demonstrate the contributions their particular study makes to a larger body of knowledge.

Similarly, a literary critic researching a question such as, "Is there a distinctly feminine form of the *Bildungsroman*?" might conduct an investigation by consulting novels categorized as *Bildungsromane* as well as by reading books, articles, and addresses in which other literary critics have responded to the same or a similar question.

Library research deals with printed or taped sources of information that you can locate by consulting various indexes, bibliographies, and catalogs in the library. Your topic, of course, will determine which kinds of library resources are most helpful to you. For topics that are very timely—for instance, legislation currently being enacted by Congress, or the latest developments in computer technology—newspapers, periodicals, and documents are more likely sources of information than books or reference works such as encyclopedias, which require considerable time for the publication process.

PERIODICALS

Usually the most recent issues of newspapers and periodicals are shelved unbound, while older issues are bound into individually indexed volumes. Finding articles in these sources requires that you consult special guides or indexes to periodical literature. The most general of these, and one that is apt to be found in even small libraries is the *Readers' Guide to Periodical Literature.* You probably learned to use this reference work in high school or as a college freshman; if you didn't, you can easily teach yourself to use it now by following the instructions printed at the beginning of each guide, or you can ask your reference librarian for assistance. Other useful and more specialized guides and indexes to periodicals usually also include instructions for use and are valuable sources of references to information contained in specialized academic journals. Some of the major indexes of this sort are the following:

Applied Science and Technology Index
Book Review Digest
Business Index
The Education Index
Engineering Index
Humanities Index
Index Medicus
MLA International Bibliography
Public Affairs Information Service
Social Sciences Index

If your library is fairly large, it probably has many more specialized indexes and bibliographies which can be located by consulting the subject cards in a special catalog for reference works.

When you find a citation in an index or bibliography for an article that sounds helpful to you, copy down the full citation; this will not only help you locate the article itself, but will also save you time later on when you need to compile a bibliography for your paper. The same is true, of course, for citations to material from other sources as well—newspapers, documents, books, pamphlets, TV and radio broadcasts, interviews, and so forth.

While using bibliographies and indexes is an efficient way to locate periodical articles, you will find that current issues of most periodicals are usually not indexed. If up-to-date information is essential to your investigation, you can use the same indexes and bibliographies to identify those periodicals that are most likely to contain articles on your topic and check the most recent issues in the periodical display shelves.

NEWSPAPERS

The procedure for locating newspaper articles is similar to that for finding information in periodicals. The major index for newspaper articles on national and international topics is the *New York Times Index*. Other important reference works for locating newspaper articles are the *National Newspaper Index*, which lists articles from the *New York Times*, the *Christian Science Monitor* and the *Wall Street Journal*; and *The Newspaper Index*, which lists articles from four major U.S. newspapers: the *Chicago Tribune*, the *Los Angeles Times*, the *New Orleans Times-Picayune* and the *Washington Post*. In addition to national and international news, these four papers give regional news for their areas.

Some newspapers publish their own indexes, which you can use to find articles about your topic, but if this is not the case with the papers that are available to you, you can use one of the three major newspaper indexes listed above to identify the dates when your topic was being covered by the news media and check issues for those same dates in the newspapers you do find in your library.

GOVERNMENT DOCUMENTS

Most large libraries contain a special section for U.S. Government publications, a type of source that can be especially useful to you if you are writing a research paper for history, political science, law, or social science courses. Some government publications are indexed in the public catalog and are shelved according to Library of Congress or Dewey Decimal numbers. Other, uncataloged documents are kept in the government documents section of the library, arranged according to Superintendent of Documents numbers. Still others are kept on microform in collections called microform sets. These too are filed according to Superintendent of Documents numbers.

The following are a few of the major indexes you can use to locate government-document publications. In many libraries you will find a number of other indexes as well, and you should ask a librarian for assistance if you have difficulty using them.

Monthly Catalogue of United States Government Publications
The Federal Index
Index to U. S. Government Periodicals
C. I. S. U. S. Serial Set Index
Washington Information Directory

BOOKS

Books or sections of books can also be extremely valuable sources of information for research papers on a wide range of topics. Sometimes you will find entire books listed in the specialized indexes and bibliographies that you consult, but you can compile a more extensive list of potentially helpful books by consulting the card catalog or on-line search terminal in your library. Books are indexed according to subject, title, and author, but generally speaking, the subject category will be the most useful to you. To find out how your topic is likely to be indexed in the catalog, you may want to consult the two-volume *Library of Congress: Subject Headings*, which lists all the subject headings and their subdivisions that appear in the catalog. When you have identified the subject headings under which you are most likely to find useful information, begin searching for book titles first under the headings that most specifically describe your subject.

COMPUTER SEARCHES

Many college libraries now have the computerized indexes and data bases that will let you do computer searches as part of your research. Ask your reference librarian about what facilities are available and how you get started. Fortunately, computer indexes in libraries are almost always accompanied by detailed instructions and user's guides. Usually you can learn the rudiments very quickly. Do ask about costs, though. Some libraries charge for searches, and you'll want to know ahead of time how much you may have to invest.

Like traditional indexes, computerized data bases are arranged by author, title, and subject, but a computer index has these advantages.

- It can be continually updated.
- It can be searched quickly.
- It can give you a printed copy of what you find.

Computer data bases work by key words, or *descriptors,* as librarians call them. So if you were doing research about prenatal care among teenage mothers, the descriptors to punch in for your search would be *prenatal care* and *teenage mothers.* If you were particularly interested in the correlation between adequate prenatal care for teenage mothers and the high school attendance record of these mothers, you could add a third descriptor: *high school attendance.* The computer then does a three-way search, narrowing its search to articles that deal with all three issues. Sometimes you have to be imaginative about your descriptors. For instance, if adding the term *high school attendance* doesn't seem to work, try *high school drop-outs.*

Listed below are some useful computerized indexes. If none of these meets your needs, ask the librarian if others have been added recently. More indexes are becoming available all the time.

Topic	Computer index
Astronomy	INSPEC
Business	ABI/INFORM; Info Trac
Contemporary events	NewsBank
Contemporary periodicals	Academic Index; Info Trac; PAIS (Public Affairs Information Service)
Economics	PAIS
Education	ERIC
General information	Wilsondisc (covers same material as *Reader's Guide*)
Humanities	Info Trac
Literature	MLA Bibliography
Mathematics	MATHFILE
Psychology	PsycLit
Public affairs	PAIS
Social science	Info Trac

When you have the information you want on the screen, you can print a copy, and you're in business.

FOLLOWING UP ON BIBLIOGRAPHY ENTRIES

A good way to expand your search for sources is to follow up on the citations you find in the bibliographies of articles and books that you have found to be relevant to your study. This method of conducting research has a number of distinct advantages that make it common practice among veteran scholars. First, the book or article where the citations appear will usually give you a fairly good idea of their content, so you may be spared some of the time you might otherwise have to spend deciding if a particular source would be helpful to you or not. Second, the frequency with which you find a work cited by others is often an indication of that work's reliability. If you find a particular book or article cited by more than one of your sources, you can be fairly sure that it is itself a credible source, even an important one for you to consult. And finally, following up on bibliographies of useful sources is a fast and efficient way of expanding your search. It is very possible that a single bibliography will yield numerous citations that are useful to you, and you will have been spared the trouble of poring over bibliographies and other indexes to find them.

However you do your search, remember to cultivate serendipity (Chapter 3). Because experienced researchers know the value of such lucky accidents, they stay alert for them, glancing at the titles of books shelved next to the ones they are seeking, or running their eyes over the table of contents in a periodical that has the article on their prepared list. Your best piece of information may be the one you stumble onto while you are looking for something else.

Taking Notes

Sometimes the chore of taking notes for a research paper looms so large that you are tempted to photocopy everything you find, then worry about making sense of it after you leave the library. That's not a good idea, however, unless for some reason you have only limited access to the library. Not only is it expensive, but it also delays the selective skimming you need to do in order to decide which material is usable. Moreover, if you use photocopies you will very likely be tempted to simply underline rather than take notes on what you have read. This practice encourages you to rely too heavily on the original words of your sources before you have digested their ideas and can articulate them in your own words. Photocopying, then, is often a shortcut that actually defeats the whole purpose of research, and in addition can result in inadvertent plagiarism.

Many people prefer to take notes on index cards because cards are easier to sort and reorganize than sheets of notebook paper. Others, however, prefer to keep all of their notes in a notebook because in this form they are easier to carry around and are less likely to get lost. Whichever method is most comfortable for you is the one you should use. In either case, you should be sure that you always include the source along with the substantive information you record in your notes. And get in the habit of writing down the page numbers for *all* the information you record, whether you directly quote that information or simply refer to it in a summary or paraphrase. If you don't keep track of page numbers at this stage of your research, you will find yourself spending a lot of time going back to the library to hunt for page numbers.

In general, your notes will be of two kinds: summaries and quotations. For the most part, you should keep direct quotations to an absolute minimum. Overusing them means that you are letting your sources speak for you rather than synthesizing their information into a unified and coherent presentation of your own. Two questions to ask yourself when you are trying to decide whether to quote your source directly or summarize its content are

- Are the *words* themselves important to the development of my argument or to the clarity of my information?
- Do the words or phrases of this source have a special rhetorical effect that will strengthen my presentation?

Only if you can answer yes to at least one of these questions should you consider quoting the material directly. In any other situation you should summarize the information in your own words. Usually it is best to summarize material when you have finished reading the source and can set it aside. In this way you avoid the temptation to slip into the author's own words or to change them so slightly that for all practical purposes you are quoting directly. There is an educational advantage to this kind of note taking as well; if you are able to summarize the important points from your source without having to look at the text, then you know that you have assimilated and understood the text's information and made it your own. You will therefore not run the risk of producing a research paper that is merely a patchwork quilt of other people's words and ideas with little of your own thinking to tie it all together.

When you write summaries in your notes, you might use the abbreviated form in which you take notes for your classes, but don't condense them so much that you will be puzzled when you try to read them a week later. The time you take to put your information into a sentence instead of a phrase might save you a trip to the library later on. When you want to use direct quotations, be sure to copy them down *exactly* as they appear in the original text, preserving all punctuation marks, spelling, and capitalization. Use quotation marks around them in your notes so that you'll know later on that they are someone else's words. It's also a good idea to indicate in your notes who is responsible for the quote and why, where, and when the words were spoken or written. This kind of contextual information will be helpful to have when you need to integrate the quotation into your own text. Remember also to put in the ellipsis points if you leave out any part of the quotation.

You will also need to set up a system for organizing your notes. At the very least, number them as you work so you will be able to arrange them in the same order in which you did your research. Or you may develop a system of classifying them according to subtopic, perhaps by using code words to remind you which part of the paper various notes will apply to. Having your notes arranged in such divisions will help you to see how the parts of your paper are going to develop and may be the first step you take toward deciding on a plan of organization for your material.

WRITING

Choosing a Plan of Organization

The best plan for organizing the material for your paper is the one that most directly answers the research question you set out to investigate. Usually you will begin to develop a sense of how this can be accomplished as you are collecting material from your outside sources. But regardless of how well you have your plan in mind at this point, it is probably best to make some sort of "road map" that reminds you where you are going as you write your paper. This in turn will help you keep your readers from getting lost or wondering what point you are trying to make.

Probably the best way to get all of your material under control is to make a rough outline based on the categories you have set up for your notes. If you do this, you will establish the broad classifications that you are going to cover in your paper and find a logical way to order them within the paper. Write those classifications down. Then make notes about subpoints you want to cover in each category. As you work, develop a series of general assertions that can serve as the framework for your paper. And as you outline, think about what subheadings you might use to keep your reader on the track.

You can also create a plan of organization by capsuling, summarizing, or writing an abstract for your paper (see section on abstracts in Chapter 12). If well done, an abstract or summary can give you substantial guidance for organizing your paper and for beginning to articulate some of the points you want to make as a result of your research. Supplemented by a list of secondary or supporting points, a comprehensive abstract will serve you just about as well as an outline. And it gives an added advantage; after you finish, you can incorporate it wholly or in parts into your paper, or you can include it as a sort of preface to your paper to give your readers advance signals about what they will be reading. Do not, however, rely on an outline preface to do the work of a good introduction—that is, to inform your reader of your research question, your reasons for attempting to answer it, and your methods of searching for that answer.

Mastering the Conventions of Documentation

If you have used the bibliographies or endnotes provided in books and articles to expand your own search for information, you already know how helpful clear documentation can be to a fellow researcher. As you document your own paper you need to keep two main purposes in mind: First, you must let your readers know where you found your material, and second, you must make it possible for them to locate and use that material if they wish.

USES OF DOCUMENTATION

Documentation is not merely a matter of using the correct forms of footnotes and bibliography entries or the right form of citation in your text. The text of your paper itself can also contribute to the clear documentation of sources. When you do research you gather *ideas* from your sources as well as direct quotations and statistical information, and your readers should always be able to tell exactly which contributions are your own comments, interpretations, and evaluations, and which are reports of someone else's words and ideas. The text of your paper should enable a reader to make these distinctions easily.

In the case of direct quotations, where you use someone else's exact words, you supply this information partly by using quotation marks (for quotes that are shorter than four or five lines) or block indentation (for quotes of five lines or more). But you also need to supply an introduction to material gathered from outside sources, whether you are paraphrasing that material or quoting it directly. Introductory comments should precede the cited material even though the material itself may be enclosed in quotation marks or indented, and even though you provide a footnote or parenthetical citation. Such introductory comments not only make it clear exactly which information is being documented, they also help to integrate quotations smoothly and gracefully into the text of your paper.

The following example is flawed by a number of documentation errors:

> Until very recently it was thought that penguins were unique among the members of the animal kingdom, being the only birds to exhibit altruistic behavior. "In order to test the icy waters for seals, the penguin's deadliest enemy, one penguin risks her own life by plunging off the ice floe to where her predators possibly lie in wait."[1] If this penguin survived and the area thus appeared to be free of seals, the rest of the flock would follow her into the water. Later on, however, ornithologists came to believe that they had misinterpreted this particular aspect of penguin behavior.[2] "It appears now that the lead penguin is not willing to sacrifice herself for the survival of her group. Quite the contrary, our observations have led us to believe that she does not even jump into the water of her own accord, but rather that she is actually *pushed* into the water by the other members of her flock."[3]

The writer uses direct quotation where simple paraphrase or summary would easily suffice. In neither of the two direct quotations in this passage is it necessary to preserve the original wording of the sources cited and in fact, there are points at which the original wording is awkward when combined with the text of the paper—because of sense shifts, for example, or shifts in point of view. In addition, a reader cannot tell where the information in the paragraph comes from. The quotation marks around the second and the last sentences indicate that someone other than the writer of the paper is responsible for these sentences, but who is that someone? Is he or she a reliable source? Is the same source responsible for both of these quoted sentences? Or are there two different sources? Or are there three sources—one for each of the directly quoted sentences and one that is referred to by the superscript number 2? If more than one source is involved, how are they related, and why is the writer of the paper using them together in this paragraph? Who are the "we" referred to in the last sentence which relates "our" observations?

The reader might be able to find the answers to these questions by studying the footnotes at the bottom of the page or the endnotes that follow the paper, but such an interruption in the reading of the text is awkward, annoying, and unnecessary. The next example eliminates the unnecessary use of direct quotation and incorporates the missing information smoothly into the text. Citations are still needed, of course, because the writer of the paper is presenting information that originally appeared in another source, and because readers may need full citations in order to conduct follow-up research.

Until recently it was thought that penguins were unique among the members of the animal kingdom, being the only birds to exhibit altruistic behavior. Arctic explorers Nichole and Sam Thigpen reported in the log of their 1951 expedition that the lead penguin from a flock would apparently risk her own life for the survival of the flock by jumping off the ice floe into the water where arctic seals, the penguin's mortal enemy, were possibly lurking. If this penguin survived, the other birds in the flock would follow her into the water, assured that no predators were lurking there (Thigpen and Thigpen, 1951). Fifteen years later, however, when the Thigpens, accompanied by ornithologist Jordan Jones, made a second arctic voyage, they revised their earlier assessment of penguin behavior, claiming that the lead penguin was not at all willing to sacrifice herself but rather that the group seemed willing to sacrifice *her* to insure their survival. This conclusion resulted from the explorers' observation that the lead penguin apparently did not jump into the potentially seal-infested water but instead was actually pushed by her followers (Jones, Thigpen, and Thigpen, 1966).

STYLES OF DOCUMENTATION

Styles of documentation vary considerably across disciplines, so you will need to find out which style is preferred in the field for which you are writing. If you are writing your research paper for a college course, your professor will probably indicate which type of documentation he or she wants you to use and which style manual you should consult if you have questions. Another way to find out this kind of information, particularly if you do not have a professor's guidance, is to check the form of notes and bibliography entries in articles published in scholarly journals in the field you are researching.

The two most common styles of documentation currently being used in academic writing are those endorsed by the MLA (Modern Language Association) and by the APA (American Psychological Association). Both of these organizations advocate the use of *internal documentation* with an accompanying bibliography. This means that brief citations appear in parentheses in the text immediately after the cited material. (See the citations that appear in the second example of the penguin text, above.) These parenthetical citations contain enough information to enable the reader to identify the cited sources from the bibliography, where full bibliographic information is given for all of the sources the writer has consulted in order to write the paper. According to this documentation method, footnotes, at the bottom of the page, or endnotes, at the end of the paper, are only used to give explanatory material that is somehow tangential to the text. For instance, a footnote to the penguin text might be something like this:

> Until recently it was thought that penguins were unique among the members of the animal kingdom, being the only birds to exhibit altruistic behavior.[1] Arctic explorers . . .

1. The possibility that parrots might also demonstrate altruistic behavior by alerting their owners to potential dangers has often been put forward by parrot owners, but has been discounted (1982) as anthropomorphism on the owners' part by zoologist Soraya Mashat.

The information about parrots is included in the paper because the author feels that it may be of interest to readers who themselves might argue that parrots are altruistic birds or who have a more general interest in animal behavior than is addressed by the paper. Nevertheless, the parrot information does not appear in the text proper because the focus of the paper is penguins, not parrots or birds in general.

The major differences between APA and MLA styles are matters of punctuation, capitalization, and arrangement of material in bibliographic entries. The following examples demonstrate how the same source would be cited in a paper using APA style and one using MLA style:

APA   This approach corresponds to the frequently cited theory that scientific revolutions come about through paradigm shifts (Kuhn, 1970, p. 79).

MLA   This approach corresponds to the frequently cited theory that scientific revolutions come about through paradigm shifts. (Kuhn, p. 79).

Notice that the APA system uses the date of publication in the parenthetical citation, whereas the MLA usually does not. MLA style would cite the publication date only if it were necessary to distinguish this work by Kuhn from another included in the bibliography—let's say, one that was published in 1962. Regardless of which system you were using, you would need to provide a full citation to Kuhn's text in the bibliography at the end of your paper.

BIBLIOGRAPHIC ENTRIES

A bibliography is a list of all the sources that helped you formulate the content of your paper, whether or not you have cited them specifically in your text. Bibliography entries for both MLA and APA systems are arranged alphabetically according to the first word of the entry, which is usually, but not necessarily, the last name of the author. The following bibliography entries for Kuhn's book illustrate the major difference between APA and MLA styles:

APA   Kuhn, T. (1970). *The structure of scientific revolutions*. Chicago: Univ. of Chicago Press.

MLA   Kuhn, Thomas S. *The Structure of Scientific Revolutions*. Chicago: Univ. of Chicago Press, 1970.

Notice that MLA uses the author's full first name and middle initial, whereas APA uses the first initial only. Also, the placement of the publication date is different for each style; APA places it in parentheses immediately after the author's name, while in the MLA format the date is the final piece of information given, followed only, in some cases, by the page numbers of articles or chapters within the book being cited. Finally, MLA style uses the same capitalization conventions that you would use if you referred to a title in a prose passage, whereas APA style eliminates all capitalization in titles except for first words, words following a colon or period in the title, and proper nouns and adjectives. Similarly, titles of "short" works such as articles, poems, or short stories are enclosed in quotation marks in MLA style entries; in APA entries, the quotation marks are omitted.

Obviously, when internal documentation is used, there is no need for a separate set of endnotes containing bibliographic information. If you use a documentation system that uses superscript numbers in the text and provides bibliographic information in separate footnotes or endnotes, remember that there are a number of differences between notes and bibliographies. Most important is the fact that bibliographies are full listings of all sources consulted, whereas footnotes or endnotes contain citations for only those sources that are directly referred to in the text. Alphabetization provides the organization for bibliography entries, whereas superscript numbers provide the order by which notes are arranged. This means that bibliographies only list each source once, whereas the same source appears in footnotes or endnotes as often as it is cited in the text of the paper. Finally, depending on the documentation style you are using, you will find various differences between the format and mechanical conventions of endnotes and bibliography entries. Because these distinctions are often minor and difficult to remember, you would be wise to use a handbook that gives you examples of note and bibliography-entry forms to follow.

The sample bibliography entries listed below illustrate the current MLA-endorsed form. For more unusual types of entries, you should consult the 1988 edition of the *MLA Handbook for Writers of Research Papers*. For APA-approved forms, consult the *Publication Manual of the American Psychological Association* (3rd ed., 1983).

A BOOK WITH A SINGLE AUTHOR:
King, Martin Luther. *The Trumpet of Conscience*. New York: Harper and Row, 1968.

A BOOK WITH TWO AUTHORS:
Clark, Kenneth and Harold Howe. *Racism and American Education*. New York: Harper and Row, 1971.

A SIGNED PERIODICAL ARTICLE:
Walters, Samuel K. "Survival Tips for Third World Travelers." *Journal of the American Travel Association* 12 (1985): 32–40.

AN UNSIGNED MAGAZINE ARTICLE:
"The Saga of Boston." *Ebony*, Oct. 1974: 110–114.

AN ARTICLE IN AN ANTHOLOGY:
Britton, James. "The Composing Processes and the Functions of Writing." *Research in Composing*. Ed. Charles Cooper and Lee Odell. Urbana, Ill.: NCTE, 1978. 13–28.

A TRANSLATION:
Vygotsky, Lev. *Thought and Language*. Trans. Eugenia Hanfmann and Gertrude Vakar. Cambridge: MIT Press, 1962.

A PAMPHLET:
Subterranean Termite Control Proposal. Key no. 33020. Terminix International, 1985.

GOVERNMENT DOCUMENT:
United States. Congress. Joint Committee on the Investigation of Alternative Energy Resources. *Hearings*. 104th Cong., 1st sess. 11 vols. Washington: GPO, 1983.

MATERIAL FROM AN INFORMATION SOURCE SUCH AS ERIC:
Agha, Shahid Ali, ed. *Academic and Cultural Exchange Programs Between the U.S. and Asian Countries*. International Education Conference Proceedings, 1985. ERIC ED 247 6855.

LETTER TO THE EDITOR:
Pruitt, Oscar K. *Raleigh Gazette* 43 (1984): 11–12.

TELEVISION PROGRAM:
Ludwig von Beethoven: A Musical Biography and a Salute to Genius. Narr. Nancy Ratner. Writ. and Prod. Patricia Vivian. NBC. Famous Figures in the Arts. KCRG, Portland, Oregon. 27 May, 1984.

AN INTERVIEW:
Tepley, Peter. Telephone Interview. Aug. 30, 1989.

HELP WITH DOCUMENTATION

If you must write a complex and important research paper, you may want more help than you can find in this comparatively short section on the forms of documentation. If so, in almost any library you can get books that treat the topic comprehensively and will give you additional sources that you can consult. Perhaps the best complete and useful book is

Barzun, Jacques and Henry Graff. *The Modern Researcher*, 4th ed. New York: Harcourt Brace Jovanovich, 1985.

Other possible sources are the following:

Lester, James D. *Writing Research Papers: A Complete Guide*, 5th ed. Glenview, IL: Scott, Foresman, 1987.

Memering, W. Dean. *Research Writing: A Complete Guide to Research Papers*. Englewood Cliffs, NJ: Prentice Hall, 1983.

Spatt, Brenda. *Writing from Sources*, 2nd ed. New York: St. Martin's Press, 1986.

Walker, Melissa. *Writing Research Papers: A Norton Guide*, 2nd ed. New York: W. W. Norton, 1987.

12 ◇ Writing on the Job

Among the most common kinds of writing that you may have to do if you work for an agency, an institution, or a corporation are grant proposals, nontechnical reports, case studies, abstracts, and papers for oral presentations.

GRANT PROPOSALS

In recent years a kind of writing that must be both informative and persuasive has become increasingly important, the grant proposal. Most scientific researchers find that they must know how to write grant proposals if they expect to get their projects funded; so do educators who want to improve the teaching of writing, welfare workers who want to help their clients practice better nutrition, or librarians who want to encourage reading in their community. In fact, in many fields, almost any person who wants to start a project that involves more than routine activity will find that he or she can do so only by successfully applying for a grant.

A small industry has even grown up to help people master the art of "grantsmanship." Self-styled experts contract to write grants for people, professional journals advertise expensive two- or three-day seminars on writing grants, and bookstores stock manuals with detailed instructions and indexes to a variety of funding agencies.

But you do not have to be an expert or a specialist to write a satisfactory grant proposal. The format is not mysterious, and the information you need is generally available from libraries or institutional offices. The agencies and foundations that give grants usually provide specific instructions about what you should include and provide a checklist and cover sheet to help you put the proposal together. So all the applicant really needs to have, besides patience and determination, is the ability to write clear, well-organized prose and some appreciation of the psychology of grant writing.

Purpose of the Proposal

When you write a grant proposal, you have one overriding purpose: *to persuade someone to give you money.* In order to do that, you are going to have to convince the reviewers at the foundation or agency to which you are applying that you have a good idea for solving an important problem, that you have or can get the facilities and equipment for handling the task, and that significant benefits will result when you do solve the problem. In short, you have to do a major selling job, but you have to do it with rhetorical restraint and with an abundance of evidence and sound reasoning to support your request. Your task is made easier, however, because the conventions for grant proposals are well established and not difficult to follow.

Preliminary Planning

Your first concern in writing a grant proposal should be to give yourself plenty of time. The research, legwork, writing, budget preparations, and so on will take longer than you think. Next, find out what kind of agency or foundation might be interested in funding it. If you are going to apply to a local organization, you need only get its application form and instruction booklet, but if you are unsure about where you should send the proposal, go to the library and ask for a directory of organizations that award grants. Not only the names are listed, but also the specific areas of interest and special requirements of the grant-award agencies. If you are connected with or close to a university or college, you can also get an abundance of information from its office for research.

Narrow the list of possibilities by noting the kind and size of grants that foundations make, and choose the funding organizations whose records show that they have been supporting projects similar to yours. Learn as much as you can about those organizations because their reviewing committees are going to make up the audience for which you will be writing.

Your next step should be to rough out a plan for your proposal. Although the sequence of items for the proposal is probably prescribed by the funding institution, write yourself some notes about how your are going to present that sequence. The key items you should think about are

(1) the description of and rationale for the project, (2) the procedures to be followed in carrying out the project, (3) a description of facilities available for working on the project or research, (4) the credentials and experience of the people who will work on the project, and (5) the budget. You are not ready to start writing the proposal until you can draft a paragraph or two for each of those items, and until you can summarize what other people have already done in the specific area you plan to work in. And you should have done the research for such a summary before making your decision to apply for the grant. This planning is important because even though you will undoubtedly be doing some creative thinking and revision as you write the proposal, grant proposals must be carefully structured documents. One cannot depend on inspiration to guide their development.

The Body of the Proposal

Although the forms provided by most grant-giving agencies specify that your proposal should begin with the title and an abstract, you will probably want to postpone writing those items until later. Begin your proposal with the description of your project, your reasons for proposing it, and a discussion of what you hope to accomplish with it. Obviously this introductory section of the proposal needs to make a good impression on your readers so as you write it keep in mind those cardinal virtues of good writing: significance, unity, clarity, economy, and vigor. Get to the point immediately by stating what you intend to do. Follow up with an explanation of why you think it is worth doing, what other people have done in similar work, and what you expect your project to accomplish that has not previously been done. You may need several paragraphs or several pages to cover all these points adequately, but try to write as succinctly as possible.

Suppose, for example, that you are an architect who has joined with a historian, an engineer, and a landscape architect to get funds to restore an old deteriorated market-area to its original condition. In the introductory section of your proposal you would identify and objectively describe the building you want to restore, describe the work that needs to be done and the approximate cost, give reasons for restoring the building—historic value, effect on surrounding area, attraction for tourists, and so on—describe and cite the effects of similar projects in other cities, and explain your belief that a restoration project that emphasizes the city's heritage can become the focus of an economic renaissance of the inner city. Your should strive for a vigorous and confident tone in this section, and should include pertinent details and enough references to previous or similar projects to sound competent and knowledgeable.

If the first section of the proposal is important because it describes what you want to do and explains why you want to do it, the second section is equally important because it must explain *how* you plan to accomplish your goal. Now you need to prove that you are competent and knowledgeable by outlining practical procedures for carrying out your plan and giving a realistic timetable for the work. If your proposal involves research, specify how you are going to collect your data, how you will control variables, and what analytical methods you will use. Experienced reviewers will take a particularly close look at this part of the proposal because they do not want to waste money supporting a project that sounds worthy but is poorly designed.

When you describe the facilities available to you for working on the project or carrying out the research, and give the credentials and experience of your coworkers, you are also establishing your credibility as an applicant. This section needs to be written carefully and honestly to show that you have the qualifications to spend the foundation's money productively. It is a good idea to include a biographical data sheet for each person who will be working on the project.

How you conclude your proposal depends on the kind of format prescribed by the organization giving the grant. If it gives no specific guidelines use your best judgment. If the proposal runs to fifteen or twenty pages, you may need to help your reader by reiterating the key points in a summary section and stressing the innovative features of your proposal. Reviewers of such proposals tend to favor projects that explore new territory or suggest fresh approaches.

Making a Budget

The first time you estimate a budget for a grant proposal you should seek help if you can because such budgets must include hidden costs that are easily overlooked, items like contributions to retirement funds and to the operating expenses of the institution whole facilities you will be using. Almost every college has employees whose job it is to help applicants with their grant proposals; don't hesitate to use them. If you are drawing up a complicated budget and you do not have access to such people, try to find a professional consultant and pay for an expert opinion. At the very least, get a book on preparing grants and look at sample budgets.

But no one else can actually make a budget for you. Only you can estimate how long your project is going to take and consequently what the outlay for salaries will be; how much computer time you may need and how much should be allotted for travel expenses; what kind of equipment you will need and what it costs to operate it. And don't make vague estimates. Finding out what things cost takes leg work and lots of phone calls, but you need to figure all your expenditures as accurately as possible before you take your tentative budget to a consultant. Remember too that you should explain and justify any large item that does not seem self-explanatory.

Resist the temptation to underestimate your costs because you feel that an accurate statement seems so high that you would not have a chance of getting the grant. The people who review grants have a good idea what expenses on a project should run, and if you turn in a budget that is unrealistically low they will question your professional competence. If necessary, it would be better for you to scale down the scope of your proposal than to look financially naive.

Writing the Abstract and Title

When you have finished the budget and finished any other sections that the grant announcement may specify, you are ready to write your abstract and title. Because they will introduce your proposal to the reviewers, you need to write them very carefully so that they will succinctly and accurately state your case. The title should be as brief as you can make it and still be explicit. For example, "A Proposal to Make an Authentic Restoration of the Farmers' Market and Surrounding Square in Dayton, Ohio," or "A Study of the Effect of Syntactical Arrangement on the Readability of Nonfiction Prose."

The following excerpt from a grants announcement pamphlet from the National Institute of Education sums up the guidelines you should follow in writing your abstract.

> Abstract: The narrative should be a succinct, nontechnical description of the research. It should not exceed 250 words, and should be so clearly written that the following questions could be answered by reading it.
> Paragraph (a) What is the specific purpose of this study? What information is being sought?
> Paragraph (b) Who needs it? Why is it desirable to do this?
> Paragraph (c) How is the study to be conducted (a nontechnical description of the general methodology)?
> Paragraph (d) What difference might the results make?—to whom?

See pp. 234–37 for more detailed information about writing abstracts.

Getting a Second Opinion

When you have finished writing the proposal and have revised it into a second draft, give a copy to a knowledgeable person whose judgment you trust. Ask that person to put himself or herself in the role of a reviewer and to read your proposal with a skeptical eye, looking particularly for omissions, oversimplifications, or unwarranted claims. Also ask that person to mark any places where the language is vague or confusing or where the writing is biased or inflated. If you can get two qualified and patient people to read the proposal, so much the better.

The Final Draft

When you have the proposal in final form, have it professionally typed, leaving good margins, making sure to follow to the letter the instructions provided in the grant applications. Mark the internal divisions with headings and subheadings and make sure charts and diagrams are labeled. Proofread the final copy meticulously to be sure that it looks as good as it can, and get the necessary number of copies made by a reliable service so that they will not be streaked or dim. In other words, make sure that the packet of paper that is going off to represent you makes the best possible appearance.

Evaluation Criteria

Reviewers for granting agencies and foundations judge proposals they receive on these criteria:

- Is the research or project relevant to the goals of the agency?
- Is the proposal innovative?
- Is the problem the proposal addresses important?
- Do the applicants show knowledge of previous work in this area?
- Is the proposal project adequately designed?
- Are the people who will work on the project competent?
- Can the project be carried out in the estimated time?
- Is the budget accurate and reasonable?
- Are the facilities and equipment for the project adequate?

If your grant proposal meets all these criteria and is clearly and carefully written, you stand a good chance of getting your money.

NONTECHNICAL REPORTS

Just as scientists, architects, or anthropologists who thought they were going into nonwriting professions often find themselves spending a surprising amount of time writing grant proposals, so nurses, social workers, bankers, or psychiatrists—in fact, perhaps the majority of professional people—find that they spend an unexpected amount of time writing reports. The report is the essential document of the business and professional world, the instrument used to inform and instruct colleagues and customers and to furnish data on which people can make decisions. So important are business and technical reports that many specialists give courses and write textbooks on technical report writing; if you think you will do a great deal of writing, you will probably want to take such a course in college or after you go to work in your profession. But people who are called on to write occasional nontechnical reports, such as a summary of a public opinion survey or an analysis of customer complaints, can learn to write successful reports by following the ordinary procedures for writing good prose.

Characteristics of Reports

Reports are about facts. The person who reads the report you have written does not expect to find out what you feel, think, believe, fear, or hope; he or she expects to find out what you have investigated, observed, experienced, or read about. Meteorologists giving a weather report to a pilot do not say that it's a "nice day." Rather they say, "Clear skies, visibility unlimited, no turbulence in this area." From those facts they may draw an inference and add, "Should be a good day to fly," but strictly speaking, the inference is not part of the report.

Reports are based on data; we use them as we use reference books to find out information. Consequently the person who writes them should

* Focus on the material under discussion.
* Not express personal emotions or opinions.
* Not argue or seek to persuade.
* Not use a literary style that calls attention to itself.[1]

Writing a good report becomes an exercise in restraint. It also becomes an exercise in practicing subtle communication skills, because although writers must seem not to be thinking about their audiences, they must be acutely aware of the audience. Equally, though they must not draw attention to themselves directly, in an indirect way they must convince their readers that they are conscientious and reliable reporters.

---

1. Guidelines adapted from James Kinneavy, *A Theory of Discourse* (Englewood Cliffs, NJ: Prentice-Hall, 1971), 88.

The Audience for Reports

People who write reports usually do so on assignment and for a specific audience. For example, a biologist might write a report on an environmental study for the state Fish and Game Commission; a nurse might write a report on her study of a pregnant diabetic woman for the instructor of her course in clinical practices; a navy officer might write a report on needed ship repairs for the head of the U.S. Bureau of Ships. Or a report might be as simple as a one-paragraph summary of snow conditions at Taos written for people who want to go skiing. The authors of any of these reports need to identify the intended audience as precisely as possible to decide just what it is they want to get from reading these reports. Because writers do not want to waste their audience's time by telling them more than they want to know, they need to assess carefully their audience's level of expertise. They also need to think about how much specialized vocabulary they can use; for the right audience it can act as a kind of shorthand, but for the wrong one it can impede communication.

Moreover, a writer needs to think about how many people will read the report and how much influence they have, how long it will last, and what actions might be taken on the basis of its contents. The snow report becomes useless after a day and is thrown away; the environmental study will reach readers at several levels of power, will serve as the basis for recommending action, and will almost certainly be filed and stored. For those reasons it should be comprehensive, documented, and written in a language nonspecialists can understand.

The language of the report should have an objective tone that puts considerable distance between reader and writer and avoids the pronoun *you* unless it seems required by the context. But writing this way should not mean writing stuffy, dull, or pedantic prose, nor should it mean writing an inflated and passive style loaded down with derived nouns and prepositional phrases.

The writer stays in the background with this kind of fact-centered, objective style. This effect is enhanced by using neutral language and by using few adjectives. But writers who try to sound objective simply by not using the pronoun *I* may create more problems than they solve. For one thing, they can wind up with a contrived and awkward style: for example, "This investigator visited Padre Island on June 25" or "The author of this report interviewed the patient." The writer trying to avoid *I* may also fall back on passive constructions and abstract subjects that can confuse the reader: for example, "The feasibility of the study was determined by the investigator" or "This material was decided to be relevant." Nearly any reader would prefer that an author write, "I interviewed the patient" or "I collected the data."

Moreover, using *I* in a report identifies you as a writer who deserves credit for having complied and written a good report. And you can strengthen that impression by routinely citing and consistently documenting all your sources. You can furnish your documentation either with footnotes written according to the style prescribed by a reputable style sheet or by giving your references in parenthesis within the body of the text (see pp. 216–17).

The Structure of Reports

Reports usually function as documents that are meant to convey information to readers so that those readers can do a job. Therefore, the report should be organized to serve the reader.[2] How can you put it together so that the reader can grasp the contents as quickly and efficiently as possible? When you are writing reports on assignment, often the reader has already decided on a plan of organization and gives you specific instructions on how to carry it out. For example, the instructions for major term reports in one school of nursing stipulate that those reports must be organized as follows:

Abstract:
Introduction, including statement of the problem
Review of the literature
Clinical application
Conclusions
Recommendations

A business firm or government bureau might insist that writers reporting to them follow this kind of plan:

Abstract
Introduction
    a. Statement of the problem
    b. Purpose of the report
    c. Description of method used
Body of report
    a. Detailed description of procedures carried out
    b. Explanation of findings
Conclusions
    a. Detailed summary of results

---

2. Gordon H. Mills and John A. Walter, *Technical Writing,* 4th ed. (New York: Holt, Rinehart and Winston, 1978), 292.

Such formulas can simplify your task and serve as useful models for many kinds of report writing assignments.

Sometimes, however, you must develop your own pattern of organization for a report. When you do, start with a comprehensive and accurate title that lets your reader know precisely what to expect from the report. (Remember also that the title controls how the report will be filed.) Immediately after the title page, many readers expect to find an abstract that summarizes the content of the report. Even if an abstract is not required, it is a good idea to include one for a long paper, as it helps to focus the reader's attention and makes it easier for him or her to follow your report (see pp. 233–37 on writing abstracts).

Begin the report itself with an introduction that states the issue or problem to be addressed, the purpose of the report, and the method used for carrying out that purpose. Such a businesslike opening may seem dull, but it is important nevertheless. Readers want to know from the start why they should read the report and where and how you got your evidence.

How you organize the body of the report will depend on your purpose for writing and the kind of material you are dealing with. If you are writing a research report about a diabetic pregnant woman, you would probably want to use a narrative form to recount the woman's case history, give the results of your interviews with her, and document the clinical symptoms as the pregnancy advanced. Then you would want to review the literature of what is known about the complications that diabetes causes for pregnant women, apply that information to the case you are writing about, and give your findings. In the conclusion of your paper, you would summarize what you learned.

In other kinds of reports writers usually begin by stating the most important information in the report. Although this kind of organization may not work well for persuasive or entertaining writing because it takes away the writer's chance to build to a climax, it does work well for factual explanatory writing. Readers for that kind of writing do not want to be intrigued and kept in suspense; they want to know results. If those results are important to them, they will probably read on to find out how they were obtained; if they are not, they do not have to spend any more time on the document.

After you have given the crucial information, you must then go on to discuss your procedures and findings in detail. Not everyone who is interested in the main content of your report will read the detailed discussion, but it should be written carefully nevertheless so it can be referred to if needed. Finally, most reports that run to more than a few pages should conclude with a summary that restates the main idea.

Case Studies

Professionals in many fields must spend substantial time writing reports that deal not only with impersonal data but with the behavior of people. Those reports are called *case studies* or *case histories,* and the methodology for education and research in a number of disciplines depends heavily on the case study method. Some of these fields are clinical and experimental psychology, social work, speech therapy, medicine, and the social sciences such as anthropology, sociology, and linguistics. People working in any of these fields of study need to know how to write case studies; so do nurses, policemen and emergency medical technicians.

Because most case studies are not highly technical, people who must write them do not have to take special training. They can manage quite well if they do their best to write clear, concise, economical, and unpretentious prose and keep in mind a few extra guidelines that apply particularly to case studies. The first is to learn to write objective, concrete descriptions of behavior without expressing personal opinions or biases and without judging; the second is to learn to write comprehensive reports that include all pertinent information; the third is to learn to anticipate the specific questions that the case study is expected to answer.

The first guideline is probably the most difficult to follow because most of us have trouble being neutral when we watch or talk to other people. We like or dislike them, approve or disapprove of their behavior even when we don't know them. Yet a linguistic researcher or social worker or clinical psychologist cannot afford to let emotion or bias appear in a case study that is supposed to be only a description. The professional responsibility of these people is to record what they observe, are told in an interview, or learn through a test. So a child-guidance counselor should write "Philip is below normal weight and height for his age and expresses fears about being attacked by larger boys in his grade," not "Philip is pathetically thin and intimidated by larger boys." And a cultural anthropologist should not describe an Indian tribe as "brave and proud," but should instead describe the behavior of the tribe. When a person is collecting and recording data, even data about human beings, that person must take great care not to prejudice the reader with connotative language.

Inexperienced report writers sometimes also have trouble deciding how much information they should include in their case studies. A writer does not want to waste the reader's time or mix irrelevant information with important data, but good case studies must include all *pertinent* facts. So the question becomes "What is pertinent?" and the answer must depend on the purpose of the case study.

In the case study of the diabetic pregnant woman, the nursing student needed to include information about the woman's weight, diet, economic circumstances, educational level, family history, marital status, and previous pregnancies, as all these matters affected her ability to control her diabetes. On the other hand, in behavioral psychologist Stanley Milgram's study of destructive obedience in a laboratory situation, the author gives only this much information about the subjects:

> The subjects were 40 males between the ages of 20 and 50, drawn from New Haven and the surrounding communities. Subjects were obtained by a newspaper advertisement and direct mail solicitation. Those who responded to the appeal believed they were to participate in a study of memory and learning at Yale University. A wide range of occupations is represented in the sample. Typical subjects were postal clerks, high school teachers, salesmen, engineers, and laborers. Subjects ranged in educational level from one who had not finished elementary school, to those who had doctorate and other professional degrees. They were paid $4.50 for their participation in the experiment. However, subjects were told that payment was simply for coming to the laboratory, and that the money was theirs no matter what happened after they arrived.
> —Stanley Milgram, "A Behavioral Study of Obedience," *The Norton Reader,* revised, shorter edition. Ed. Arthur Eastman et al. (New York: W.W. Norton, 1965), 195.

For the rest of the case study, Milgram reported only the subjects' actual behavior in the laboratory. Any other information about them was not relevant to the study.

Your ability to select data that are appropriate for your case study and to exclude information that is irrelevant or peripheral reveals a great deal about your competence in your field. If you cannot discriminate between useful and irrelevant data or judge how much evidence you need for a particular study, you signal to your reader that you probably don't know what you are doing. As one expert puts it:

> As to pertinence, the report writer should not collect data for its own sake, use it indiscriminately, or use it to pad or make the report appear to be more professional.
> —Jack Huber, *Report Writing in Psychology and Psychiatry* (New York: Harper & Row, 1961), 13.

Finally, people write case studies in order to answer questions that someone has asked or will ask about their work. You should be able to figure out what those questions will be if you know *why* they are being asked. For example, the emergency medical technician who is writing a case history of a patient brought in from an automobile accident knows that the doctor wants information that will help in treating the patient, so the technician reports on blood type, location of injuries, temperature, blood pressure, treatment given, and so on. However, a rehabilitation counselor who is writing a case history in order to help that same person qualify for a state training program knows that the screening committee wants to know whether the person can be helped and why the state should subsidize rehabilitation. To answer those questions the counselor needs to include information on the person's injuries, educational level, financial status, and so on. The kind and amount of information the audience needs will vary with the task; thus people who write case studies may need to develop their sense of audience and purpose even more highly than other writers do.

ABSTRACTS

The Uses of Abstracts

People who write regularly in business, industry, technology, medicine, or the academic profession learn to write abstracts early in their careers because the abstract is an essential part of the communication system in their field. A good abstract summarizes an article or report so succinctly and accurately that readers can quickly infer from the abstract the essential content of the longer work. Ideally, an abstract should have the same relationship to an article or report that an architect's model of a building has to the completed building. Just as one should be able to tell from an architect's model what a building is going to look like, one should be able to tell from an abstract what a report is going to say. And both the model and the abstract should be self-contained units, independent miniatures that make sense even when separated from the piece they represent.

Promissory Abstracts

Abstracts are important because they can serve both writers and readers in a number of different ways. First, a writer can draft a preliminary abstract of a paper as a way of beginning to think about the topic and as a device for organizing those ideas. This kind of abstract is preliminary and flexible, more like a working sketch for a building than like a model, and usually it will be substantially revised or discarded altogether when the paper is completed.

Second, a person may write an abstract that is a kind of promissory note or prospectus to a program chairman or an editor. In this kind of abstract the writer sketches out the paper or report he or she plans to write and submit it for consideration. If the editor or chairman thinks the projected piece of writing is worth publishing or presenting, and if the person submitting the abstract has good credentials for writing such a piece, the abstract may be accepted, and the writer is then asked to produce the paper. People who submit abstracts of this kind must follow them faithfully when they write their final paper because they have made a contract on the basis of the abstract.

People who will be working in fields in which one earns rewards by publishing or presenting papers should master the art of writing these promissory abstracts as a part of their professional training. For one thing, you can often meet a deadline for papers or program proposals if you can submit an abstract by the deadline rather than a completed paper. Second, once an editor or program chairman accepts your proposal on the basis of an abstract, you have made a commitment and established a deadline that will force you to write the paper. Many of us need that kind of motivation.

Summary Abstracts

Abstracts written after a report has been completed can also serve several purposes. First, they may appear at the beginning of a report and function as a kind of preview that lets the reader know what to expect; this is particularly useful for long reports. Second, they can serve as a summary that will give an administrator or executive necessary information in a capsule form. Third, they can be used as a quick reference—for example, an abstract could appear in the program for a professional meeting to help participants decide if they want to hear the full paper, or it could be published in a journal or catalog of abstracts so that people searching for material on the topic could determine whether they want to read the full-length paper.

Because an abstract serves so many functions, you can see why it is so important that it be well written. One authority claims that it is the most important part of the paper:

> The first significant impression of your report is formed on the reader's mind by the abstract; and the sympathy with which it is read, if it is read at all, is often determined by this first impression.
> —Christian K. Arnold. "The Writing of Abstracts,"
> in *The Practical Craft*, ed. Keith Sparrow and
> Donald Cunningham (Boston: Houghton
> Mifflin, 1978), 264.

Writing the Abstract

Good abstracts are hard to write because they must accurately compress so much information into compact form, and because they should be written in easy-to-understand, nontechnical language. Moreover, your method of writing an abstract will differ when you are writing a promissory abstract and when you are writing a summary abstract. The first is creative, the second analytical.

WRITING THE PROMISSORY ABSTRACT

When you are writing a promissory abstract, you need to go through a process similar to the one you use at the preparatory stages of writing a paper. First write down the main idea or thesis that you want to present; then brainstorm and take notes on all the possible points you might want to make about that thesis. On a new page jot down the sources and examples that you might use to illustrate your thesis. Finally you might write down why you think the paper you propose is worth presenting or why an audience would be interested in reading or listening to what you have to say.

Then, beginning either with a statement of your main idea or a listing of the main evidence on which you base your thesis, write a first draft that answers these questions: What are you going to say? Who needs to know it or what is the information good for?

Don't worry too much about the length on this first draft. Get down as much information as you think the program chairman or editor needs in order to make a judgment about the paper. You can trim it to size later. In the second and third drafts cut if necessary, and simplify and polish your writing because this abstract will not only represent the content of your paper but will also be a sample of your prose style. You can present your credentials for giving the paper on a separate sheet or in a letter.

Here is a sample of a promissory abstract that I turned in for a conference:

ABSTRACT

By using interviews, questionnaires, the examination of drafts, and conference with editors and by drawing from work already done on the writing process, I plan to investigate the writing processes of ten professional writers of nonfiction. From this research, I hope to validate and expand tentative hypotheses that I have constructed about how such writers work and to gather a body of information about the craft of writing that will be available in itself and will also benefit other scholars working in this very new area. These data may also be useful to scholars interested in more general theories of creativity.

The program chairman accepted the paper, and four months later I wrote it.

WRITING THE SUMMARY ABSTRACT

In writing the summary abstract, you need to start by carefully reread-ing your paper and underlining the main points. Write brief summaries of each section in the margins as you would if you were studying for an exam on the paper; star the most important points you make. Then make a rough outline of the paper so that you see your plan of development at a glance; you may realize, for instance, that although you spent twice as long developing point one as you did in developing point two, the points are equally important and you do not need to give twice as much space to point one in the abstract. It is because of concerns of this kind that you should not try to write an abstract by stringing together sentences that summarize each paragraph.

One way to write an analytical abstract would be to put down the most important idea in your paper in the first sentence and in two or three more sentences develop that idea. Then decide how you arrived at your thesis, giving specific details if it seems useful. Finally, summarize the implications of your thesis or hypothesize about what its value might be. Another ap-proach might be to begin by stating the problem you are writing about, then describe the approach you used to work on it, and finally give your results. And there are other ways to write an abstract. You do not have to organize abstracts in the same way that you organize your papers, but that method may be easier when you first start to write them.

As you write the abstract, think of the audience that may read it. Use terminology that an intelligent nonspecialist could understand and try to make your summary so complete that someone outside your field could understand what you are talking about. Keep reminding yourself that this abstract should be a self-contained piece of writing that can stand on its own when it is separated from the paper it represents. And when it is sepa-rated, it represents your thought, so you want it to be an intelligible, cohe-sive piece of writing.

For example, here is how a summary abstract of the proposal for the university day-care center mentioned in earlier chapters might look:

> The university needs to sponsor and subsidize an on-campus day-care center for the children of university faculty and students for sev-eral reasons. Such a center would help the university to attract more of the large number of women who are returning to school to finish their educations or improve their professional credentials. It would also help the university to attract and hold young men and women faculty who favor working for institutions that offer good family-related fringe benefits. In addition, providing good on-campus child care would im-prove the performances of both students and faculty by reducing their anxiety about their children not being adequately cared for.
>
> The university should provide funds for this faculty on a prorated

basis because doing so would help to compensate for its not providing paid maternity benefits or leaves of absence for faculty. Further, data from countries that provide this kind of care indicate that such facilities contribute to better infant health and to an increase in scholarly productivity among women faculty. The cost of such a center would be approximately $250,000 for the next year, and $120,000 a year after that. These costs would be met partially by tax money and partially by user fees.

Length of Abstracts

Although one might think that the length of a finished paper would control the length of the abstract that represents it, such is not usually the case. More often, directions will say that abstracts should not exceed 250 words; that is, one double-spaced page typed in pica type. If the directions say "no more than one page" rather than giving the number of words, you can squeeze in another fifty words by using elite type. It is probably best not to single-space an abstract.

When you begin writing abstracts you will continually face a conflict between keeping the abstract short enough and putting in everything that you think should be included. Inevitably you compromise and your abstracts will never come as close to being perfect miniature reports as you would like. Neither do anyone else's. But as you continue to write them and to realize what a necessary professional tool they are, you will develop an instinct about what to include in an abstract, and your task will gradually become easier.

PAPERS FOR ORAL PRESENTATION

Many young professionals find early in their careers that they must often write papers for oral presentations. When they give such papers, they are not necessarily giving speeches; rather they are apt to be reading a paper to explain a concept or theory, offer a solution to a problem, or present the results of their research. They want to make a good impression, but too often they do not succeed because they have written their papers for a reading audience rather than for a listening audience. The need of the two audiences are significantly different.

Length of Papers

The first concern of any person writing a paper to be given orally should be its length. How much time are you going to have? Ten minutes? Twenty-five minutes? You need to find out and take the limit very seriously. If you are asked to be on a ninety-minute panel with two other speakers, don't assume that you will have thirty minutes to read your paper. Almost certainly the panel will start late, the moderator will need time to introduce the panelists, and time should be allowed for questions and discussions. You should really only count on twenty minutes to present your paper, and you should plan accordingly. And even if you are the only person who will be delivering a paper at a meeting, usually you should condense what you have to say into thirty minutes or less. Only the most charismatic speakers can hold their audience's attention much longer than that.

The best way to be sure your paper is not too long is to read it into a tape recorder, and time it as you play it back. That way you can judge the pace and decide whether you are reading too quickly. Probably you will be. Most of us tend to forget that the audience needs time to absorb our points as we make them. If you don't have a tape recorder, read your paper out loud and time it. Then start cutting if you have to. If, however, the paper doesn't quite fill up your allotted time you should probably resist the temptation to expand it.

When you are writing a paper for oral presentation, you should figure on at least two minutes to read one double-spaced, 250-word page in pica type. (For elite type, adjust accordingly.) If you can read 125 words in a minute—and that's a fairly brisk pace—you can plan on twenty minutes for a 2,500-word, 10-page paper. And if your finished paper runs 11½ pages, you should not plan to rush through it to meet your deadline. Better to cut it back to the proper length and read it effectively.

Structure for Oral Presentations

Once you know the allotted time for your paper, you can decide how to restrict your topic to one that you can treat adequately in the 2,500 or 3,000 words to which you are limited. You have to make your points clear the first time; therefore you should have fewer points. Because an oral presentation usually requires that you explain and illustrate your points more fully, you need to insert signal sentences to preview or summarize for your audience or to keep them headed in the direction you want to go. Remember that your audience cannot go back and reread earlier paragraphs.

Whether you choose to begin your oral presentation with a lead-in paragraph to catch your audience's attention, or with a direct statement announcing your thesis depends partially on the occasion and partially on your personal style. I usually prefer a direct opening statement that announces my thesis and starts any audience off in the right direction. For example:

> Students who are struggling to become writers can profit in several ways from learning about the behavior of professional writers.

I would then go on to list those ways in order to give my audience a preview of what they are about to hear. After the preview I would work my way through my points, being careful to use words such as *first, second,* and *next,* and strong signal words such as *therefore* and *consequently* to help my audience anticipate what is coming. And I would downshift frequently, particularly when I wanted to illustrate an abstract statement.

By using these obvious devices you help your listening audience move with you through your paper. You map it for them and provide directional signals. You can even reinforce your signals by writing your main points on a blackboard as you go. You can also punctuate your presentation with slides or charts shown with an overhead projector. These visual aids not only reinforce the content of your paper, but they give your listeners intermittent breaks in which to absorb the content.

Oral Style

When you begin to work on the second or third version of a paper that you will be reading aloud, try to think in terms of an oral style. As one authority points out, that means several things:

> In other words, a style adapted to the ear instead of the eye means that the language will be simpler to grasp; unusual terms will be used more sparingly, and when they are used will be spoken more clearly and defined more fully; ideas will be paced more slowly; and the development will be less condensed than in writing.
> —Roger P. Wilcox, *Communication at Work* (Boston: Houghton Mifflin, 1977), 454–455.

Three more strategies that will make your prose more listenable have already been discussed in earlier chapters as ways of making your writing more readable. The first is to construct sentences in which there is frequent closure. That is, try not to write long strung-out sentences whose meaning cannot be grasped until one reaches the end.

Second, when possible rearrange many of your sentences into the agent/action pattern. Because the pattern gives readers strong signals about what to anticipate, it should also help listeners. If your agent is a concrete or personal subject, so much the better.

Third, check your writing to see if it is overburdened with derived nouns—words ending in *ity, -ness, -tion,* and so on—or with a disproportionate number of prepositional phrases.

In addition, a listening audience will particularly appreciate a speaker who uses metaphors and analogies as explanatory devices. Probably nothing helps an audience grasp a vague or elusive concept as quickly as having a writer clarify it by a graphic comparison. In fact, listeners may remember the central point of a paper primarily because of the visual image triggered by an apt analogy. Thus if you were to form an image for your listeners by comparing the process of transmitting documents over telephone lines to someone transmitting braille impressions through the fingers you help them to understand a complex process.

Finally, it seems useful to point out that "reading a paper" should not mean that you stand before your audience with your eyes focused only on your paper. People do not like to feel that they are being read to. To counteract that impression, you should study your paper ahead of time so that you can look up from it frequently. Make eye contact with your audience to let them know that it is important to you that they understand what you are saying. And if you have written your paper specifically with that listening audience in mind, probably they will.

EXERCISES

1. In a paragraph of about 100 words, analyze the audience you would have for the following writing tasks. How knowledgeable would they probably be, and what would they want to get from reading your writing?

    A. A grant proposal to the National Endowment for the Arts to ask for $165,000 to support a project to give dancing lessons to children whose families cannot afford such lessons.

    B. A report to the commanding officer at the Air Force Academy on cadets' attitudes toward the honor code of the academy.

    C. A case study to the probation officer about a thirteen-year-old child who is on probation from the juvenile court for stealing a car.

    D. A speech for the California Bar Association on the possible effects of legislation to limit liability in medical malpractice suits.

2. Choose articles from three magazines that vary widely in their focus, for instance, *National Geographic*, *Rolling Stone*, and *U.S. News and World Report*. Read the articles carefully and take notes on points in each one that should be included by a person writing a summary abstract of the articles.

3. Analyze the purpose you would have in writing a promissory abstract for a paper you propose to give with one of the following titles:

The Declining Use of Migrant Labor in the Food Processing Industry
Existential Despair in the Novels of Joan Didion
Using the Care of Pets to Raise Self-Confidence in the Mentally Retarded

4. In a paragraph of no more than 150 words, analyze the specific problems you would anticipate in giving an oral presentation under the following circumstances:

   A. Presenting a report on the effect of high interest rates on real-estate sales in your area.

   B. Presenting the results of a psychological experiment on factors found to produce writing anxiety in high school students.

   C. Presenting to the directors of a corporation a report on new underwater oil drilling operations completed in the past year.

SUGGESTED WRITING ASSIGNMENTS

For each paper, begin by defining and analyzing your audience and your purpose. Specify the characteristics of your audience that are important to keep in mind as you write, and state the specific points that your audience would want to get from reading your paper. Also state clearly and in some detail what you hope to accomplish by writing the paper. When appropriate, give your paper an accurate and descriptive title.

TOPIC 1: Choose a foundation or government agency that gives money for research projects that will contribute to knowledge in a particular field or help to solve a serious problem. Some of the best-known foundations are these:

Ford Foundation
Rockefeller Foundation
Exxon Corporation
Sloan Foundation
National Institute for Education
National Endowment of the Humanities
National Endowment for the Arts
National Science Foundation

Write a grant proposal for one of these projects:

   A. A film on nutrition for young mothers in poverty areas.

   B. An expedition to New Mexico to record oral history of a tribe of Indians.

C. An educational film on the most effective methods of birth control. Specify a particular audience.

D. Outreach project to teach illiterate adults to read.

E. Research project to develop a chemical to eradicate mesquite from pasture land.

F. A film to teach high school students how to establish and use credit.

TOPIC 2: Write a report in response to one of these assignments:

A. A credit report on a family applying for a home loan. Give the wife's and husband's ages, employment, income, education, and whatever other features you think may be pertinent.

B. A report for an urban planning class showing how population patterns in your area have changed in the past ten years.

C. A report for the state legislature showing the comparative salaries and ranks of men and women in higher education in your state.

TOPIC 3: Write a case study about one of the following individuals. Specify the purpose of the study:

A A twenty-one-year-old man who was blinded in an industrial accident on his summer job is applying for a tuition grant and financial assistance in order that he may return to college.

B. A family who wants to adopt a child from an ethnic group different from its own.

C. A forty-five-year-old displaced homemaker whose husband has died, leaving her with no insurance and only a small income. She has no marketable skills so she is applying for admission to a city retraining program offered for women who want to return to school. The program offers subsidies to ten such women each year.

TOPIC 4: Choose an article from a magazine in which you are particularly interested and write a 250-word abstract that reflects the tone and emphasis of the article and functions as a miniature model of it. Attach a copy of the article to your paper.

TOPIC 5: Write a promissory abstract to go with one of the oral presentations suggested under Topic 6.

TOPIC 6: Write a talk on one of these topics, to be presented under the circumstances specified for each one:

A. A talk for a summer orientation meeting on campus. Try to get incoming students interested in working in campus organizations and politics.

B. A radio talk to persuade young people of the benefits of individual exercise programs and show why they are superior to team sports.

C. Prepare a talk for a local service club—Rotary, Optimists, Altrusa, or American Association of University Women—and outline your plan for increasing voter participation among eighteen- to twenty-five year-old people.

D. As education officer for your corporation, give a talk to a group of executive trainees on the value of learning to write clearly and effectively.

E. Present a ten-minute summary of the results of your research on how the typical middle-income family in your area spends its food budget.

INDEX